The 'Secret' Family Court
Fact or Fiction?

His Honour Clifford Bellamy

With a Foreword by
Sir James Munby

BATH PUBLISHING

Published March 2020

ISBN 978-1-9164315-8-4

Text © Clifford Bellamy

Typography © Bath Publishing

All rights reserved. No part of this publication may be reproduced in any material form (including photocopying or storing it in any medium by electronic means and whether or not transiently or incidentally to some other use of this publication) without the written permission of the copyright holder except in accordance with the provisions of the Copyright, Designs and Patents Act 1988 or under the terms of a licence issued by the Copyright Licensing Agency (www.cla.co.uk). Applications for the copyright owner's written permission to reproduce any part of this publication should be addressed to the publisher.

Clifford Bellamy asserts his rights as set out in ss77 and 78 of the Copyright Designs and Patents Act 1988 to be identified as the author of this work wherever it is published commercially and whenever any adaptation of this work is published or produced including any sound recordings or films made of or based upon this work.

The information presented in this work is accurate and current as at March 2020 to the best knowledge of the author. The author and the publisher, however, make no guarantee as to, and assume no responsibility for, the correctness or sufficiency of such information or recommendation. The contents of this book are not intended as legal advice and should not be treated as such.

Bath Publishing Limited
27 Charmouth Road
Bath
BA1 3LJ
Tel: 01225 577810
email: info@bathpublishing.co.uk
www.bathpublishing.co.uk

Bath Publishing is a company registered in England: 5209173

Registered Office: As above

For Thomas and Charlotte from Grandpa

Contents

Acknowledgments		vii
Foreword		xi
Preface		xv
Table of cases		xix
Chapter 1	Introduction	1
Chapter 2	Open Justice	11
Chapter 3	Open Justice in the Family Court	23
Chapter 4	Opening up the Family Court	43
Chapter 5	Next Steps	67
Chapter 6	Practice Guidance on Transparency	79
Chapter 7	The Impact of the Practice Guidance	93
Chapter 8	Who Should Be Named in Judgments?	113
Chapter 9	The Media – the Facts of Life	131
Chapter 10	The Media – Trust and Truth	143
Chapter 11	Legal Blogging	167
Chapter 12	Research and the Voice of the Child	171
Chapter 13	Open Justice in Other Countries	193
Chapter 14	The Child's Right to Privacy	211
Chapter 15	Reflections	233
Recommendations		243
Appendix A		255
Bibliography		259
Index		265

Acknowledgments

Although this book has my name on the front cover the process of writing it has, in truth, been a collective effort. There are a number of people whom I need to thank for their support and encouragement.

I am grateful to the President of the Family Division of the High Court, Sir Andrew McFarlane, for giving me encouragement to write this book.

I owe a great debt of thanks to Sir James Munby, immediate past President of the Family Division. He has cast his expert eye over drafts of each chapter. He has made some invaluable suggestions. His positive comments have been a great source of encouragement.

In March 2019 I was pleased to accept an invitation to become the Patron of the Transparency Project[1]. I am immensely grateful to Lucy Reed (Chair of the Transparency Project), Dr Julie Doughty (a trustee of the Transparency Project), and Louise Tickle[2] (a freelance journalist who regularly writes for *The Guardian* and for the Transparency Project) for their unstinting support; each of them has made a huge contribution.

Mavis Maclean CBE has carried out socio-legal research in Oxford since 1974. She served as an academic advisor to the Lord Chancellor's Department (now the Ministry of Justice) from 1990 to 2009. She continues to be actively involved in research. Her contribution to the discussion, in Chapter 5, of the Family Court Information Pilot and the Children, Schools and Families Act 2010 has been invaluable.

In Chapter 13, I consider the present position relating to media attendance at and publication of information concerning hearings in the family courts in Australia, New Zealand, Canada (Nova Scotia and British Columbia), Scotland, Northern Ireland and Eire. I am indebted to Professor Patrick Parkinson (Dean of Law, T C Beirne School of Law, The University of Queensland, Brisbane), Professor Mark Henaghan (Professor of Law in the

---

[1] The Transparency Project is a registered charity. Its aims and objectives are to explain and discuss family law and family courts in England & Wales, and signpost to useful resources to help people understand the system and the law better. The Transparency Project works towards improving the quality, range and accessibility of information available to the public, both in the press and elsewhere, concerning the family justice system and the Family Court.

[2] In 2016 Louise Tickle won the Bar Council Legal Reporting award for work undertaken in respect of care proceedings. That same year she was also shortlisted for the Orwell Prize for Journalism for her reporting on family law issues.

Law Faculty at the University of Auckland, New Zealand), Professor Rollie Thompson (Professor of Law, Schulich School of Law, Dalhousie University, Halifax, Nova Scotia), Professor Nicholas Bala (Professor of Law at the Faculty of Law, Queen's University, Kingston, Ontario) and Dr Gillian Black (Senior Lecturer in Family Law at the University of Edinburgh) for the help they have given me to enable me to understand something about the role of transparency in the family courts of those other countries. I am also grateful for the help I have received from Virginia Wilson (Deputy Principal Registrar and National Family Law Registrar in the Family Court of Australia in Canberra), Glenda Frew (Judgments Publication Manager) and Katie Boyd (Judgments Co-ordinator in the Federal Court of Australia).

With the President's permission, and with the help of Louise Tickle, I have interviewed ten journalists including Louise herself. I am grateful to Sanchia Berg[3] (Reporter, the Today programme, BBC News), John Sweeney[4] (Freelance writer and broadcaster), Mike Dodd[5] (Legal editor, PA Media), Mark Hanna[6] (Senior University Teacher in the Department of Journalism Studies at the University of Sheffield), Brian Farmer (Journalist, PA Media), Josh White (Journalist, the *Daily Mail*), Polly Curtis[7] (Tortoise Media), Emily Dugan[8] (BuzzFeed News) and Claire Hayhurst (Regional reporter, PA Media) for giving me their time and the benefit of their experience and insights.

As I completed each chapter my two sons, Christopher and Jonathan, cast an eye over it, pointing out errors and making suggestions for improvement. The book is the better for their suggestions and constructive criticism. I am very grateful to them both. I am also grateful to Her Honour Judge Sally

---

[3] In 2011, the Bar Council gave special praise for Sanchia Berg's piece about the Family Court, Legal Aid and Domestic Abuse reform. In 2015 she won the Bar Council Legal Reporting award for two pieces of work relating to the Court of Protection and the Family Court. In 2016, she was long-listed for the Orwell Prize, "Exposing Britain's Social Evils".
[4] In 2005, John Sweeney won the Royal Television Society and the Paul Foot awards for his investigation into miscarriages of justice relating to cases of shaken baby syndrome.
[5] Mike Dodd is a co-editor of the leading text book *McNae's Essential Law for Journalists*. He is also a member of the Law Board of the National Council for the Training of Journalists.
[6] Mark Hanna is a co-editor of *McNae's Essential Law for Journalists*. He is also Chair of the National Council for Training of Journalists Media Law Examination Board.
[7] Polly Curtis' project on family separation was nominated for a British Press Awards special journalist award 2019. The full project can be found at: *https://www.tortoisemedia.com/casefiles/separated*.
[8] Emily Dugan was the winner of the 2018 Bar Council Legal Reporting Award for her access to justice campaign exposing failings in the UK's legal system and the 2019 Private Eye Paul Foot Award. In 2019 she was short-listed for the News Reporter of the Year at the National Press Awards.

Acknowledgments

Dowding, Designated Family Judge for Wolverhampton and Telford, and to Kaye Howells, senior lecturer in law at The University of Derby, for reading the final draft.

In writing this book I have entered what, for me, has been the new and unknown world of publishing. I am delighted that Bath Publishing have agreed to publish this book. I am extremely grateful to David Chaplin and Helen Lacey for their support and encouragement and for giving me the benefit of their many years' experience in the publishing world.

Some while ago I was diagnosed with Parkinson's disease. Since then life has been one long round of hospital appointments of one kind or another. The NHS and the Family Court have one thing in common: they are both regularly the subject of criticism – very often unfair criticism. The care I have received has been very impressive. I owe the NHS a great debt of thanks. I want to single out one of those professionals for particular praise. Emma Shaddock is a dedicated and highly competent neuro-physiotherapist with a special interest in Parkinson's disease. She epitomises the very best of the NHS. It is in large measure thanks to her skill and care that I have been able to keep as mobile as I am. She has kept the wheels turning and that has been invaluable as I have been writing this book.

Parkinson's disease is an unpleasant, degenerative disease which, over time, affects every area of your life. I am confident that research will eventually lead to more effective treatments. I have informed the publishers that any royalties from the sale of this book are to go to Parkinson's UK for research.

Last, but by no means least, throughout this journey my wife, Christine, has been my rock. She has been a constant source of patient support and encouragement as I have continued, through this book, to pursue my long-standing passion for justice for those who find themselves involved in proceedings in the Family Court. Christine has been at my side throughout the whole of my professional career. Whatever has been achieved has been achieved together. Words are inadequate to express my thanks and love.

Notwithstanding the help I have had from so many people, full responsibility for the text is mine alone.

Clifford Bellamy

February 2020

Foreword

His Honour Clifford Bellamy was, until his recent retirement, a distinguished Designated Family Judge on the Midland Circuit, and a judge notable for his intellectual curiosity and thoughtfulness as well as his formidable industry. He was also an ardent practitioner of transparency in the Family Court, for, although he is too modest to say so, he heads the list of Circuit Judges as the most prolific publisher of judgments on Bailii.

Now, from his active retirement, he has given us as the matured autumnal fruits of his time on the Bench. We are indeed lucky, for he has given us an extended but incisive meditation on one of the most pressing issues which the family justice system currently faces: transparency.

Our author tells us that this is not intended to be a text book. Modestly, he describes his objectives as more limited: *"to undertake a critical review of the attempts that have taken place to try to improve transparency in the Family Court over the last 15 years, to try to explain why those attempts have either failed or have not been as successful as was hoped, and to make suggestions about a way forward."* That is an important task, in which he triumphantly succeeds, made all the more useful because it is, as he tells us, written from the perspective of a Circuit Judge. His treatment of these undoubtedly controversial topics is, throughout, as one would expect of our author, insightful, fair, balanced and judicious.

He highlights the *"very deep fault line"* between supporters and opponents of greater transparency. *"On one side of the divide there are those who believe that the transparency agenda has not gone far enough and that more needs to be done to open up the Family Court. On the other side of the divide there are those who believe that the transparency agenda has already been pushed too far."* Indeed.

His conclusion is clear: *"In my opinion it is no longer credible to seek to argue that open justice in the Family Court must be sacrificed on the high alter of guaranteed absolute privacy for children in order to ensure that justice is done. A more proportionate and balanced approach is required."* In this he reiterates the orthodox view, surely correct, that in the context of transparency the child's welfare is *not* the court's paramount consideration.

Very usefully, he covers both the views of the Academy, where his analysis is both penetrating and, on some aspects, justly critical, and the experience in a number of other common law jurisdictions, both in this country and further abroad. In relation to this he makes the important point that: *"none of these different models has been so convincing that other countries have been queu-*

ing up to follow them." As he observes, for example, of the courts in Victoria and South Australia: *"their approaches to transparency could not be more different."*

Addressing the question posed in his title, *The 'Secret' Family Court – Fact or Fiction?* our author notes, surely accurately, that the argument *"has descended into a semantic debate about whether the Family Court should be described as 'secret' or 'private'."* His comment is trenchant: *"That debate is nothing more than a distraction. It is arid and pointless."*

He says that it *"is neither accurate nor appropriate to describe the Family Court as a 'secret' court."* He goes on: *"... in my opinion, the greatest achievement of the use of the word 'secret' has been to undermine public trust and confidence in the family justice system ... that description is a fiction which diverts attention away from the real point."* What matters, he says, is that: *"there is a lack of adequate scrutiny of what goes on in the Family Court."*

In an illuminating passage, which I take the liberty of quoting at length because it is so important, he elaborates:

> *"What really matters, surely, is that much of what happens in the Family Court is not 'open justice' in the sense in which that expression has been used and understood for more than a century? That needs to change. The whole focus of the debate needs to change. There needs to be greater openness, greater transparency, about the work of the Family Court. Transparency should be the default position for cases heard in the Family Court as much as for cases heard in any other court. 'Transparency' means one of two things – either that hearings are heard in open court or that the media be given the right to report what goes on in the Family Court – the right which they mistakenly believed was being given to them in April 2009. In any situation in the Family Court where transparency and openness are deemed not appropriate there needs to be clear, rational, cogent reasons, publicly stated, why that should be the case."*

This leads to an important conclusion, that the key to meaningful progress is the repeal of section 12 of the Administration of Justice Act 1960:

> *"The charge of 'secrecy' is, in truth, a full-frontal attack on section 12 ... Viewed in that way, the media's attack is fully justified. If only the media had spent the last 15 years campaigning for that section to be repealed rather than continually banging the drum of secrecy we may not now be in the position we are in, responsible reporting may*

Foreword

be much easier and public trust in the Family Court may be significantly higher than it is."

The publication of this stimulating book is most timely, for the President of the Family Division is currently consulting on transparency. It is a book to be read and most carefully considered by everyone interested, from whatever perspective, in transparency, past, present and future, indeed by everyone concerned with the future of our family justice system. It is written in a clear and engaging style which, most happily, makes it equally accessible to lawyers and non-lawyers, journalists and non-journalists, alike.

We are all much indebted to Clifford Bellamy. I wish his book all the success it so richly deserves.

James Munby

February 2020

Preface

Eighteen months ago, in the autumn of 2018, in front of an audience of lawyers and judges at the Derby Family Justice Board annual conference, I gave a lecture that offered a trenchant critique of what I said were failures of transparency, scrutiny and accountability in the family justice system. At the end, as I looked out a little anxiously at the faces staring back at me, a grey-haired man came up and held out his hand.

"I'm Clifford Bellamy, the designated family judge for this area" he said quietly. Oh crikey, I thought as we shook hands. I'm about to be told off.

"Well," he said, breaking into a smile. *"That has certainly given us all a lot to think about."*

This book comes in the wake of the author's acceptance of the role of patron of The Transparency Project, a charity which seeks to increase public understanding of family law. It was written during a year in which there has been increasingly vociferous criticism of the family justice system, and renewed debate in Parliament and society more widely about whether – and how – the "secret" family courts should be open to more independent scrutiny.

There are compelling, laudably child welfare-centred views that sit in diametric opposition to these calls for change. But nonetheless, I am one of those who believe that our privacy laws relating to family hearings mean they take place, to all intents and purposes, in secret. Those working in the family justice system find the charge that they operate in secret courts very hard to stomach. And clearly we are not talking about the kind of pseudo tribunals that take place in conflict-torn countries or dictatorships where the locations of courts are unknown and summary "justice" is meted out in anonymous cellars. But that is a dismally low bar. Our justice system aims to achieve a level of openness many magnitudes better. So yes, we may know where family courts are located, and yes, journalists are allowed to observe most family hearings. And yes, appeals are heard in public. The secrecy comes in what the media may – actually may not – do with the information we learn as a result. Without making often expensive, and always in my experience, time consuming and risky applications, neither reporters nor families may say a word about the substance of what happens in court, or disclose what is contained in case documents. There is no other situation I know of other than national security (where the government has to convince a judge of its argument for secrecy, rather than being allowed to gag reporting from the off) whereby the prohibition on citizens being allowed to know what has taken place in their name is so extensive, so widespread, and ultimately so damaging to public acceptance of the courts' legitimacy.

It is a testament to Clifford Bellamy that he has been willing seriously to engage with and explore the validity of this perspective – but perhaps it should be no surprise. Until his recent retirement, he was the most prolific circuit judge publisher of family court judgments in England and Wales, and therefore, it might be said, a transparency champion. So he is absolutely the right person to write this book, which explores whether or not our strict privacy laws damage the functioning of our family justice system, and whether they impact disproportionately on freedom of expression – not simply for journalists wishing to report in the public interest, but for family members wishing to protest at their treatment, whose lives are changed forever by the decisions made in family courts.

In deciding on some of the most sensitive, difficult and complex matters that ever come before our courts, family judges promise to uphold laws that make the best interests of vulnerable children their paramount consideration. In doing so, their duty is to remain unbiased, open and objective throughout hearings that are often distressing and sometimes traumatic. It is an approach, a discipline – and, I'm sure, a hard-earned skill – that is evident throughout this book. The author's meticulous research, evident in every chapter, demonstrates the highest qualities a judge can aspire to. Because real people, suffering greatly, who have been in his courtroom, matter; because the law matters; because genuine enquiry in good faith matters, he has sought out a range of perspectives on the knotty issue of transparency and opened the scope of this book to views that robustly challenge aspects of the justice system to which he has dedicated his professional life. He has not flinched from listening to and addressing them; in doing so I wonder if he may have found the unvarnished opinions of some of my journalist colleagues amusingly different to the restrained legal language of the courtroom.

As well as drawing on his own extensive knowledge of family law and practice, he has not just ventured, but *ad*ventured out of the familiar confines of the court to investigate how our privacy legislation came about, enquired into contemporaneous opposition to the way it was framed, and interrogated lawyers', journalists' and academics' reasoning for the various positions they hold. Reading each chapter, I was fascinated and often surprised by what I learned. The rigorous analysis one would expect from a judge makes for uncomfortable reading at times, both for those desiring more transparency and, I would expect, for those who want to retain the privacy status quo, or even extend it.

Now retired from the bench, Clifford Bellamy is able to express views of his own. I wonder if it feels liberating? It is entirely admirable to me that he does not sit on the fence. He says what he thinks. He offers constructive ideas for reform. And building something better is always so much harder than simply criticising what has gone wrong.

This book is not just an absorbing read for anyone who cares about the family justice system; it plays an important role in the creative attempts now being made to ensure that more robust and accountable decisions are made for the people who pass through the doors of the family court.

Louise Tickle

February 2020

Table of cases

A G (Nova Scotia) v MacIntyre [1982] 1 SCR 175	1
B and P v United Kingdom [2001] ECHR 298	13, 221
Baron & Ors (4 Defective Divorces) [2019] EWFC 26	74
BBC v Rochdale Metropolitan Borough Council and X and Y [2005] EWHC 2862 (Fam)	117
Bergens Tidende v Norway (2001) 31 EHRR 16	158
British Broadcasting Corporation v Cafcass Legal and others [2007] EWHC 616 (Fam)	125
Clayton v Clayton [2006] EWCA Civ 878	17
Clibbery v Allen [2002] EWCA Civ 45	11
Diennet v France (1995) 21 EHRR 544	11
Dorset Council v A [2019] EWFC 62	178
Dr A v Ward [2010] EWHC 16 (Fam)	117, 126
Gillick v West Norfolk and Wisbech Area Health Authority and Another [1985] UKHL 7	211, 230
In re Guardian News and Media Ltd [2010] UKSC 1	76
In re S (A Child) (Identification: Restrictions on Publication) [2004] UKHL 47	17, 220, 226
In the matter of A (A Child) [2015] EWFC 11	119
In the matter of an application by Gloucestershire County Council for the committal to prison of Matthew John Newman [2014] EWHC 3136 (Fam)	118
In the matter of the B children, X Council v B and others [2004] EWHC 2015 (Fam)	114

In the matter of X (A Child) (No 2)
[2016] EWHC 1668 (Fam)   55, 102, 103

JH v MF [2020] EWHC 86 (Fam)   146

Justyna-Zeromska-smith v United Lincolnshire Hospitals NHS Trust
[2019] EWHC 552 (QB)   239

London Borough of Barnett v Y and Z [2006] EWCC 1 (Fam)   34

M v Derbyshire CC & Ors [2018] EWHC 3734 (Fam)   30

Manchester University NHS Foundation Trust v Midrar Namiq, Karwan
Mohammed Ali and Shokhan Namiq [2020] EWHC 181 (Fam)   123

Norfolk County Council v Webster [2004] EW Misc 3   183

Norfolk County Council v Webster [2006] EWHC 2733 (Fam)   183

Norfolk County Council v Webster
[2006] EWHC 2898 (Fam)   35, 183

PNM v Times Newspapers Ltd & Ors [2017] UKSC 49   13, 15

Prager and Oberschlick v Austria (1996) 21 EHRR 1   32

RBC v J-M [2014] EWFC B174   106

Re A (Children) [2015] EWCA Civ 133   239

Re B (A Child) [2004] EWHC 411 (Fam)   32, 48, 59

Re Brandon Webster [2007] EWHC 549 (Fam)   183

Re B, X Council v B [2007] EWHC 1622 (Fam)   115

Re D (A Child) [2006] UKHL 51   217

Re F (A Minor) [2016] EWHC 2149 (Fam)   30

Re G (Children: Fair Hearing) [2019] EWCA Civ 126   239

Re J (A Child) [2013] EWHC 2694 (Fam)   234

Case	Page
Re J (A minor) [2016] EWHC 2595 (Fam)	189
Re K (Infants) [1965] AC 201	13
Re L (A Child: Media Reporting) [2011] EWHC B8 (Fam)	161
Re L and M (Children) [2013] EWHC 1569 (Fam)	29
Re M and N (Wards) (Publication of Information) [1990] 1 FLR 149	54
Re M (Declaration of Death of Child) [2020] EWCA Civ 164	124
Re P (A Child) [2013] EWHC 4048 (Fam)	134
Re RB (Adult) (No 4) [2011] EWHC 3017 (Fam)	57
Re Roddy [2003] EWHC 2927 (Fam)	158, 228
Re S (A Child) [2010] EWCA Civ 219	156
Re S-W (Children) [2015] EWCA Civ 27	239
Re W (Children) [2016] EWCA Civ 113	220
Re W (Wardship: Discharge: Publicity) [1995] 2 FLR 466	32
Re X (Non-Accidental Injury: Expert Evidence) [2001] EWHC Fam 6	30
Re X, Y and Z (Children) [2010] EWHC B12 (Fam)	81, 136
Reynolds v Times Newspapers Ltd [1999] UKHL 45	159
RP v Nottinghamshire County Council and the Official Solicitor [2008] EWCA Civ 462	81
R v Sarker [2018] EWCA Crim 1341	45
Scott v Scott [1913] UKHL 2	13, 14, 18
Secretary of State for the Home Office, ex p Simms [2000] 2 AC 115	62

Seven Network (Operations) Limited v Aaron Philip Cockman and Attorney General of Western Australia [2018] FCWA 108   212

Shoesmith v Ofsted and Others [2011] EWCA Civ 642   120

Shoesmith v Ofsted, Secretary of State for Children, Schools and Families [2010] EWHC 852 (Admin)   120

Webster v Norfolk County Council [2009] EWCA Civ 59   26, 183

West Australian newspapers Ltd and Channel 7 Perth Pty Ltd and Cuzens (2016) FLC 93-690   212

X, Y, and Z & Anor v A Local Authority [2011] EWHC 1157 (Fam)   81, 128, 136, 224, 226

Z County Council v TS & Ors [2008] EWHC 1773 (Fam)   157

ZH (Tanzania) v Secretary of State for the Home Department [2011] UKSC 4   217

1: INTRODUCTION

> *"In the darkness of secrecy, sinister interest and evil in every shape have full swing. Only in proportion as publicity has place can any of the checks applicable to judicial injustice operate. Where there is no publicity there is no justice".* (Jeremy Bentham)[1]

On three occasions in May 2019 the Victoria Derbyshire show, a daily magazine programme on BBC 2, explored concerns about family judges putting children at risk by allowing their fathers to have contact with them even though the fathers were known to be abusive. In these three programmes the Family Court was repeatedly referred to as the 'secret' Family Court. Is that a fair description?

After nine years sitting as a District Judge at the Combined Court Centre in Leeds, in October 2004 I was sworn in as a Circuit Judge. The previous month the House of Commons Constitutional Affairs Select Committee had begun an inquiry into the work of the Family Court. That inquiry led to the publication of the report: *Family Justice: the operation of the family courts*. One of the issues addressed in the report was that of transparency in the Family Court.

In his written evidence to the committee, submitted on 8 November 2004, BBC reporter, John Sweeney, said:[2]

> *"I believe that the Family Court system is systematically unfair to parents accused of child abuse. This is because, firstly, the system is closed and takes place very much behind closed doors. Secondly, because the 'primacy of the child' effectively over-rides and indeed reverses the presumption of innocence. Thirdly, because 'expert' evidence outweighs that of lay people who know the family. As a result of these three failures, my colleagues and I have been horrified to discover a series of what we believe have been a whole category of miscarriages of justice in the Family Courts...Secret courts are bad courts."*

---

[1] Quoted by Dickson J in *A G (Nova Scotia) v MacIntyre* [1982] 1 SCR 175 at page 183.
[2] House of Commons Constitutional Affairs Committee, *Family Justice: the operation of the family courts*, Fourth Report, Session 2004 – 2005 Vol II page 206, 8 November 2004.

In his oral evidence to the committee, Mr Justice Munby[3] said that:[4]

> *"The fact is, and I believe it is a fact, that the family justice system is under criticism today because it is perceived as being a secret justice system, and in that sense we are crippling public debate. As the President has indicated, a lot of the criticisms, whether they come from Fathers4Justice or the NSPCC, are necessarily anecdotal and nobody is able to see the relevant material. I think it is doing us serious harm, and I do not think that the existing system, the existing rules, are necessary."*

"Secret" family courts? Surely, what goes on in the family courts is private, not secret, isn't it? These cases deal with sensitive confidential information about families – about children abused or neglected by their parents (referred to as 'public law' cases) and about children who are the subject of disputes between their parents or other family members (referred to as 'private law' cases). Information relating to such disputes should be discussed in private behind closed doors and not, like the criminal courts, open to the full glare of the media and the public. Shouldn't it?

The committee's report was published in March 2005. On this issue of transparency, the report concluded that:[5]

> *"Lack of transparency has been a major factor in creating dissatisfaction with the current Family Justice system on the part of those involved in cases... Some of the evidence we received was that the lack of openness prevented proper scrutiny of the work done by family judges or court officials, and made it impossible to prove or disprove perceived unfairness. While there is disagreement as to whether all the criticism of the system of Family Justice is justified, it is widely agreed that reform is needed."*

On 28 February 2019, I retired as a Circuit Judge. I sat as a family Circuit

---

[3] Sir James Munby features large in this book. He was appointed a High Court Judge of the Family Division in May 2000. His judicial title then was Mr Justice Munby. In October 2009 he was appointed a Lord Justice of Appeal. His judicial title then was Lord Justice Munby. In January 2013 he was appointed President of the Family Division of the High Court and Head of Family Justice. His judicial title then was Sir James Munby P. He retired in July 2018. To assist readers of this book who are non-lawyers I shall refer to him throughout, at all stages of his judicial career, as Sir James Munby.

[4] House of Commons Constitutional Affairs Committee *Family Justice: the operation of the family courts* Fourth Report of Session 2004 – 2005 Vol 1 at page 38, paragraph 138, 9 November 2004.

[5] Ibid at page 43, paragraph 154.

Judge for more than 14 years. Throughout the whole of that time the Family Court was regularly and routinely described, especially in the media, as a 'secret' court. It is clear that the use by journalists of the word 'secret' was not intended to be merely descriptive. The word 'secret' was being used in a pejorative sense. The description of the Family Court as 'secret' was intended to – and did – cause great public concern; it undermined the public's confidence and trust in the family justice system, a problem that was exacerbated by some disturbing miscarriages of justice.

One of the down sides of retirement is the exposure to daytime television. It was shortly after I retired that I watched part of the Victoria Derbyshire programmes to which I referred earlier. This particular trilogy of programmes referred to occasions where a separated father had murdered his children whilst having contact with them, contact which had been approved by the Family Court in private law proceedings. None of these were recent cases but all of them were poignant and tragic – and devastating for the families concerned. When dealing with a private law case, the risk of something like that happening after giving permission for unsupervised contact to take place is a family judge's worst nightmare. It brings home in stark form the fact that however hard the judge tries to arrive at an outcome that is in the best interest of the child's welfare, that decision-making process inevitably involves a degree of risk. The judge may have got it wrong. Whilst it is the responsibility of witnesses to tell the truth; the responsibility of expert witnesses to give sound, reliable, professional advice; the responsibility of lawyers to prepare cases thoroughly in order to ensure that the judge has all the evidence he or she needs to be able to make an informed decision; the responsibility of advocates to present cases fairly and honestly; the ultimate responsibility for making the decision rests with the judge. The buck stops with the judge. Any risks involved in making that decision are the responsibility of the judge.

The judge makes his or her decisions based on the totality of the evidence before the court, faithfully applying the law and after giving each case the most anxious consideration. Section 1(1) of the Children Act 1989 is always the judge's start point and end point in considering his or her decision about that child. Section 1(1) provides that:

> *"When a court determines any question with respect to ... the upbringing of a child ... the child's welfare shall be the court's paramount consideration"*

No judge is infallible. Sometimes the judge will get it wrong; very occasionally with tragic consequences.

It is appropriate to note that one journalist recently acknowledged the level of responsibility on family court judges. Writing in *The Guardian* on 25 January 2020, journalist Sonia Sodha observed that:

> *"Family court judges have an unenviable responsibility: they have to make balance-of-probability rulings about what happened between two parents behind closed doors, sometimes on limited evidence, that determine how much, if at all, contact those parents have with their children, whose safety is paramount."*

In 2012 the judge's task became even more challenging. As part of its austerity measures, in 2012 the Coalition Government introduced the Legal Aid Sentencing and Punishment of Offenders Act. One intentional effect of that Act was to remove the entitlement of a large number of parents to legal aid for private law Children Act cases no matter what their means and no matter what the merits of their case.[6] There are limited exceptions for parents who are able to prove that they and/or their child are the victim of, or are at risk of being the victim of, domestic violence and the applicant and the perpetrator or potential perpetrator are 'associated with each other'.[7] The person who is alleged to have perpetrated, or to present a risk of perpetrating, that violence is not entitled to legal aid. The consequences of this pernicious piece of legislation include a significant increase in the number of parents who have had to deal with their case without legal representation (i.e. as 'litigants in person'). This includes the need to prepare and issue their own application, to comply with any directions the court may make to get the case ready for a final hearing, to present their own case in court and to cross-examine their former partner in court. This has led to a significant increase in the length of hearings in court. It is questionable whether this

---

[6] Ever since it came into force LASPO has been much criticised by judges and practitioners alike. In a talk given in Edinburgh on 10 February 2020 (*The Crisis in Private Law in the English Family Court*), Sir James Munby said that: "The effect of LASPO, with its withdrawal of legal aid from most private law disputes, has been to make the family court an increasingly lawyer-free zone, with ever-increasing numbers of litigants having to appear unrepresented and without legal advice." Amongst the consequences of that, as he pointed out, has been that "there is less advice to prospective appellants and therefore, one fears, fewer appeals being brought which might be successful and less knowledge within and feedback from the professions as to what is truly going on."

[7] The Civil Legal Aid (Procedure) Regulations 2012 as amended specify the type of evidence required to prove that the applicant has been, or is at risk of being, the victim of domestic violence.

Act has led to significant financial savings for the government.[8]

The process of judging public law cases also involves risk. Sanctioning the removal of a child from the care of his or her parents and ordering that he or she be placed for adoption is a Draconian order to make.

Such an order changes the course of the lives of that child and his or her parents for ever. So far as the child is concerned there is no guarantee that such changes will necessarily prove to be for the better. Making a care order involves taking a risk. Equally, ordering the return to his or her parents of a child who has been removed because of concern about past harm and/or risk of future harm also involves taking a risk. If the judge's risk assessment of the parents is flawed the judge could be returning the child to a situation in which he or she will be at real risk of harm. When that happens, here, too, there can very occasionally be tragic consequences.

As I watched the Victoria Derbyshire programmes and listened to the repeated references to the 'secret family court' I reflected on the fact that that description has been in continuous use throughout the whole of my career as a family Circuit Judge. It has still not gone away. It continues to thrive. It continues to shape and colour the public's view of the Family Court and to undermine public confidence in the Family Court. It has taken root in public consciousness.

In the early days when this expression came to be used by the media, the public was not interested in judges seeking to give reassurance that the family court sits in private and not in secret. The public was not interested in abstract concepts of privacy and confidentiality. Encouraged by the media, the public was concerned – genuinely, and in my opinion understandably, concerned – that this was not open justice. The public were locked out.

---

[8] See *The impact of LASPO on routes to justice* (Research Report 118) published by the Equality and Human Rights Commission in September 2018: *https://www.equalityhumanrights.com/sites/default/files/the-impact-of-laspo-on-routes-to-justice-september-2018.pdf*. So serious is the impact of LASPO that, according to an article in *The Sunday Times* on 9 February 2020: "The country's most senior family judge has urged private law firms to make regular donations to keep the crisis-hit court system functioning…Sir Andrew McFarlane, President of the Family Division for England and Wales, wants law firms to fund a charity to provide support for about 160,000 people clogging up the system by appearing in court without a lawyer. The charity needs extra donations of at least £1.5m a year." The headline given to this article was *Judge begs for donations to ease family court crisis*. Later in this book, in Chapter 10, I am critical of the print media for sensationalising headlines and stories about the work of the Family Court. I do not consider this headline to be sensationalist or open to criticism in any way. On the contrary, to the shame of those whose responsibility it is to ensure that this country has a properly funded family justice system that is fit for purpose, this headline is both accurate and true. It is – or at least it ought to be – a wake-up call.

The media were locked out. There were very significant limits on what parents could say publicly about their experience of the family court without putting themselves at risk of being made the subject of an application for committal to prison for contempt of court.

Something had to be done. Identifying what that 'something' should be has proved to be extremely difficult. It is a topic about which many people hold very strong – and often strongly conflicting – views. What could be done to improve transparency in the Family Court that would command widespread public, professional and academic support and approval?

The senior judiciary were neither unaware of, nor unconcerned about, the repeated references to the 'secret' Family Court. On the contrary, they were acutely aware of the damage this was causing, not least to public confidence in the work of the Family Court.

This is a problem that has challenged each of the last four Presidents of the Family Division – Sir Mark Potter (2005 to 2010), Sir Nicholas Wall (2010 to 2012), Sir James Munby (2013 to 2018) and Sir Andrew McFarlane (appointed in July 2018). Each of them has taken steps to try to address the problem. And yet, despite their best efforts, there still remains concern about the failure to achieve adequate transparency in the Family Court. The search for a solution goes on; the search must go on.

It is because of my deep concern about the importance of the issue of transparency that I decided to write this book. It is important that I should emphasise at the outset that though written by a former family Circuit Judge about the work of the Family Court, this is not, and is not intended to be, a text book on the law relating to transparency in the Family Court. There is already an excellent recently published book on that subject, *Transparency in the Family Courts: Publicity and Privacy in Practice*,[9] which I have no hesitation in commending to anyone who has an interest in the law in that area. My objectives are more limited. I propose to undertake a critical review of the attempts that have taken place to try to improve transparency in the Family Court over the last 15 years, to try to explain why those attempts have either failed or have not been as successful as was hoped, and to make suggestions about a way forward.

Throughout this book I shall refer to the Family Court in the singular. I

---

[9] Julie Doughty, Lucy Reed, Paul MaGrath, 2018, published by Bloomsbury Professional, Haywards Heath. Julie, Lucy and Paul are all trustees of the Transparency Project - *www.transparencyproject.org.uk*.

do so for the sake of convenience though that description is not strictly accurate. Prior to April 2014 there was no single, unified Family Court in England and Wales. It was more accurate to refer to 'family courts' than to a 'Family Court'. Family law work was dealt with in the Family Division of the High Court, the County Court and the Family Proceedings Court. The Family Procedure Rules 2010 came into force in April 2011. Until then different rules governed the work in each of the three tiers of court which dealt with family law cases. The Family Procedure Rules apply to all three tiers. Their implementation was an important step along the road towards the creation of a single Family Court in April 2014.[10]

The work of the Family Court covers a wide range of different types of case including, for example, public and private law cases relating to children, cases relating to marriage, divorce and dissolution of civil partnerships, applications for financial remedies following divorce and dissolution of civil partnerships, applications for domestic violence injunctions, for forced marriage protection orders and for female genital mutilation protection orders. The issue of transparency arises in many areas of the work conducted in the Family Court. In this book I am only concerned with the issue of transparency in public and private law Children Act cases dealt with in the Family Court.

Cases in the Family Court are heard by Judges of the Family Division of the High Court, by Circuit Judges, by District Judges and by lay justices (magistrates). Cases are allocated to a particular tier of judge according to complexity. This book is written from the perspective of a Circuit Judge.

Family Court judgments that are published are normally anonymised so that the child concerned and his or her family cannot be identified. Anonymisation is likely to include not only withholding the name of the child and his or her family but, for example, not giving details of the place or area where the family lives or the name of the school which the child attends or the name of the hospital where the child is being treated. Omitting that kind of information is not controversial. But what about the identities of local authorities, social workers, Children's Guardians, health care staff and expert witnesses? Must they always be named in judgments or are there circumstances in which it is appropriate for their identity, too, to be anonymised? This is an important issue which I address in Chapter 8.

The next part of my review deals with the role of the media. I have been greatly assisted by discussions with ten journalists: Sanchia Berg (Reporter,

---

[10] This was established by section 17 of the Crime and Courts Act 2013.

the Today programme, BBC News), John Sweeney (Freelance writer and broadcaster), Brian Farmer (PA Media formerly known as the Press Association based at the Royal Courts of Justice), Louise Tickle (Freelance journalist who regularly writes for *The Guardian*), Mike Dodd (Legal Editor, PA Media), Mark Hanna (Senior University Teacher in the Department of Journalism Studies at the University of Sheffield), Josh White (journalist with the *Daily Mail*), Polly Curtis (editor of and partner in Tortoise Media), Claire Hayhurst (Regional Reporter for the PA Media) and Emily Dugan (a Senior Reporter for BuzzFeed News). Between them, these ten journalists have a wealth of experience. It has been enlightening to have the opportunity to discuss and, on occasion, challenge their views.

Concerns have been expressed by some, including by some judges, about the reliability and trustworthiness of the media. Putting it shortly, they raise a question about whether the media can be trusted. The media continues to have concerns about the family courts – as is apparent from the frequency with which they still refer to the Family Court as a 'secret' court. Is it possible to build trust between the media and the judges? How might that be achieved? How important is it that working relationships built on trust are achieved? Analysing the problem is easier than proposing a solution. I shall deal with these issues in Chapters 9 and 10.

When considering what further developments there should be (if any) in increasing the openness and transparency of the Family Court in England and Wales, it is important that the voice of the child should be heard clearly in that debate. That has been the subject of research which has focussed primarily on the views and fears of children. I shall consider that research in Chapter 12.

Research has also considered what can be learned from the experiences of other countries (Australia, New Zealand, Canada (Nova Scotia and British Columbia) and Scotland) as they have addressed the issues of openness and transparency in their own family justice systems. The research was undertaken more than a decade ago. In Chapter 13, I consider the changes that have taken place in those other countries during the last decade in order to see what more can be learned as we continue to grapple with these challenging issues in England and Wales. In addition to the countries considered in that earlier research I have also explored developments in Northern Ireland and Eire.

An issue of central importance in cases heard in the Family Court is the need to protect the identity and privacy of the children concerned. The greatest concern that has been expressed about further increasing transparency in the Family Court is the consequent increase in risk to children's privacy. Difficult questions arise with respect to the balancing of the rights set out in Articles 6 and 8 of the European Convention on Human Rights (the right to a fair trial and the right to respect for a person's private and family life) and those set out in Article 10 (the right to freedom of expression). There are also issues to be considered concerning the scope of the rights set out in Articles 12 and 16 of the United Nations Convention on the Rights of the Child. I shall deal with these issues in Chapter 14.

In the final chapter I will set out my reflections on this review of the last 15 years of debate and disagreement concerning the 'secret' Family Court. The title of this book asks a question. I will set out my answer, recognising that others will disagree.

Finally, I will make recommendations about how, in my opinion, we might move forward in addressing the eternal and seemingly unresolvable tension between privacy and publicity, confidence and confidentiality in the Family Court.

Although I write from my perspective as a retired family Circuit Judge, I do not claim to speak on behalf of all family Circuit Judges. I have been able to draw on helpful observations from those judges who were kind enough to respond to the survey I describe in Chapter 7. However, it is important to stress that all views expressed in this book are mine and mine alone. I acknowledge at the outset that some (including some judges) will disagree with my analysis. Some will disagree with my conclusions and recommendations. However, if this book stimulates thoughtful debate, and in particular if that debate should lead to a way forward to improve transparency in the Family Court that commands general support from all interested stakeholders whilst also safeguarding the welfare and privacy of children, the time and effort in writing it will have been worthwhile.

2: OPEN JUSTICE

> *"We live in a country which is committed to the rule of law. Central to that commitment is that justice is done in public – that what goes on in court and what the court decides is open to scrutiny... Public awareness of what happens in our courts serves to bolster public confidence in the administration of justice...."* (Lord Neuberger)[1]

'Open justice' is one of the most important hallmarks of a democratic society and a fundamental aspect of our commitment to the rule of law. Over many years that point has been made repeatedly by judges both in court and out of court.

Secret courts are unacceptable in a democracy. In 1995 the European Court of Human Rights said that:[2]

> *"The Court reiterates that the holding of court hearings in public constitutes a fundamental principle enshrined in Article 6.[3] This public character protects litigants against the administration of justice in secret with no public scrutiny; it is also one of the means whereby confidence in the court can be maintained. By rendering the administration of justice transparent, publicity contributes to the achievement of the aim of Article 6(1), namely a fair trial, the guarantee of which is one of the fundamental principles of any democratic society".*

That case was not a family case. It did not concern the welfare of children. However, the same point has been made about hearings in the Family Court. In 2002 the then President of the Family Division of the High Court, Dame Elizabeth Butler-Sloss, said that:[4]

> *"The starting point must be the importance of the principle of open justice. This has been a thread to be discerned throughout the common*

---

[1] *Open justice unbound?* – Judicial Studies Board Annual Lecture, 16 March 2011.
[2] *Diennet v France* (1995) 21 EHRR 544 at paragraph 33.
[3] Article 6 of the European Convention for the Protection of Human Rights and Fundamental Freedoms, Rome, 4.XI.1950 (hereafter abbreviated to 'the ECHR'), signed by the UK on 4 November 1950.
[4] *Clibbery v Allen* [2002] EWCA Civ 45 at paragraph 16.

law systems...Consequently...the exclusion of the public from proceedings has objectively to be justified. It is not good enough for it to be said that we have always done it this way so it has to be right. That principle of open justice applies to all courts and in principle the family courts are not excluded from it, although for good reasons which I shall set out later, many family cases...require confidentiality."

Open justice comprises two key components. The first is the right of the media and the public to be present in court to observe justice being done. The second, which follows naturally from the first, is the right of those who are the subject of the judicial process to discuss their experiences, freely and openly, outside court. In the Family Court, both of these rights have been severely circumscribed by a mixture of practice, statute and rule. If such restrictions are lawful, that raises two very important questions for the family justice system. First, what does 'open justice' mean? Second, what are its limits? Our understanding of open justice and of the limits of open justice are central to the issues with which this book is concerned.

In 2014 an authoritative analysis of the principle of open justice was given by the Supreme Court.[5] It is appropriate to quote from the judgment of Lord Reed at some length:

"23. It is a general principle of our constitutional law that justice is administered by the courts in public, and is therefore open to public scrutiny. The principle is an aspect of the rule of law in a democracy...society depends on the courts to act as guardians of the rule of law...

25. The principle that courts should sit in public has important implications for the publishing of reports of court proceedings...[It] is by an application of the same principle that it has long been recognised that proceedings in open court may be reported in the press and by other methods of broadcasting in the media...

26. The connection between the principle of open justice and the reporting of court proceedings is not however merely functional. Since the rationale of the principle is that justice should be open to public scrutiny, and the media are the conduit through which most members of the public receive information about court proceedings, it follows that the principle of open justice is inextricably linked to the freedom

---

[5] *A v British Broadcasting Corporation (Scotland)* [2014] UKSC 25 – see in particular paragraphs 23-41.

of the media to report on court proceedings.

27. Since the principle of open justice is a constitutional principle to be found in the common law, it follows that it is for the courts to determine its ambit and its requirements, subject to any statutory provision. The courts therefore have an inherent jurisdiction to determine how the principle should be applied...

29. Exceptions to the principle of open justice were considered in the well-known case of Scott v Scott,[6] in which the House of Lords emphasised in the strongest terms the importance of the general principle, but also recognised that there were circumstances in which it was necessary to depart from it...

30. ...[The] issue was considered in detail in In re K (Infants)[7]... Lord Devlin noted...that the ordinary principles of a judicial inquiry included the rules that justice should be done openly, that it should be done only after a fair hearing, and that judgment should be given only upon evidence that is made known to all parties...He continued:

> *"But a principle of judicial inquiry, whether fundamental or not, is only a means to an end. If it can be shown in any particular class of case that the observance of a principle of this sort does not serve the ends of justice, it must be dismissed; otherwise it would become the master instead of the servant of justice. Obviously, the ordinary principles of judicial inquiry are requirements for all ordinary cases and it can only be in an extraordinary class of case that any one of them can be discarded. This is what was so clearly decided in Scott v Scott....That test is not easy to pass. It is not enough to show that dispensation would be convenient. It must be shown that it is a matter of necessity in order to avoid the subordination of the ends of justice to the means.""*

The importance of the principle of open justice remains as strong today as it was a century ago. The justification for the principle also remains the same. It is a "means whereby confidence in the courts can be maintained".[8] As the Supreme Court has recently noted:[9]

---

[6] [1913] UKHL 2.
[7] [1965] AC 201.
[8] *B and P v United Kingdom* [1985] UKHL 7, at paragraph 36.
[9] *PNM v Times Newspapers Ltd & Ors* [2017] UKSC 49 paragraph 13 per Lord Sumption.

> "Its significance has if anything increased in an age which attaches growing importance to the public accountability of public officers and institutions and to the availability of information about the performance of their functions."

It is the case, however, that for as long as the fundamental importance of this principle of open justice has been acknowledged, so, too, has it also been acknowledged that there are exceptions. For example, in *Scott v Scott*[10] Lord Shaw said that the principle of open justice did not apply to proceedings relating to wards of court (children). He said:

> "[their] affairs are truly private affairs; the transactions are transactions truly intra familiam; and it has long been recognized that an appeal for the protection of the Court in the case of such persons does not involve the consequence of placing in the light of publicity their truly domestic affairs."

That argument still holds good today. In 2017, giving judgment in the Supreme Court, Lord Sumption reaffirmed that:

> "The principle of open justice has, however, never been absolute. There have been highly specific historic exceptions, such as the matrimonial jurisdiction inherited from the ecclesiastical courts, the old jurisdiction in lunacy and wardship and interlocutory hearings in chambers, where private hearings had become traditional. Some of these exceptions persist. Others have been superseded by statute, notably in cases involving children. More generally, the courts have an inherent power to sit in private where it is necessary for the proper administration of justice…Traditionally, the power was exercised mainly in cases where open justice would have been no justice at all, for example because the dispute related to trade secrets or some other subject-matter which would have been destroyed by a public hearing, or where the physical or other risks to a party or a witness might make it impossible for the proceedings to be held at all. The inherent power of the courts extends to making orders for the conduct of the proceedings in a way which will prevent the disclosure in open court of the names of parties or witnesses or of other matters, and it is well established that this may be a preferable alternative to the more drastic course of sitting in private…But the court retains the power which it has always possessed to allow evidence to be given in such a way that the identity of a witness or other matters is not more widely

---

[10] [1913] UKHL 2.

disclosed in open court, if the interests of justice require it."[11]

It is clear that for many years the court has considered that cases relating to children are properly to be regarded as an extraordinary class of case such that the usual principle of open justice can be, even if not completely dispensed with, applied with less than its usual full rigour. It was because of the extraordinary nature of cases relating to children that it became the practice for hearings relating to children to take place in private (or 'in chambers' to use the technical expression).[12] Since 1991 that practice has been confirmed by rules of court.[13] Today, cases relating to children continue, normally, to be heard in private.

It is perhaps somewhat ironic that at a time when there is such public concern about the supposedly 'secret' Family Court that the Supreme Court should acknowledge that the exceptions to the rule of open justice have recently widened and their application become more frequent. As Lord Sumption noted in 2017:[14]

> *"More recently, two factors have combined to broaden the scope of the exceptions to the open justice rule and the frequency of their application. One is the growing volume of civil and criminal litigation raising issues of national security. This calls for no comment on the present appeal. The other is the recognition of a number of rights derived from the European Convention on Human Rights, which the courts as public authorities are bound by section 6 of the Human Rights Act 1998 to respect. The Convention right most often engaged in such cases is the right under article 8 to respect for private and family life. Article 8 rights are heavily qualified by the Convention itself, and even when they are made good they must be balanced in a publication case against the right to freedom of expression protected by article 10....These countervailing interests have become significant, not just because they have come to be recognised as legal rights, but because the resonance of what used to be reported only in the press and the broadcasting media has been greatly magnified in the age of the internet and social media."*

So it is that today the court must take account not only of the exceptions to the common law principle of open justice which have been identified and

---

[11] *PNM v Times Newspapers Ltd & Ors* [2017] UKSC 49 paragraph 14.
[12] See, for example, Rayden and Jackson on Divorce and Family Matters, 16th edition, Vol 1, paragraph 40.36.
[13] FPR 1991 and FPR 2010.
[14] *PNM v Times Newspapers Ltd & Ors* [2017] UKSC 49 paragraph 15.

accepted over the course of the last century, but must also take account of the exceptions derived from the European Convention on Human Rights, most notably, in cases relating to children, Articles 6, 8 and 10.

Article 8(1) provides that:

> *"Everyone has the right to respect for his private and family life, his home and his correspondence."*

'Everyone' includes children as well as adults.

It is generally accepted, even by those who seek greater transparency in the Family Court, that the identity of children involved in proceedings in the Family Court should be protected and that in any public reporting of a case relating to a child appropriate steps should be taken to ensure anonymity for the child. However, that does not mean that the media should not be entitled to attend and report hearings relating to children or that the judge should refrain from publishing his or her judgment, suitably anonymised. The rights of the media are not inherently incompatible with the rights of the child under Article 8. Indeed, the media is very well used to ensuring the protection of the identity and privacy of children when reporting criminal cases heard in the Crown Court in which children give evidence either as the victim of crime or as a witness to a crime.

It is also clear that the Convention itself does not seek to make a child's rights under Article 8(1) absolute. Those rights are subject to the qualifications set out in Article 8(2):

> *"There shall be no interference by a public authority with the exercise of this right except such as is in accordance with the law and is necessary in a democratic society in the interests of national security, public safety or the economic wellbeing of the country, for the prevention of disorder or crime, for the protection of health or morals, or for the protection of the rights and freedoms of others."*

It is now trite law that a child's rights under Article 8(1) must be balanced against the media's rights under Article 10. Article 10(1) provides that:

> *"Everyone has the right to freedom of expression. This right shall include freedom to hold opinions and to receive and impart information and ideas without interference by public authority and regardless of frontiers. This Article shall not prevent States from requiring the licensing of broadcasting, television or cinema enterprises."*

As with the rights under Article 8(1), so, too, the rights under Article 10(1) are qualified rights. Article 10(2) provides that:

> *"The exercise of these freedoms, since it carries with it duties and responsibilities, may be subject to such formalities, conditions, restrictions or penalties as are prescribed by law and are necessary in a democratic society, in the interests of national security, territorial integrity or public safety, for the prevention of disorder or crime, for the protection of health or morals, for the protection of the reputation or rights of others, for preventing the disclosure of information received in confidence, or for maintaining the authority and impartiality of the judiciary."*

There is no presumption that rights under Article 8 outweigh rights under Article 10 or vice versa. In every case where the point arises the arguments under Article 8 and Article 10 must be balanced. In 2005, in a case in the House of Lords,[15] Lord Steyn endorsed four propositions:

> *"17. ...First, neither article [8 or 10] has <u>as such</u> precedence over the other. Secondly, where the values under the two articles are in conflict, an intense focus on the comparative importance of the specific rights being claimed in the individual case is necessary. Thirdly, the justification for interfering with or restricting each right must be taken into account. Finally, the proportionality test must be applied to each. For convenience I will call this the ultimate balancing test..."* (emphasis supplied).

The following year the then President of the Family Division, Sir Mark Potter, summarised the position in this way:[16]

> *"...each Article propounds a fundamental right which there is a pressing social need to protect. Equally, each Article qualifies the right it propounds so far as it may be lawful, necessary, and proportionate to do so in order to accommodate the other. The exercise to be performed is one of parallel analysis in which the starting point is presumptive parity, in that neither Article has precedence over or trumps the other. The exercise of parallel analysis requires the court to examine the justification for interfering with each right and the issue of proportionality is to be considered in respect of each. It is not a mechanical exercise to be decided on the basis of rival generalities.*

---

[15] *In re S (A Child) (Identification: Restrictions on Publication)* [2004] UKHL 47.
[16] *Clayton v Clayton* [2006] EWCA Civ 878 at paragraph 58.

An intense focus on the comparative importance of the specific rights being claimed in the individual case is necessary before the ultimate balancing test in the terms of proportionality is carried out."

In addition to the rights set out in Articles 8 and 10, it is also necessary to have regard to the parties' rights under Article 6 of the Convention. Article 6 guarantees the right to a 'fair and public hearing'. Article 6(1) provides that:

"In the determination of his civil rights and obligations or of any criminal charge against him, everyone is entitled to a fair <u>and public hearing</u> within a reasonable time by an independent and impartial tribunal established by law. Judgment shall be pronounced publicly <u>but the press and public may be excluded from all or part of the trial in the interest of morals, public order or national security in a democratic society, where the interests of juveniles or the protection of the private life of the parties so require, or the extent strictly necessary in the opinion of the court in special circumstances where publicity would prejudice the interests of justice.</u> (emphasis supplied)."

As the underlined words indicate, the Convention acknowledges that there can be legitimate and justifiable reasons for allowing an exception to the requirement to hold a hearing in public.

The position in law is, therefore, more complex than may at first appear. It is simply not possible to contend that because open justice is a fundamental aspect of our commitment to the rule of law it inevitably follows that every court hearing must take place in public. There have always been exceptions – principled exceptions – that are not inconsistent with the importance of the general principle of open justice. As was said by Viscount Haldane L.C. in *Scott v Scott*,[17] the exceptions to the principle of open justice:

"are themselves the outcome of a yet more fundamental principle that the chief object of Courts of justice must be to secure that justice is done."

If it can be shown that in any particular case applying the principle of open justice would be likely to defeat the ends of justice, the need to ensure that justice is done overrides the principle of open justice.

Expressing the position in that way suggests that the decision about

---

[17] [1913] UKHL 2.

whether a case should be heard in open court and not in private is a decision that should be made on a case by case basis. However, it has long been accepted that there is no reason in principle why a particular class of case – for example, cases relating to children – should not routinely be heard in private unless, in any particular case, the court directs that that case should be heard in open court.

In a lecture given in 2018,[18] Baroness Hale explained the complexities involved in determining when, and if so to what extent, there should be an exception to the general principle of open justice. She said:

> *"We strive for coherence and principle across the whole legal field. So we have to ask, first, what the general principles are, and second, whether the family justice system is different from any other part of the legal system, and if so why and how.*
>
> *There are three relevant principles: First, there is the common law principle of open justice…This leads on to the second important principle, which flows from the principle of open justice. There is not much point in allowing the media into the court room if they cannot then report upon what they have seen and heard… [There] is a third principle at stake here, and that is the right to respect for private and family life, guaranteed by article 8 of the European Convention. As with article 10, this is not an absolute right."*

Notwithstanding the above analysis, it remains the case that the holding of Family Court hearings in private still leads to trenchant criticism by commentators, most notably the media, who insist that what happens in the Family Court is not justice but 'secret justice', by which is meant something less than justice. That is a significant criticism which cannot simply be ignored.

The following passage, though written by journalist Heather Brooke more than a decade ago, still represents the views of many journalists:

> *"One group…[which has] been particularly disadvantaged by the closed system are the hundreds of parents whose children have been taken away in secret care hearings. The default position for all court hearings should always be for openness…If the courts are concerned about privacy, then a judge already has the power to impose naming restrictions; there is no need for an entire branch of the justice system*

---

[18] *Openness and privacy in family proceedings*, the Sir Nicholas Wall Memorial Lecture.

> *to be hidden from public view. Public confidence in the justice system can only be assured if the courts and the evidence used in those courts are fully open to the public".*[19]

Similar views continue to be expressed by journalists. They are not alone in holding those views. Even some family judges – and in particular some senior judges – have acknowledged the need to open up the Family Court and make its workings more transparent. Whilst it is, of course, essential that appropriate and robust safeguards are in place to protect children's privacy and to ensure that the chances of them being identified are minimal, that does not mean that the restrictions currently imposed by section 12 of the Administration of Justice Act 1960[20] are either necessary or desirable. In my opinion it is no longer credible to seek to argue that open justice in the Family Court must be sacrificed on the high alter of guaranteed absolute privacy for children in order to ensure that justice is done. A more proportionate and balanced approach is required.

In passing I note, as others have pointed out many times, that it seems odd that whereas hearings in the Family Court relating to children are held in private, appeals to the Court of Appeal and to the Supreme Court in cases relating to children are held in public. Indeed, appeals to the Supreme Court are broadcast live and the recordings are available to view for 12 months after the date of the appeal hearing.[21] True it is that unlike the Family Court, the appellate courts do not normally hear oral evidence (an appeal is a review of the decision of the lower court not a rehearing) but that does not detract from the point that appellate hearings demonstrate that appeal hearings in cases relating to children can be (and normally are) heard in public. So far as I am aware, there is no research evidence which demonstrates that any appellate court hearings have led to a child being identified or to a breach of a child's privacy.

In my opinion, the reality today is that whilst there continues to be a compelling argument in favour of protecting the identity and privacy of children involved in litigation in the Family Court, it does not follow, either as a matter of logic or as a matter of practical necessity, that that means that such cases must always be heard, from start to finish, in private, or that

---

[19] *Your right to know* (2007) published by Pluto Press, London, pages 125 and 130.
[20] I shall consider section 12 of the Administration of Justice Act 1960 in detail in Chapter 4.
[21] On 14 January 2020, the Law Society Gazette reported that, speaking at an event organised by the UK association of Jewish Lawyers and Jurists, the Master of the Rolls, Sir Terence Etherington, announced that: "We are hoping to get a change to regulation which will allow us to live stream family cases in the Court of Appeal. At the moment you cannot do that at all."

media reporting of such cases should be as limited as has been the case in the past. There must be a half-way house which protects the anonymity of children whilst at the same time enabling the media to shine a light into the workings of the Family Court in order to dispel once and for all the myth that the Family Court is a 'secret' court. Only when that happens will the public see and understand how the Family Court works, gain some insight into the challenges that family judges have to deal with and be able to see for themselves the care that is taken by all those professionals working in the Family Court to try to ensure that justice is done.

The remainder of this book is largely concerned with exploring and evaluating the steps that have been taken over the last 15 years to make the Family Court more open and transparent and to consider what more, realistically, can be done to improve the situation.

3: OPEN JUSTICE IN THE FAMILY COURT

> *"Imagine a country where parents accused of child abuse are assumed guilty unless proven innocent. Where secret courts need no criminal convictions to remove their children, only the word of a medical expert, and rarely let parents call their own experts in defence. Where even parents who are vindicated on appeal cannot see their children again, because they have been adopted. And where the 'welfare of the child' is used to gag them from discussing the case ever after. I live in that country."* (Camilla Cavendish)[1]

In this chapter I shall consider the rules relating to the communication of information in Children Act proceedings and the admission of duly accredited representatives of news gathering and reporting organisations to certain hearings in the Family Court. Before I do that, it is necessary, first, to set out some of the background history.

Communication of information
As a parent involved in court proceedings relating to your child, whether public law or private law proceedings, human nature is such that you are likely to want to discuss the stressful situation you are going through with family and friends. You will need to discuss the issues with your legal team. You may want to discuss them with your doctor. You may be so concerned about the way you feel you are being treated by social workers that you want to speak to your local councillor, or your MP or perhaps even to a journalist. You may want to show them some of the court papers – for example, social work statements and expert medical reports. What is permissible?

Until 2005 the answer to that question was 'very little'. There were wide ranging restrictions on the disclosure of information relating to cases heard in the Family Court concerning children. The scale and complexity of those restrictions and the urgent need for change were highlighted by the senior judiciary. Action was needed to address this issue and was needed quickly. In December 2004 the Government published a consultation paper, *Disclosure of Information in Family Proceedings Cases Involving Children*.

---
[1] *How can this happen here?* - Camilla Cavendish, *The Times* (London) 18 May 2006.

In March 2005, whilst that consultation was still taking place, the House of Commons Constitutional Affairs Select Committee published its report, *Family Justice: the operation of the family courts revisited*.[2] One of the issues dealt with in the report concerned the unsatisfactory position relating to the disclosure of information. The report stated that:

> "154. ...the current rules relating to communication of the details of particular cases are too strict. The restrictions on communicating details of family cases to those not involved (which may apply to Members of Parliament handling constituency cases) have served to fuel the perception of bias and unfairness. Some of the evidence we received was that the lack of openness prevented proper scrutiny of the work done by family judges or court officials, and made it impossible to prove or disprove perceived unfairness."

The government took steps to bring section 62 of the Children Act 2004 into force. Section 62 made important changes to section 12 of the Administration of Justice Act 1960 and section 97(2) of the Children Act 1989.[3] In particular those changes meant, firstly, that it would no longer be a criminal offence for a party to family proceedings involving children to disclose information to other individuals or bodies so long as disclosure was not made to the general public or to any section of the general public or to the media, and, secondly, that it would no longer be a contempt of court to disclose information in the circumstances permitted by the rules.

It was expected that the outcome of the consultation would lead to a rule change in respect of disclosure of information. The results of the consultation, together with the government's response and proposals for change, were published in July 2005. The Family Proceedings Rules 1991 were amended[4] to include a completely new rule[5] which set out the circumstances in which information relating to proceedings could be disclosed without the prior permission of the court, and specified who could make that disclosure, to whom that disclosure could be made and the purpose for which that disclosure could be made. The new rule did not permit disclosure of information to be made to the media.

---

[2] *https://publications.parliament.uk/pa/cm200405/cmselect/cmconst/116/11601.htm.*
[3] I deal with section 12 of the Administration of Justice Act 1960 and section 97(2) of the Children Act 1989 in Chapter 4.
[4] See the Family Proceedings (Amendment) (No 4) Rules 2005.
[5] Rule 10.20A.

This new rule was replaced in 2009.[6] This second new rule was even more detailed and comprehensive than that introduced in 2005. However, once again the media were not included in the category of persons or bodies to whom disclosure of information could be made without the prior permission of the court. There was yet further amendment to the rule when, in April 2011, the Family Proceedings Rules 1991 were replaced by the Family Procedure Rules 2010. The position relating to the communication of information to the media remained unchanged.[7]

It remains the position today that disclosure to the media of 'information relating to proceedings held in private'[8] is a contempt of court unless the court has given express permission for that information to be disclosed. A person held to be in contempt of court can be committed to prison for a maximum of two years or be ordered to pay a fine.[9]

Transparency
The report of the House of Commons Constitutional Affairs Select Committee published in March 2005 also dealt with the issue of transparency. The report made recommendations concerning the admission of the media and the public into Family Court hearings. In particular, the committee recommended that:

> *"25. A greater degree of transparency is required in the family courts. An obvious move would be to allow the press and public into the family courts under appropriate reporting restrictions, and subject to the judge's discretion to exclude the public. Anonymised judgments should normally be delivered in public unless the judge in question specifically chooses to make an order to the contrary. This would make it possible for the public to have a more informed picture of what happens in the family courts, and would give the courts the 'open justice' which characterises our judicial system, while protecting the parties."*

It was to be another four years before any change was made. During those four years the press, and in particular *The Times*, repeatedly criticised what it asserted to be the secrecy of the Family Court. At the same time, some

---

[6] See the Family Proceedings (Amendment) (No 2) Rules 2009. In April 2011 the Family Proceedings Rules 1991 were replaced by the Family Procedure Rules 2010.
[7] The current rule relating to the communication of information is to be found in the Family Procedure Rules 2010, Part 12, Practice Direction 12G.
[8] Family Procedure Rules 2010, Rule 12.73(2).
[9] Section 14 of the Contempt of Court Act 1981. In the magistrates' court the fine is limited to £2,500 but in the higher courts there is no limit.

senior judges acknowledged that there had been miscarriages of justice and expressed concern about the increasing lack of public confidence in the Family Court.

The Times' campaign

Between May 2006 and April 2009, *The Times*' journalist Camilla Cavendish (now Baroness Cavendish of Little Venice) wrote a number of articles in which she condemned the secrecy of the Family Court and highlighted some of the injustices that were coming to light. These are just a selection of the headlines given to her articles: *Guilty until proved innocent; the grotesque reality of family courts* (17 June 2006); *Blind justice without a name* (19 October 2006); *The forces of secrecy are prevailing* (29 March 2007); *The rank hypocrisy of family court judges* (24 May 2007); *A decent family ruined. That's justice?* (21 February 2008); *The secret state that steals our children* (7 July 2008); *Your word against theirs – family justice* (9 July 2008); *A secret state is operating in which families are being torn apart – Behind the story* (20 October 2008).

It is unnecessary to go into the detail of those articles. It is, though, appropriate to note some of the key issues that caused Cavendish concern. These included, for example, her concern that the court places too much reliance on expert medical evidence some of which may later be shown to be flawed. There have been occasions when, in reliance on such evidence, children have not only been placed in the care of the local authority but have been placed with prospective adopters and made the subjects of adoption orders in favour of their new 'parents'. They will have been told that their new family is their "forever" family.

That is exactly what happened in the case of *Webster v Norfolk County Council* (the *Webster* case).[10] In 2004 three young children (referred to anonymously as A, B and C) were made the subject of care orders following a finding by the court that the parents had physically abused one of the children. The children were freed for adoption and placed with prospective adopters. Adoption orders were made. Two years later the birth parents had a fourth child, Brandon. The local authority began care proceedings. Their care of the fourth child raised no concerns. The parents were allowed to continue caring for him. The birth parents appealed against the adoption order. The appeal was dismissed. In the Court of Appeal, Lord Justice Wall said,

> "149. This is a case in which the court has to go back to first principles. Adoption is a statutory process. The law relating to it is very clear. The scope for the exercise of judicial discretion is severely curtailed.

---

[10] [2009] EWCA Civ 59.

> *Once orders for adoption have been lawfully and properly made, it is only in highly exceptional and very particular circumstances that the court will permit them to be set aside..."*

The more poignant judgment was given by Lord Justice Wilson. He said:

> *"202. Like Wall L.J., I have spent a professional life-time working in our family justice system. With reservations, I remain reasonably content with the way in which it usually operates and I am proud to have a role in it. This application, however, makes me profoundly uncomfortable. For, although the medical evidence remains by no means unanimous, there are substantial grounds for doubting whether, at a re-hearing, Norfolk would again succeed in establishing what they established on 21 May 2004, namely that the injuries suffered by child B in October/November 2003 were non-accidental. There are substantial grounds for considering, on the contrary, that they were accidental in that they were sustained in the course of normal parental handling by a child whose bones had been weakened by a particular diet productive of a gross deficiency of vitamin C (scurvy) and of iron.*
>
> *203. Yet the finding of non-accidental injury to child B was the foundation of the permanent removal from the applicants of himself and indeed of their two other children, achieved by three sets of orders, namely the care orders, the freeing orders and finally the adoption orders.*
>
> *204. Unfortunately for them, it is far too late for the applicants to bring appeals in which to press that these orders be set aside and that the applications for them be reheard. It is far too late at each of two levels. The first is the level at which the interests of the three children fall to be considered: almost four years ago they moved into alternative homes which they were told would be permanent and of which they would be full, legal members; and at that time they ceased even to see the applicants. The second is the level which demands recognition of the vast social importance of not undermining the irrevocability of adoption orders."*

This case well illustrates the point that it is only in the most exceptional of circumstances that an adoption order will be set aside. An adoption order is normally final and irreversible.

It might be thought that cases like this underline Cavendish's concerns and provide strong support in favour of greater transparency in the Family Court.

Cavendish also expressed concern that even in those cases where the judge agreed to an anonymised version of his judgment being published invariably the local authority, the social workers and the expert witnesses were not named, giving the impression of protecting those witnesses from being held accountable for their evidence and the consequences which flowed from it (which in many instances, as in the *Webster* case, included the permanent separation of a child from his or her birth parents).

Cavendish went on to express concern about the severe limitations placed on parents – as also on journalists – about what information relating to the case they are permitted to disclose to third parties and the risk they face of being committed to prison for contempt of court if they should go beyond what is permissible. She argued that parents were effectively being gagged. Worse, they were being gagged in circumstances where they faced a life sentence not, as in the criminal courts, of imprisonment but of separation from their child, their own flesh and blood.

The reference to 'a life sentence' is wholly appropriate. In 2002 Sir James Munby made the point that:[11]

> *"It must never be forgotten that, with the state's abandonment of the right to impose capital sentences, orders of the kind which this Division are typically invited to make in public law proceedings are amongst the most drastic that any judge in any jurisdiction is evere empowered to make. It is a terrible thing to say to any parent – particularly, perhaps, to a mother – that he or she is to lose their child for ever."*

Cavendish makes the point that: "The opponents of openness claim that their concern is the 'welfare of the child'". That is a fair, albeit brief, summary of the key reason most frequently advanced by those who are opposed to any further opening up of the Family Court. Cavendish counters by saying that, "the true interests of the child lie in protecting him or her from a miscarriage of justice. At the moment we are simply protecting the professionals."

I acknowledge that there is substance in all of these criticisms. The only one with which I would wish to take some issue is the first – the weight

---

[11] *Re L (Care: Assessment: Fair Trial)* [2002] EWHC 1379 (Fam) at paragraph 150.

given to expert medical evidence. Cavendish gives the impression – and this may, indeed, be her belief – that judges routinely accept the evidence of an expert witness no matter what other conflicting evidence there may be. In one article, for example, she says:

> *"'Expert' evidence almost always takes precedence over evidence from relatives and people who actually know the family."*

With respect, I do not accept that to be the case. Over the years, in cases heard and decided by senior judges, clear guidance has been given about the way the court should approach the evidence of expert witnesses. That guidance is followed by judges, up and down the land, on a daily basis. Not to follow that guidance in any particular case would be likely to lead to an appeal. The correct approach to expert medical evidence includes, for example:

(i) a requirement to consider expert evidence in the context of all of the other evidence in the case, the point having frequently been made that the court is under a duty to evaluate the totality of the evidence;[12]

(ii) an emphasis on the fact that the evidence of the parents and any other carers is of the utmost importance and that it is, therefore, essential that the court forms a clear assessment of their credibility and reliability;[13]

(iii) a reminder that judges must never forget that today's medical certainty may be discarded by the next generation of experts or that future scientific research may throw a light into corners that are at present dark; that what may be unexplained today may be perfectly well understood tomorrow.[14]

That list is illustrative, not exhaustive. Judges understand all of this and factor it into their decision-making. So, when Cavendish says that expert evidence almost always takes precedence over evidence from relatives and people who actually know the family, based on my experience as a family Circuit Judge, I believe this to be a sweeping generalisation in respect of which Cavendish has not produced any evidence in support. There are several illustrations in published judgments of occasions when an expert's evidence has not been accepted and also of occasions when experts have

---

[12] Baker J, *Re L and M (Children)* [2013] EWHC 1569 (Fam) at paragraph 50.
[13] Baker J, *Re L and M (Children)* [2013] EWHC 1569 (Fam) at paragraph 52.
[14] Baker J, *Re L and M (Children)* [2013] EWHC 1569 (Fam) at paragraph 50.

been criticised by judges – sometimes severely criticised.[15]

After that small detour, I return to Cavendish's articles. On every weekday during the week beginning Monday 7 July 2008, *The Times* published an article by Cavendish concerning the 'secret' Family Court. Monday's article ended with this paragraph:

> *"Over the next few days I hope to paint a more detailed picture of the pieces of the secret state, offer some explanations as to why mistakes are made, and to outline some solutions. The Times' interest is more than theoretical: we will continue to challenge various injunctions in the courts. But we also need your help by asking you to write to your MP. We will not give up. Because to sever a child from its family without due cause is licensed state oppression of the worst kind. It is, in fact, child abuse."*

At the beginning of Cavendish's next article, on Tuesday 8 July, she said:

> *"The Times' call to end secrecy in family courts has produced a huge reaction – except from the man who could change it"* (a reference to the then Lord Chancellor, Lord Falconer).

The articles continued for the remainder of that week.

On the Friday of that week, 11 July, *The Times* published an article by Sir Mark Potter, then the President of the Family Division of the High Court. In it he mounted what *The Times'* then legal editor, Frances Gibb, described as a "vigorous defence of the 'closed' family justice system."

Sir Mark said that Cavendish's main criticism of the judicial process, set out in her article on Monday 7 July, related:

> *"to the 'secrecy' of proceedings and that a lower standard of proof is required than in the criminal courts. The 'secrecy' is, of course, the 'privacy' that the law accords to the conduct of proceedings and the documents filed in them…Whatever the views of the media (or the*

---

[15] See, for example, the decision of Mr Justice Singer in *Re X (Non-Accidental Injury: Expert Evidence)* [2001] EWHC Fam 6, the decision of Mr Justice Hayden in *Re F (A Minor)* [2016] EWHC 2149 (Fam) and the decision of Mr Justice Keehan in *M v Derbyshire CC & Ors* [2018] EWHC 3734 (Fam). For a comprehensive list of 10 factors the court must always have in mind when dealing with a finding of fact hearing, see the judgment of Mr Justice (now Lord Justice) Baker in *Gloucestershire County Council v RH and others* [2012] EWHC 1370 (Fam) at paragraphs 36 – 47.

judiciary), the vast majority of parents and children in care cases want privacy, rather than the 'washing of dirty linen' and the exploring of deeply emotional and personal issues in public.

Here judges operate in a minefield of complexity and emotion in which they must take into account the evidence not only of professionals (whether social workers or medical experts), but of family members and, when old enough, the children themselves. Judges adopt a critical approach to the professional evidence of that of anyone advocating the removal of the child from the family, but in the end they are obliged to take a decision based on the child's [best] interests."

That special pleading cut no ice with *The Times*. Although it was technically correct to describe proceedings in the family courts as 'private' and not 'secret', *The Times* was not concerned with semantics and legal niceties but with practical realities. To the non-lawyer, it did appear that hearings in the Family Court were being held in secret. In light of the rules relating to the communication of information, which I dealt with earlier, it is difficult to disagree with Cavendish's concern that parents were effectively being gagged. *The Times*' campaign continued.

In an article the following week, Cavendish said that she was "awed by the response" to *The Times*' campaign. She reported that:

"So many readers have e-mailed their MPs that I am getting calls from all three main parties. Several MPs have also raised their private concerns about how their own local authorities behave. It is uplifting to see democracy in action."

In an article published in *The Times* on 28 April 2009 the headline read: "At last, we go behind the closed doors". Cavendish began her article by saying:

"Yesterday morning I finally walked through a door that used to be marked 'keep out'."

For her investigative work on this subject, Cavendish won the 2008 Paul Foot award for journalism. She also won the Campaign of the Year at the 2009 British Press Awards. Both awards were well earned. And yet two other articles in *The Times* in April 2009 gave the impression – correctly as it turned out – that the battle was not won. Both were published on 10 April 2009. In one, Cavendish notes that:

"The detail of the Ministry of Justice reforms, published this week,

makes clear for the first time that although the family courts will be opened to the press on April 27, they will not be quite as open as we had expected."

The headline to the other article, by Frances Gibb, then the Legal Editor for *The Times*, was blunter. She said:

"Openness of family courts is a 'con trick'"

The campaign waged by *The Times* and Camilla Cavendish did not fully succeed in its primary objective which was, through the media, to open up the Family Court so that the public could be informed about what goes on there. That objective has still not been fully met.

Judicial concerns

As I noted earlier, some senior judges shared the concerns that lay at the heart of *The Times'* campaign. One voice stands out. In a judgment given in 2004,[16] Sir James Munby said:

"97. ...of great importance, as it seems to me, in the present context, is what I have referred to as the public interest in maintaining the confidence of the public at large in the courts. Article 6[17] is intended, amongst other things, to promote the confidence in the judicial process. This is a point that has repeatedly been stressed by the Strasbourg court. In Prager and Oberschlick v Austria[18]... the court said:

"Regard must...be had to the special role of the judiciary in society. As the guarantor of justice, a fundamental value in a law-governed State, it must enjoy public confidence if it is to be successful in carrying out its duties."

99. There are many voices raised in this debate, and they often stand in stark conflict. Parents – like the mother in the present case – often want to speak out publicly...In my judgment, the workings of the family justice system and, very importantly, the views about the system of the mothers and fathers caught up in it, are "matters of public interest which can and should be discussed publicly"[19]...Many

---

[16] *Re B (A Child)* [2004] EWHC 411 (Fam).
[17] This is a reference to the right to a fair trial set out in Article 6 of the European Convention on Human Rights.
[18] (1996) 21 EHRR 1 at paragraph 34.
[19] Quotation from the judgment of Lord Justice Balcombe in *Re W (Wardship: Discharge: Publicity)* [1995] 2 FLR 466 at page 474.

of the issues litigated in the family justice system require open and public debate in the media...I repeat what I said in Harris v Harris, Attorney General v Harris [2001] 2 FLR 895 at paras [360]-[389] about the importance in a free society of parents who feel aggrieved at their experiences of the family justice system being able to express their views publicly about what they conceive to be failings on the part of individual judges or failings in the judicial system. As Lord Steyn pointed out in R v Secretary of State for the Home Department ex p Simms [2000] 2 AC 115 at p 126,

> *'freedom of speech is the lifeblood of democracy. The free flow of information and ideas informs political debate. ... It facilitates the exposure of errors in the governance and administration of justice of the country.'"*

The following year, in October 2005, Sir James delivered a lecture at the Jordan's Family Law Conference. He outlined all of the restrictions on the reporting of family proceedings noting that the intention of these restrictions was to impose a 'curtain of privacy' intended to protect the child. He set out the reasons said to justify that approach. He makes this key point:

> *"There is much wrong with our system and the time has come for us to recognise that fact and to face up to it honestly. If we do not we risk forfeiting public confidence. The newspapers – and I mean newspapers generally for this is a theme taken up with increasing emphasis by all sectors of the press – make uncomfortable reading for us. They suggest that confidence is already ebbing away. We ignore the media at our peril. We delude ourselves if we dismiss the views of journalists as unrepresentative of public opinion or as representative only of sectors of public opinion we think we can ignore. Responsible voices are raised in condemnation of our system. We need to take note. We need to act. And we need to act now."*

He also expressed the point – a very important point – that:

> *"where the State is seeking to exercise such drastic powers as are engaged when it seeks a full care order or a freeing order, it might be thought that the arguments in favour of publicity – in favour of openness, public scrutiny and public accountability – are particularly compelling."*

He said that the failure to be sufficiently open to public scrutiny:

"feeds into and fuels another problem: that misunderstandings about how the family justice system operates are allowed to grow and fester unchecked and uncorrected."

In May 2006, Sir James gave evidence to the House of Commons Constitutional Affairs Select Committee which was again considering the issue of transparency. He said:

"...when I first became a judge of the division I was an outsider. I had not spent the whole of my professional life at the family bar. I had done a certain amount of family work but much of my professional life had been spent in other divisions where the rule of open justice prevailed. Perhaps for that reason I have always had a slightly more sceptical view of this than those who have spent their entire professional lives steeped in the system. I have come over the years since I began to sit firmly to the view that the balance that is currently held between the confidentiality and privacy interests of the parties and the public interest in open justice is badly skewed in the sense that the arguments in favour of confidentiality and privacy have left what I believe to be a very serious diminution of public confidence in the system. It seems to me that something has got to be done to restore confidence in the system...My own view – and I speak purely personally...is that any advantages that can be gained in terms of the confidentiality and privacy of proceedings are outweighed, and I believe heavily outweighed, by the constantly eroding damage to public confidence in the system...So far as public law care proceedings are concerned, it seems to me...indefensible for such proceedings to be heard in private. They are proceedings where the state is seeking take away somebody's child...I have to say it seems to me to be quite indefensible that there should be no access by the media and no access by the public to what is going on in courts where judges are day-by-day taking people's children away."

Speaking for myself, as a family judge I find it difficult if not impossible to disagree with any of those sentiments. Those points were made out of court. Sir James made the same points in court that same year. He said:[20]

"166. ...In my view the public generally, and not just the professional readers of the law reports or similar publications, have a legitimate – indeed a compelling – interest in knowing how the family courts exercise their care jurisdiction. Moreover, if leave [to publish

---

[20] *London Borough of Barnett v Y and Z* [2006] EWCC 1 (Fam).

> *a judgment] is confined in practice to those cases which are, for some reason, thought to be worthy of reporting in a law report, the sample of cases which will ever come to public attention is not merely very small but also very unrepresentative.*
>
> *167. My own view, and I make no bones about this, is that, subject of course to appropriate anonymisation, the presumption ought to be that leave should be given to publish any judgment in any care case, irrespective of whether the judgment has any particular interest for law reporters, lawyers or other professionals. It should not be necessary to show that there is some particular reason to justify why leave should be given in the particular case, let alone any need to justify leave on the basis that the judgment deals with some supposedly interesting point of law, practice or principle. For my own part, I should have thought that the proper approach ought to [be] the other way round. It is not so much for those who seek leave to publish an anonymised judgment to justify their request; surely it is for those who resist such leave to demonstrate some good reason why the judgment should not be published even in a suitably anonymised form."*

It has long been the convention that judges do not discuss the detail of their judgments outside the confines of the court room. They do not seek either to explain or justify their decisions to the public at large save to the extent that in some cases they give permission for their detailed, reasoned judgments (prepared primarily for the benefit of the parties themselves) to be published and thereby made public. As Sir James pointed out in the *Webster* case, this long-established rule of confidentiality has the unfortunate consequence that where a judgment is not published this:

> *"facilitates the dissemination of false and tendentious accounts of proceedings in family courts, which in turn tends to further undermine public confidence in the system."*[21]

He also made the point that:

> *"87. ...in a case where the parents allege that they are the victims of a miscarriage of justice, it is more than usually important that the truth – the full truth – should out. If, as the parents allege, they have lost three children and stand at risk of losing a fourth due to deficiencies in the system, then there is a pressing need for the true*

---

[21] *Norfolk County Council v Webster* [2006] EWHC 2898 (Fam) at paragraph 105.

facts to be exposed.'[22]

Lest it should be thought that Sir James was fighting a one-man crusade, that was not the case. During those same years, Lord Justice Wall was also expressing similar concerns. For example, in a lecture given in 2006,[23] he said that:

> "...*my simple and fundamental point is that if the family justice system is to shake off the canard of 'secret justice', there is only one way to do it; and that is to admit the press into the courtroom. In my judgment, this is what we should do. But plainly we need to have clear rules about what the press can, and cannot report, and in particular we need to have clear rules about anonymity and confidentiality.*
>
> *The balance which has to be struck, it seems to me, is clear. On the one side, there is the undoubted need to protect family privacy and to encourage frankness. On the other is the need to have a system which is understood by, and accountable to, the public. Speaking for myself, I see no reason why the tension between the need for a media presence and the need to respect privacy and confidentiality cannot be satisfactorily resolved...*
>
> *I am persuaded that the time has come to open up the family courts to the Press. Judgments should routinely be given in open court in anonymised form. Judges should prepare and use press releases in controversial cases, so that the public can understand the reasons for the decisions they have reached. There should be ongoing dialogue with the press and the media generally about family justice and how it is administered. We, the judiciary and the practitioners have nothing to fear from public scrutiny: indeed, we should welcome it."*

Government consultations
The general view was that any steps taken towards opening up the Family Court were steps that would have to be taken by Government. It quickly became clear that this was an issue that the Government was struggling with. In broad terms, there appeared to be two possible ways forward. The first was to let more people come into the Family Court to observe what goes on. The second was to get more information out of the Family Court so that

---

[22] Writer and journalist, John Sweeney, subsequently made five documentaries for the BBC concerning the *Webster* case. See his account of the case at *http://news.bbc.co.uk/1/hi/programmes/panorama/6254354.stm*.
[23] *Opening up the Family courts: a personal view* – Association of Lawyers for Children annual lecture in memory of Allan Levy QC and David Hershman QC, 29 June 2006.

people could read about what goes on. In essence, these were the proposals that were the subject of the Government consultations to which I referred earlier. Perhaps one of the most remarkable features of these consultations was the apparent ease and speed with which the Government changed its mind – not once, but twice.

The first consultation was published in July 2006 under the title '*Confidence and confidentiality: Improving transparency and privacy in family courts*'. The consultation paper acknowledged both the need for public confidence in the Family Court and the need to maintain confidentiality for those families whose cases come before the Family Court. The challenge was to balance confidence and confidentiality. Of the eight proposals for change, one in particular was clearly the centrepiece:

> "*Allow the media, on behalf of and for the benefit of the public, to attend proceedings as of right, though allowing the court to exclude them when appropriate to do so and, where appropriate, to place restrictions on reporting of evidence.*"

The requirement 'to place restrictions on reporting of evidence' seems a little strange. There was already a statutory restriction on the reporting of evidence contained in section 12 of the Administration of Justice Act 1960 which made 'the publication of information relating to proceedings in private' a contempt of court. Was the Government considering amending – or perhaps even repealing – section 12? There was no suggestion of such a radical step in the consultation paper.

The Government set out its revised proposals in a response to the consultation published in March 2007. Its proposals did not command universal support. As a result, the Government came to the conclusion that the original proposals could not be pursued. Under the heading 'Conclusion and Next Steps' the response document said:

> (1) *The proposals in Confidence and Confidentiality were a genuine attempt to make the family courts more open, and still continue to protect the privacy of those families involved in family proceedings.*
>
> (2) *While some of the proposals received strong support, others raised concerns amongst large sections of stakeholders, including children and young people. We have considered the responses to this consultation very carefully and we will be bringing forward our proposals in due course.*

Those proposals were set out in a second consultation paper, '*Confidence and confidentiality: Openness in family courts – a new approach*'. This was published in June 2007. In his foreword to this consultation the then Lord Chancellor, Lord Falconer, said:

> *"We have decided not to proceed with proposals to allow the media in to family courts as of right. I understand that this will disappoint some people – especially media organisations themselves. But I believe it is the right decision...*
>
> *We have listened to what people said in response to our original proposals. We have carefully considered the responses. And we have changed our mind. I believe that in this case with the welfare of children at stake, that this is clearly the right thing to do."*

The new proposal was to focus on improving the openness of family courts not by counting the numbers or types of people going *in* to the courts, but by the amount and quality of information coming *out* of the courts. How was this to be achieved? The paper was light on detail. It proposed to:

(a) provide better information to people involved in family proceedings and to the public;

(b) pilot the provision of information to families through making either the judgment of a family court decision or a brief summary of that decision available;

(c) change the rules about disclosure of information relating to proceedings.

As for the media, it was now proposed to 'provide for the media not to attend family court proceedings as of right, but to apply to attend on a case by case basis'.

This last proposal was, frankly, absurd. Unlike criminal proceedings, no adequate or meaningful public notice is given of the cases coming before the Family Court. That has been considered necessary in order to maintain privacy and confidentiality. However, in the absence of that information how were the media to be expected to know when a case was about to come before the court which would be newsworthy? Was it expected that they would take pot luck by coming to court on a daily basis and ask for permission to sit in? If that was the expectation, was any serious thought given to whether the media had the resources to operate in that way? I don't think so. This proposal came perilously close to keeping the media out of the family courts altogether. This was more than the 'change of mind' referred to by the Lord Chancellor. It was a step almost guaranteed to ensure that the Family Court would continue to be perceived as a secret court. Had that proposal been implemented – and fortunately it was not – the trenchant criticisms of Camilla Cavendish and other journalists would inevitably have continued. That proposal was not a step forward. It was a step backwards.

The final Government publication to which reference must be made is *Family Justice in View*. This was a response to the second consultation published in December 2008, 18 months after the publication of the consultation paper. By now, Jack Straw had replaced Lord Falconer as Lord Chancellor and Secretary of State for Justice. In the foreword to this document, Jack Straw and Bridget Prentice MP (Minister for Family Justice) repeated the Government's commitment to keep confidence and confidentiality in balance. They said that the Government had decided to merge the two sets of proposals set out in the earlier consultation papers. The result would be that:

> *"The media will be allowed to attend family proceedings, but the court will have the power to restrict both attendance and what can be reported. We will increase and improve the quality of the information being made available. We will ensure a child cannot be identified, even after the conclusion of a case. And we will allow those involved in proceedings to share information to get help and support they need."*

Again, there is reference to giving the court power 'to restrict … what can be reported' but no reference to section 12 of the Administration of Justice Act 1960. Indeed, the only time that Act was referred to during the course of these consultations was in the second consultation paper published in June 2007. Even then there was no reference to the impact section 12 would have on any reporters who took advantage of the newly won right to attend hearings in the family courts. Surprisingly, the media appears not to have picked this up. I say 'surprisingly' because *The Times* has ready access to expert legal advice and one might have expected that this was an issue that would have been picked up before *The Times* became too enthusiastic about the Government's proposal to change the rules.

It was left to Mr Justice McFarlane (later to become President of the Family Division) to highlight the point. In his Key Note Address to the *Resolution National Conference* in March 2009, referring to Cavendish's articles, he said that:

> *"The impression given by these articles is that, from April the press will be able to attend and freely report upon family court proceedings, and parents will be at liberty to discuss their case before a wide public audience. This view seems to be widely shared by the media in general with the result that from an early stage after the Lord Chancellor's announcement, court offices have been receiving calls from journalists seeking information about any newsworthy family cases that are due for hearing after the beginning of April...*
>
> *With regard to 'reporting restrictions' the MOJ statement points out that there are at least 10 current statutes that set out what the media may or may not report in different types of proceedings. In due course the aim is to revise the law so as to make reporting restrictions consistent across all tiers of court for all types of proceeding, and to do so in a manner which would simplify the legislation so that it is readily accessible and easily understood. Whilst the MOJ commit themselves to undertake this revision of the statute law on reporting restrictions 'as soon as parliamentary time allows', it is plain that that is not going to happen prior to April and that therefore the current law on reporting restrictions will remain in force and un-amended to accommodate the insertion of the media into the courtroom."*

Ten years on and the promised revision of statute law on reporting restrictions has still not come to pass. We therefore have to interpret a modern rule, which came into force ten years ago, in the light of a very old statute, which came into force almost 60 years ago.

The 2009 rule change – media attendance at hearings in the Family Court

It was not until 27 April 2009 that new rules came into force which permitted accredited representatives of news gathering and reporting organisations into the Family Court (Rule 10.28) without obtaining prior permission either from the parties or from the court.

Although that was the default position, Rule 10.28 provided that at any stage of the proceedings the court may direct that any media representative shall not attend the proceedings or any part of them. Before the judge may make such an order he or she must first be satisfied that it is necessary,

- in the interests of any child concerned in, or connected with, the proceedings; or

- for the safety or protection of a party, a witness in the proceedings, or a person connected with such a party or witness; or

- for the orderly conduct of the proceedings; or

- if the judge is of the opinion that if a media representative is present in court justice will be impeded or prejudiced.

The question that arises now is a very simple question: has the rule change introduced in April 2009 achieved its objective of improving transparency in the Family Court? That is the question to which we must now turn.

4: OPENING UP THE FAMILY COURT

"The aim of media attendance is that family justice is not only done, but seen to be done. This open and visible justice aims to ensure accountability through professional and public scrutiny of the decisions of the court and increase public confidence in the way the Family Court works."[1]

If the above statement correctly sets out the aims of allowing media attendance at some hearings in the Family Court then it is clear that those aims have not been fully met. The study of the impact of changes to court rules governing media attendance in family proceedings, published by the Ministry of Justice in January 2010, was based in part on an online questionnaire completed by family court managers. Almost 75% of those who responded were not aware of an accredited media representative ever having attended a hearing in their court. In the ten years between the rule change and my retirement I can only recall a journalist coming into my court on one occasion. A survey of more than 50 family Circuit Judges[2] indicates that my experience is common.

One of the consequences of journalists not coming to court on a regular basis is that court staff are often taken by surprise when a journalist does attend and uncertain what to do. Some are uncertain whether to allow the journalists into the court room at all. I have heard from several different sources of occasions when journalists have initially been told they are not allowed to go into court.

In my opinion, the rule change allowing accredited journalists to attend hearings in the Family Court has contributed little to the objective of improving transparency in the Family Court. That is also the view of the journalists I have spoken to. Neither has it led to any real improvement in public confidence in the Family Court.

---

[1] *A study of the impact of changes to court rules governing media attendance in family proceedings* – Summary of responses to stakeholder feedback, published by the Ministry of Justice, January 2010.

[2] I conducted the survey in the summer of 2019. I deal with the results in more detail in Chapter 7.

The Ministry of Justice report suggests that the reason for the very low take-up by journalists of their right to attend hearings in the Family Court is 'because of the lack of interest from the media'. I do not accept that to be the case. There are at least five main reasons why the media have not taken up this opportunity to attend Family Court hearings more frequently.

First, journalists are fearful of the consequences of publishing a story relating to the Family Court. Mark Hanna[3] makes the point, with some force, that one of the key reasons why journalists do not go into the Family Court is that, in the light of section 12 of the Administration of Justice Act 1960, there is great uncertainty amongst journalists about what (if anything) they can lawfully publish when they leave court and great fear about the risk of getting it wrong and being fined or even committed to prison for contempt of court.[4] They are also concerned about the risk of publishing something which might be regarded as irresponsible.

Second, when journalists attend a hearing in the Family Court they are uncertain at the beginning of the hearing whether they will be able to publish a story at the conclusion of the hearing. There is a risk, for many journalists and editors an unacceptable risk, of a journalist spending hours (or even days) sitting in the Family Court with nothing to show for his or her efforts because the judge's judgment is not published and the judge does not lift the automatic reporting restrictions. This problem was articulated very clearly by Louise Tickle when I interviewed her. She asked, rhetorically, "why would you, as an editor, send a journalist to any event where they wouldn't be able to report on it? It makes absolutely zero sense, even in a media world where the streets were running with gold." It is clear, certainly at regional level, that the streets are not running with gold – quite the reverse. Another journalist, Emily Dugan, made a similar point. She said that the biggest problem with journalists attending the Family Court is that "you go into court and then you discover there isn't an awful lot you can write. For

---

[3] Senior University Teacher, Department of Journalism Studies, Sheffield University, co-author of *McNae's Essential Law for Journalists* and Chair of the NCTJ Media Law Examinations Board.
[4] The last editor to be committed to prison for contempt of court was Silvester Bolam in 1949. He was committed to prison for contempt for publishing a story describing the defendant in a murder trial as 'a murderer' whilst the trial was still in progress.

resource strapped media that is not really a very viable way of working."[5]

Third, is the lack of journalistic resources. Just over 50 years ago, Lord Denning wrote what to our twenty-first century eyes appears to be a rather quaint account of court reporting in his day. He said:

> *"A newspaper reporter is in every court. He sits through the dullest cases in the Court of Appeal and the most trivial cases before the magistrates. He says nothing but writes a lot. He notes all that goes on and makes a fair and accurate report of it. He supplies it for use either in the national press or in the local press according to the public interest it commands. He is, I verily believe, the watchdog of justice."*[6]

Another of the journalists I spoke to was Brian Farmer of PA Media (formerly the Press Association). Farmer is based at the Royal Courts of Justice in London. Asked for his opinion why, ten years after the amendment to the rules which permitted journalists to attend most hearings in the Family Court, so few journalists take advantage of this entitlement, Farmer said that:

> *"The change has coincided with a decline in the newspaper industry, especially the local newspaper industry. Editors have had to think about covering a type of court which was never on the menu before at a time when newspapers have fewer and fewer reporters. I started my career on The Westmorland Gazette, a weekly newspaper in Kendal, Cumbria, in 1982. We had seven or eight reporters, a news editor, two sub-editors, three photographers, and an editor. We had enough staff to cover every magistrates' court, Carlisle Crown Court, inquests, county court, council meetings. No doubt we'd have grappled with family courts too if they had been available. There was also enough slack to let a reporter spend a day or two looking for stories. The last time I checked the paper had two reporters and one photographer. I daresay the 2019 Westmorland Gazette struggles to cover Kendal magistrates' court let alone a family court."*

---

[5] The case of *R v Sarker* [2018] EWCA Crim 1341, though it concerns a criminal case, illustrates the point. The trial judge made a reporting restrictions order on the application of the Defendant. The BBC applied for the order to be discharged. Allowing the BBC's application the Lord Chief Justice, Lord Burnett, made the point that:

> "25. ...The reality is that most local newspapers, for decades the mainstay of reporting the work of our courts, will be unable to justify the cost of applying to discharge or appealing a reporting restriction order. One need only look through the names of the appellants in this type of cases to see the rarity of appeals by local media."

[6] *The Road to Justice*, Lord Denning, Stevens & Sons, 1955 at page 64.

That graphically explains the problem.

Fourth, there is the problem of lack of prior knowledge of the cases the court deals with from day to day. Before any editor can commit dwindling journalistic resources to covering cases proceeding in the Family Court, he or she needs to know something about the cases that are to be heard. In some courts, the Crown Court for example, the list of cases to be heard on any particular day is published the previous working day. Even in the Court of Protection some advance indication is given of the nature of the cases listed. In the *Court of Protection: Transparency Pilot*, which ran until August 2017, a paper was published under the title: *Court of Protection: Transparency Pilot – Cause list descriptors (19 January 2016)*[7] which gave detailed guidance on the preparation of a daily court list.

In June 2017, a Note from the Vice President of the Court of Protection acknowledged that:

> *"It is recognised that it is important that cases are appropriately described when they are listed to provide information to the public at large of what they are about and when and where they will be heard. Comment on how this should be and is being done is welcomed. As is more general comment on how the public and the media can make themselves aware, or should be made aware, that certain types of case are due to be heard and a Pilot Order has been made in them."*

The same sentiments could equally be expressed in relation to cause lists in the Family Court. That still does not happen. Lists are not published in advance. A notice is published on a noticeboard at court each morning listing the cases that are to be heard that day. The cases will normally be listed in anonymised form – for example, *A v B*. The nature of each of the cases listed will not be provided. A journalist will not know, therefore, whether any of the cases listed are likely to be newsworthy.

For the regional media there is a fifth reason why the rule change in April 2009 did not achieve much. In public law proceedings, if a published judgment does not name the local authority concerned then publication of the story in a local newspaper would give a very broad hint that the local authority concerned (and therefore also the family) were local to the area covered by that newspaper. There is concern that that may be held to be a contempt (though I am not aware of any regional newspaper that has found itself in that difficulty).

---

[7] *https://www.judiciary.uk/publications/transparency-pilot-court-of-protection/.*

Having outlined the five reasons why the rule change in April 2009 has achieved so little, I can say with absolute confidence that lack of interest is not a reason why the media do not more regularly send journalists along to the Family Court.

Section 12 of the Administration of Justice Act 1960

Fear of contempt proceedings and concern that time spent in court may be wholly unproductive from a journalist's perspective, both have their origins in section 12 of the Administration of Justice Act 1960. That Act came into force almost 60 years ago on 27 October 1960. Between 1991 and 2014 the section has been amended on six occasions. So far as is relevant to my analysis, section 12 now provides that:

> *Publication of information relating to proceedings in private.*
>
> *(1) The publication of information relating to proceedings before any court sitting in private shall not of itself be contempt of court except in the following cases, that is to say –*
>
> *(a) where the proceedings –*
>
> *(i) relate to the exercise of the inherent jurisdiction of the High Court with respect to minors;*
>
> *(ii) are brought under the Children Act 1989 or the Adoption and Children Act 2002; or*
>
> *(iii) otherwise relate wholly or mainly to the maintenance or upbringing of a minor...*
>
> *(e) where the court (having power to do so) expressly prohibits the publication of all information relating to the proceedings or of information of the description which is published.*
>
> *(2) Without prejudice to the foregoing subsection, the publication of the text or a summary of the whole or part of an order made by a court sitting in private shall not of itself be contempt of court except where the court (having power to do so) expressly prohibits the publication...*
>
> *(4) Nothing in this section shall be construed as implying that any publication is punishable as contempt of court which would not be so punishable apart from this section.*

It is interesting to note that whereas today the media would be glad to see the repeal of section 12, in 1960, when the Administration of Justice Bill made its way through Parliament, the media were amongst its greatest supporters. The reason why they were such strong supporters of the Bill would appear to be because, in 1960, the media thought that the effect of section 12 would be to make it *less* likely that a journalist could accidentally fall foul of the contempt laws. Today, the opposite is the case. Today, the media fear, with good reason in my opinion, that section 12 makes it *more* likely that a journalist could accidentally fall foul of the contempt laws.

In a judgment given by Sir James Munby in 2004[8] he considered what can and what cannot be published in order to be compliant with section 12. His judgment highlights the complexity of section 12. He says:

> *"84. Since it is apparent that there is still widespread misunderstanding as to the precise ambit of section 12 it may be helpful if I attempt to summarise the learning. In doing so I wish to emphasise that what follows is not to be treated as if it were a statutory formulation – it is not – nor as a substitute for applying the words of section 12 itself. Moreover, any attempt to summarise an extensive and subtle jurisprudence will inevitably suffer from the inherent difficulties and defects of the exercise. There is no substitute for a careful study of the reported cases. That said, I hope that what follows may provide some practical assistance to those, unfamiliar with all the nuances of the jurisprudence, who may lack the time or opportunity to study the case-law."*

The contemporary contexts – 1960 and 2020 contrasted
In order to put this rather old piece of legislation into its historical context it is helpful to consider the Hansard[9] report of the second reading of the Bill on 1 July 1960. The debate was opened by the Solicitor General, Sir Jocelyn Simon:[10]

> *"…The Bill makes great improvements in the administration of our criminal law, and I think that it will be generally agreed that those improvements are of wide public importance. With one odd excep-*

---

[8] *Re B (A Child)* [2004] EWHC 411 (Fam).
[9] Hansard is an edited verbatim record of what was said in Parliament. It also includes records of votes and written ministerial statements. The report is published daily covering the preceding day, and is followed later by a bound final version.
[10] Sir Jocelyn Simon was later to become the President of the Probate, Divorce and Admiralty Division of the High Court (affectionately known as the Division for Wills, Wives and Wrecks). In 1971, this became the Family Division of the High Court.

tion, this Measure has been warmly and generously welcomed by the organs of enlightened opinion. In fact, I think that it was only the leader writer of The Times, with bees buzzing in his bonnet and bile swilling round his heart, who called it "an unsatisfactory Bill." In fact, he sourly said that it was a case where no bread at all might be better than the half loaf offered.

It seemed to me that that opinion stood in striking contrast to the reactions of the rest of the Press. For example, The Guardian spoke of the Bill as ...replete with liberal provisions relating to the criminal law. The News Chronicle said that it is ...the most valuable reform which will come before Parliament this session...a measure which strengthens the freedom of the individual and further entrenches the rights of the accused. The comment of the rest of the Press was to similar effect..."

I doubt there are any elements of the press which would subscribe to those views today. The Solicitor General continued:

"I present this Bill to the House. It falls into three main parts...

The second part deals with the law and procedure relating to contempt of court. That is a subject of vital interest to the Press and, therefore, to the public at large, which depends on the Press for the information necessary for the formation of opinion and thus the influencing of the conduct of national affairs...

...The common law has always taken a stern view of contempt of court. It has always been the law that a person who publishes matter that tends to prejudice pending proceedings commits contempt of court. He cannot escape liability by showing that he did not know that proceedings were pending, nor could the distributor of the matter be heard to say that he was ignorant of its contents. That has always been the law, but the sternness of these rules was, I think, forgotten until they were brought to light in two recent cases.

In one case it was held that a newspaper reporter would have been liable even if, as he alleged, he was not only ignorant of the fact that proceedings were pending but had taken all reasonable steps to find out whether or not they were pending. In the second case, the distributors of a foreign periodical were held liable although it would not have been reasonably practicable for them to have scrutinised every edition of the periodical to satisfy themselves that no contempt was committed."

It is appropriate to note that the mischief that concerned the Government in 1960 related to comments made by the press in respect of "pending proceedings". One of the main concerns about section 12 today is that, in children's cases, its reach extends beyond proceedings which are "pending" but continues after the proceedings have been concluded.

The Solicitor General continued:

> *"The law has been strongly criticised in both these respects – and not only by the Press itself, which of course has an interest in the matter. It has also been subject to adverse scrutiny by the organisation known as "Justice", which in recent years has made more than one valuable contribution towards the maintenance and improvement of the Rule of Law in this country and abroad. We are satisfied that the law as I have ventured to set it out to the House is too harsh. The common law on the subject was formulated at a time when there were no newspapers as we know them today, and when the publication and distribution of printed matter were very different from what they are now. We think that the law must be changed to accord with contemporary conditions."*

That last sentence is very important. What was "contemporary" in 1960 is no longer "contemporary" in 2020. Over the last 60 years, across all domains of daily life, society has changed considerably. That is reflected in the development of family law and in the work of the Family Court. A brief consideration of just two areas of family law emphasises the vast changes between contemporary society today and in 1960.

It was in the second half of the twentieth century that the medical profession and the NSPCC raised concerns about the issue of child abuse. The label "battered baby syndrome"[11] came to be used following work undertaken by paediatricians in the USA and orthopaedic surgeons in the UK.

The systems for child protection that are in place today are far more sophisticated than those in place in 1960. Over the last 60 years our approach to

---

[11] *The battered child syndrome* by Kempe, C H, Silverman, F N, Steel, B F, Droegmuller, W and Silver, H K (1962/1985) published in 'Child Abuse and Neglect', vol 9, pages 167 – 187; and *Multiple epiphyseal injuries to babies*, Griffiths, D and Moynihan, F J (1963) published in the British Medical Journal, vol 11, pages 1558-1561. Both of these references are taken from *Learning from Baby P – The politics of blame, fear and denial*, Shoesmith, S (2016), Jessica Kingsley Publishers, London at page 50.

child protection has been refined by the learning that has come from public enquiries following an all-too long list of children who have died at the hands of their carers – from Maria Colwell (1973) to Ellie Butler (2013) – and from public inquiries into serious system failures in child protection – from the Cleveland Inquiry (1988) to the Independent Inquiry into Child Sexual Abuse in Rotherham (2013).

In 1960 the Children Act 1948 was still in force. The preamble to the Act says that it is:

> *"An Act to make further provision for the care or welfare up to the age of eighteen and, in certain cases, for further periods, for boys and girls when they are without parents or have been lost or abandoned by, or are living away from, their parents, or when their parents are unfit or unable to take care of them, and in certain other circumstances…"*

The provision of care for a child under the Children Act 1948 rarely included the making of a care order by a court. Children were cared for by a local authority pursuant to a resolution made by that local authority. The court was not involved. The local authority did not need the consent of a parent to pass such a resolution but were required to give notice of the resolution to the parents. The parents were entitled to serve a notice upon the local authority objecting to the resolution. The resolution lapsed 14 days thereafter unless the local authority made a complaint in the juvenile court. The juvenile court had the power to order that the resolution should not lapse.

Fast forward 60 years. Today, a local authority cannot remove a child from the care of unwilling parents without an order of the court. The parents have the right to be heard. They have the right to be represented. They are entitled to free state funding for legal representation. The child will have his or her own voice by the tandem representation of Children's Guardian and solicitor. The actions of the local authority are open to rigorous scrutiny by the court. The burden of proving facts relied upon by the local authority in support of its case rests upon the local authority. The decision of the court can be appealed. It is a system that endeavours to be scrupulously fair and child focussed. It is a system in which the best interests of the child's welfare are paramount.

Adoption is another area in which the law has changed dramatically over the last 60 years, reflecting significant changes in society and societal attitudes. Cretney captures these changes well.[12] He says that the Adoption of Children Act 1926:

> *"created the institution of legal adoption in this country. For many years thereafter adoption under the Act was used primarily in the case of babies (usually illegitimate) placed with childless families who would thenceforth care for the child as if it had been born to the husband and wife, and in 1949 the Adoption Act accepted the principle that the law should treat the child as legally the child of the adoptive parents. Adoption became very popular: in 1968 the number of adoption orders made rose to a peak of 24,831...The last quarter of the century was a period of dramatic change in the perception of adoption. The ready availability of contraception and legal abortion meant that very few healthy babies born in this country, were available for adoption. Adoption accordingly ceased to be primarily concerned with babies...adoption became much more concerned with the provision of long-term care for children who had been in local authority care."*[13]

Since December 2005[14] adoption applications can be made by a married couple,[15] two people who are civil partners of each other and two people (whether of different sexes or the same sex) who are "living as partners in an enduring family relationship"[16] or on the application of a single person aged over 21.[17] In 2018, 3,820 children ceased to be looked after by local authorities as a result of being adopted, down from a peak of 5,360 adoptions of looked after children in 2015.

These two developments alone demonstrate clearly that the legal and social context in which we live today is light years away from the legal and social context in which the Administration of Justice Act 1960 was passed. To these one might also want to add the changes brought about by the revolution in forms of communication, not least the internet and social media.[18]

The Solicitor General continued:

---

[12] *Family Law in the Twentieth Century: A History*, Stephen Cretney, (2003), Oxford University Press, Chapter 17.
[13] Ibid pages 595-596. The practice of placing looked after children for adoption is controversial. It is invariably referred to by some as 'forced adoption'.
[14] When the Adoption and Children Act 2002 came into force.
[15] As a result of the Marriage (Same Sex Couples) Act 2013 'married couple' includes a same sex married couple.
[16] See sections 50 and 144(4) of the Adoption and Children Act 2002.
[17] Section 51 of the 2002 Act.
[18] I deal with issues relating to the internet and social media in Chapter 10.

"The House will, however, appreciate that it is necessary in this matter to strike a balance between the legitimate demands of a free Press on the one hand and the requirements of the proper administration of justice on the other. Both are essential contributories to the liberty of the individual. We do not want to fetter the Press. Equally, we cannot tolerate in this country anything like what has been called "trial by newspaper"...

In Clause 12 we have sought to clarify the law in another respect in which it has been criticised, again notably by "Justice" – that is, in relation to the publication of proceedings in Chambers. Proceedings in Chambers are private, in the sense that the public is not admitted to them; but it does not necessarily follow that publication of proceedings in Chambers, still less of orders made in Chambers, does any harm calling for the intervention of the law.

We have not, therefore, taken the line which has commended itself to some courts, that the publication of reports of proceedings in Chambers is in itself contempt of court. We have confined the application of the law of contempt to those cases where publication is inherently likely to be harmful. It will continue to be contempt to publish reports of proceedings where the court in exercising its parental jurisdiction over infants, or where the court sits in private for reasons of national security, or where the proceedings relate, for instance, to a secret trade process so that the publication of the details would frustrate the very purpose for which the proceedings were brought."

"But apart from those special cases, publication of the proceedings of a court sitting in Chambers is not to be contempt, unless the court has itself expressly prohibited publication of the matter. I shall return to that point in a moment. Even in those exceptional cases it is not to be contempt to publish an order made in Chambers, or an accurate summary of it, unless the court forbids it. Moreover, it must not be thought that the court has an unfettered discretion to prohibit publication of the proceedings or the order. It can do so only by virtue either of express statutory power or of its limited inherent powers, for example, where publicity would defeat the object itself of having the proceedings in private.

Perhaps I may be allowed to quote the striking words of the Guardian again in relation to this Clause. It said: Bentham's aphorism that publicity is the soul of justice has been carried out to the letter. Those two Clauses – 11 and 12 – deal with the substance of the law of contempt..."

Although the Bill was passed, some MPs sounded a note of caution. For example, Mr Gordon Walker, the MP for Smethwick, said:

"...As a layman, I am somewhat worried about the extent of litigation in private and the use of judicial powers exercised in private. Immense powers can be exercised by judges sitting alone and secretly – committing people for contempt and so forth. They have all sorts of powers which they can exercise over me and other citizens. It amazes me that so many people hold up their hands in horror at the mere suggestion that preliminary hearings before a magistrates' court should be held in camera, while they never say a word about the immense powers which are exercised in secret by judges.

That offends my sense of justice and fills me with a certain resentment against judicial arrogance, a feeling which I am entitled to have, but which should not be evoked in my breast, being a reasonable sort of man, and which is evoked in my breast by things of this sort. No judge should exercise judicial power over a citizen, except on evidence examined and cross-examined and, except in the most exceptional circumstances, in public. We should be much more careful about the powers which we allow to courts in camera and judges sitting alone and in secret."

Those are strong words which, perhaps, sound even more loudly today than they did in 1960.

It has been suggested that the need to preserve the privacy of children and families was the driving force which led Parliament to enact section 12. In a judgment given in 1990 the then Master of the Rolls, Lord Donaldson, said:[19]

"The family is essentially a private unit and this is particularly the case in relation to children of the family. The accident that, usually through no fault of their own, outside agencies, whether the courts or local authorities, are called upon to intrude into the family unit in the interests of the welfare of the children should never of itself be allowed to deprive the children of the privacy which they should and would have enjoyed, but for that intrusion. <u>This is recognised by Parliament and led to the enactment of the Administration of Justice</u>

---

[19] Re M and N (Wards) (Publication of Information) [1990] 1 FLR 149 at page 164.

Act 1960." (emphasis supplied)

I hesitate to disagree with such a distinguished and well-respected judge. However, with respect to that last sentence, the debate recorded in Hansard does not suggest that the enactment of section 12 had any link with a perceived need to protect the privacy of children involved in the family justice system. That section 12 came to be the means by which their privacy was jealously guarded, casting an almost impenetrable veil over the work of the Family Court was, it appears, a very much later development.

Since the Children Act 1989 came into force, section 12 of the Administration of Justice Act 1960 has assumed much greater importance. Yet there have been difficulties of interpretation. For example, in section 12(1) what does 'publication' mean? And what does 'information relating to proceedings' mean. In section 12(2) what is the meaning of 'the publication of the text or a summary of the whole or part of an order made by a court sitting in private'?[20] The text of an order will include the name of the court, the court reference number, the names of the parties and, if the proceedings relate to a child, the name and date of birth of the child. Does section 12(2) mean that it is permissible to publish the name of the subject child and the names of his or her parents? It does indeed mean exactly that.

Contempt of court[21]
I noted in Chapter 3 that as a result of rule changes in 2005, 2009 and 2010 there has been some relaxation in the scope of section 12 of the Administration of Justice Act 1960. The current position is set out in the Family Procedure Rules 2010, Practice Direction 12G. In three Tables that Practice Direction sets out what information may be communicated by whom, to whom and for what purpose. Those who are authorised to disclose such information include, for example, a party to the proceedings, a legal repre-

---

[20] Most hearings in the Family Court relating to children take place in private. In those cases section 12 of the Administration of Justice Act 1960 and section 97(2) of the Children Act 1989 both apply. However, it is important to note that there are occasions when the judge will decide to conduct a hearing, or part of a hearing, in open court and/or may give judgment in open court. Those two sections do not apply to any hearing (or part of a hearing) conducted in open court. Any part of a hearing which takes place in, or a judgment which is given in, open court can be reported on by the media unless the judge makes a reporting restrictions order preventing the reporting of some or all of the detail that has been given in open court. For a discussion of this topic see the judgment of Sir James Munby in *In the Matter of X (A Child) (No 2)* [2016] EWHC 1668 (Fam).
[21] A fuller discussion of the law of contempt in so far as it applies to the media, can be found in *Transparency in the Family Courts: Publicity and Privacy in Practice*, Julie Doughty, Lucy Reed and Paul Magrath, (2018) Bloomsbury Publishing, London (see especially Chapter 6) and *McNae's Essential Law for Journalists*, 24th Edition, Mike Dodd and Mark Hanna (2018), Oxford University Press (see especially Chapter 19).

sentative, an officer of Cafcass and Minister of the Crown. Those to whom the communication of certain information is permitted include, for example, a health care professional, the Secretary of State, a Tribunal dealing with an appeal under section 24 of the Child Support Act 1991, an adoption panel, The Children's Commissioner and a police officer. Journalists are not included in the categories of people who may receive information relating to proceedings and, not surprisingly in those circumstances, are also not included in the categories of people who may communicate information relating to proceedings. The media are not entitled to any of the concessions set out in Practice Direction 12G. Any breach of section 12 by the media will, therefore, be a contempt of court and capable of being dealt with as such.

That position is unsatisfactory. I have already noted the difficulties which exist in interpreting section 12. Editors and journalists may need legal advice before publishing if there is any uncertainty about whether publication might amount to a breach of section 12. In my opinion, it is undesirable (at its lowest), unfair and wholly inappropriate that the media should find themselves in a position of such uncertainty. That uncertainty is avoidable. If in any particular case there is good reason to be sure that the media has a clear understanding of what information it may not publish, arguably the better course than simply relying on section 12 is to seek a reporting restrictions order. A reporting restrictions order is an order of the court restraining the media from publishing any of the information specified in the order. Breach of a reporting restrictions order is a contempt of court. In the Family Court, a Circuit Judge has the power to imprison the contemnor for a maximum of two years or to impose an unlimited fine. The one downside when pursuing an application for a reporting restrictions order is that Family Procedure Rules 2010 Practice Direction 12I provides that:

> *"Orders can only be made in the High Court and are normally dealt with by a Judge of the Family Division. If the need for an order arises in existing proceedings in the family court, judges should either transfer the application to the High Court or consult their Family Division Liaison Judge."*

Unless the judge provides expressly to the contrary, every published judgment shall be deemed to contain the following warning (referred to as a "rubric"):

> *"This judgment was delivered in private. The judge has given leave for this version of the judgment to be published on condition that (irrespective of what is contained in the judgment) in any published*

version of the judgment the anonymity of the children and members of their family must be strictly preserved. All persons, including representatives of the media, must ensure that this condition is strictly complied with. Failure to do so will be a contempt of court."

If the breach of Article 12 occurs after the publication of an anonymised judgment and in breach of the terms of the rubric, it is thought that any breach of the terms of the rubric amounts to a contempt of court and is punishable as such. I say "thought" to be the position because I am not aware of any case in which a judge at any level has made a finding that a breach of a particular rubric amounted to a contempt of court and has gone on to punish the contemnor accordingly. The argument that breach of a rubric is a contempt of court arises from a decision of Sir James Munby in 2011.[22] In his judgment, he said:

"13. The rubric is not an injunction: see Re HM (Vulnerable Adult: Abduction) (No 2) [2010] EWHC 1579 (Fam), [2011] 1 FLR 97. It is not drafted in the way in which injunctions are usually drafted. There is no penal notice. And the procedures required by section 12(3) of the Human Rights Act 1998 and Practice Direction 12I: Applications for Reporting Restriction Orders will not have been complied with. But this does not mean that it is unenforceable and of no effect. On the contrary, it is, in my judgment, binding on anyone who seeks to make use of a judgment to which it is attached. And anyone who disobeys it is, in principle, guilty of a contempt of court. This accords with, though it goes a little further than, what is said in paragraph 82 of The Family Courts: Media Access & Reporting, published in July 2011.

Notwithstanding the impeccable source from which those comments come, until the point is tested in court it is not possible to say with absolute certainty that Sir James Munby's view will be followed.

The point made by Sir James in that case leads me on, finally, to the one remaining route to contempt proceedings. In any case where there has not been a breach of a reporting restrictions order and there has not been any breach of the rubric at the start of a published judgment (or, for the reasons just explained, a decision is taken not to test the point whether breach of a rubric amounts to a contempt of court) the party seeking committal for contempt may rely solely on an allegation that the editor and/or journalist has acted in breach of the provisions of section 12 of the Administration of

---

[22] *Re RB (Adult) (No 4)* [2011] EWHC 3017 (Fam).

Justice Act. The procedure for dealing with such an application is set out in Part 37 of the Family Procedure Rules 2010, rules 37.13 – 37.15. Before such an application for committal can be made the applicant must first obtain the permission of a High Court Judge. In other words, this is a two step process. No prior permission is required to bring committal proceedings for breach of a reporting restrictions order. That is a one step process.

Section 97(2) of the Children Act 1989

Although section 12 of the Administration of Justice Act 1960 does not make it impermissible to name the child, section 97(2) of the Children Act 1989 does. Section 97(2) provides that:

> *"No person shall publish to the public at large or any section of the public any material which is intended, or likely, to identify –*
>
> *(a) any child as being involved in any proceedings before the High Court or the family court in which any power under this Act or the Adoption and Children Act 2002 may be exercised by the court with respect to that or any other child; or*
>
> *(b) an address or school as being that of a child involved in any such proceedings."*

The combined effect of section 12 of the Administration of Justice Act 1960 and section 97(2) of the Children Act 1989 is that there is very little that can routinely be published about Children Act cases relating to a child involved in public law or private law proceedings without breaching the terms of one or other or both of those sections.

There are, though, two significant differences between those two sections. Firstly, whereas the protection provided by section 12 remains in place indefinitely the protection provided by section 97(2) ceases to have effect when the proceedings come to an end unless the court orders that the protection should continue to apply.

The second difference relates to enforcement. As explained above, the remedy for breach of the provisions of section 12 of the Administration of Justice Act 1960 is by means of a committal application. In contrast, breach of section 97(2) of the Children Act 1989 is a criminal offence. Section 97(6) provides that:

> *"Any person who contravenes this section shall be guilty of an offence and liable on summary conviction, to a fine not exceeding level 4 on*

the standard scale.'[23]

There are no reported examples of a prosecution under this section.

In terms of ease of enforcement in the event of breach, a reporting restrictions order would seem to provide a swifter and, therefore, more appropriate means of dealing with a breach than applying to the High Court for leave to apply for a committal order for breach of section 12 or waiting for criminal justice agencies to bring a criminal prosecution for breach of section 97(2).

It is important for journalists to have a working knowledge of the reporting restrictions that apply as a result of the combined effect of section 12 of the 1960 Act and section 97(2) of the 1989 Act. They need to understand what they can and what they cannot (without the permission of the judge) report at the end of the hearing. Getting it wrong could have serious consequences for the journalist.

This is where the cause of difficulty for the media has its roots. As Sir James Munby highlighted in *Re B (A Child)*,[24] to which I referred earlier, when it comes to the need to understand fully all the various subtleties of the case law relating to the interpretation of section 12:

"There is no substitute for a careful study of the reported cases."

That is an impossible task for most journalists and editors and a costly exercise should they consider it necessary to obtain the advice of a lawyer. It is in my opinion deeply unsatisfactory that a statute which plays such an important part in the reporting of family court proceedings and the pursuit of transparency should require such a high level of legal skill and understanding in order to discern how it applies from case to case. Something very much simpler is required.

Section 12 creates a burden on journalists and editors alike. It is a burden which, today, most if not all newspapers (particularly, but not exclusively, regional newspapers) simply cannot afford to bear. Even national newspapers are unlikely to consider taking on the risk and cost involved save in the most exceptional of cases. Hanna makes the point that the first question the editor of a regional newspaper is likely to ask when considering whether to send a journalist into the Family Court is 'is it worth the trouble?'

---

[23] Currently £2,500 – see section 37(2) of the Criminal Justice Act 1982.
[24] [2004] EWHC 411 (Fam).

Hanna also makes the point that most journalists – regional and national – are not steeped in family law. They have very little (if any) contact with social workers or other professionals who work in the Family Court. For them this is unknown territory. They know only enough to enable them to understand that they are not allowed to write much, if anything, about the cases they see in the Family Court and that there are strong sanctions if they get it wrong.

Hanna chairs the examination Board of the National Council for the Training of Journalists. There is an examination on court reporting. However, although journalists are taught about section 12 of the Administration of Justice Act 1960, questions about section 12 are no longer included in the exam paper. There are two reasons for this: firstly, because it is felt that this is such a minefield; secondly, because the current expectation is that it will be rare for a journalist to go into the Family Court.

Hanna's view is that section 12 should be repealed. His view, which he believes is shared by many journalists, is that journalists are very well aware both of the need for and the art of anonymisation. That alone should be sufficient to guarantee the privacy and confidentiality of the children and families involved in proceedings in the Family Court.

Hanna is in good company. In an article published in 2010,[25] Sir James Munby expressed the opinion that:

> *"The family justice system needs to make better provision – much better provision – of information to the public generally. Although I will not here explore the matter in detail, there are two steps which, I suggest, urgently need to be taken.*
>
> *The first is to make more judgments – many more judgments – publicly accessible, albeit, of course, in appropriately anonymised form...*
>
> *The second step must be to revisit section 12 of the 1960 Act. Publication of judgments is, I believe, necessary, but such a step will not of itself necessarily suffice. After all, a judgment contains only what a judge has decided to include in it. Someone may wish to argue in a public arena, relying for this purpose on matters not recorded in the judgment, that, for example, the expert evidence was flawed, that the*

---

[25] *Lost opportunities: law reform and transparency in the family courts*, an article based on the Hershman-Levy Memorial Lecture given on 1 July 2010, subsequently published in the Child and Family Law Quarterly, vol 22, No 3 pp 273-289.

judge misunderstood the evidence, or that if the judge had had access to other information the outcome might have been different. Section 12, which as noted above fails to protect the anonymity which most would endorse, is in other respects surely far too restrictive. Is it not time to make a fresh start? This might involve abandoning section 12 altogether and starting again. If that approach is thought to be too radical, would it not be possible to re-cast section 12 so that it defined a much more limited and focussed list of materials that could not be disseminated without the prior permission of the court?"

In a debate in the House of Lords in November 1979, Lord Hailsham said:

"Are we to leave on the Statute Book a Section which is really manifestly intolerable because it is unjust and anachronistic; and if tolerable at all, is tolerable only because it is unenforceable and unenforced and therefore brings the law into disrepute."[26]

That debate concerned section 2 of the Official Secrets Act 1911. Could not something very similar be said today about section 12 of the Administration of Justice Act 1960? In the Queen's Speech on 15 May 1979 the Government proposed that:

"A measure will be introduced to replace the provisions of Section 2 of the Official Secrets Act 1911 with provisions appropriate to the present time."[27]

Do we not now need to hear a Queen's Speech in which the same promise is made – and for the same reasons – with respect to section 12 of the Administration of Justice Act 1960?

Another concern for Hanna relates to the restrictions on parties to family proceedings speaking openly to the media about the proceedings and the restrictions on what the media can publish. These restrictions do not mean that parents cannot speak to the media at all. They can, for example, talk about the impact the proceedings are having upon them, about their fears, worries and hopes about the future. However, they are not permitted to provide the media with any "information relating to the proceedings", an enigmatic phrase the precise meaning of which is not absolutely clear. This is a grey area.

---

[26] Hansard, 5 November 1979, Vol 402, column 616.
[27] Hansard, 15 May 1979, Vol 400, column 9.

Even if the information the parents give to journalists is information which they are entitled to give, that does not necessarily mean that the media is entitled to publish that information. It is a criminal offence to publish to the public at large any material which is intended or likely to identify the child. To publish anything at all about the parents' story runs the risk that the parents – and therefore so, too, the child – will be identified. Invariably the media will need to seek permission from the court to publish.

This whole area lacks adequate clarity. For both parents and the media, safely navigating section 12 is somewhat like walking through quicksand. Hanna shares Camilla Cavendish's view that this amounts to gagging parents. In his experience, journalists are astonished that someone cannot speak to them in detail about a life-changing experience. There can be few experiences that are more life-changing than having your child forcibly removed from your care by the state and placed for adoption with strangers. The 2005 and 2009 rule changes relating to disclosure of information[28] made no change at all to the position concerning the disclosure of information by parents to the media.

Hanna draws an analogy with the approach taken by the House of Lords in *Secretary of State for the Home Office, ex p Simms*.[29] Two serving prisoners wished to seek permission to appeal against their convictions. They wished to enlist the help of a journalist. It was the Home Secretary's policy that prisoners have no right to have oral interviews with journalists in aid of an attempt to gain access to the Court of Appeal (Criminal Division). The policy was challenged as a breach of the prisoners' rights under Article 10 ECHR. Lord Steyn said:

> *"The prisoners are in prison because they are presumed to have been properly convicted. They wish to challenge the safety of their convictions. In principle it is not easy to conceive of a more important function which free speech might fulfil."*

He went on to speak of:

> *"the principle that the more substantial the interference with fundamental rights the more the court will require by way of justification before it can be satisfied that the interference is reasonable in a public law sense."*

---

[28] See the section headed *Communication of information* in Chapter 3.
[29] [2000] 2 AC 115.

The House of Lords concluded that the Home Office policy could not be justified. Lord Steyn said:

> *"The criminal justice system has been shown to be fallible. Yet the effect of the judgment of the Court of Appeal is to outlaw the safety valve of effective investigative journalism. In my judgment the conclusions and reasoning of the Court of Appeal were wrong."*

Hanna makes a very simple point. The family justice system has also been shown to be fallible. It is accepted that miscarriages of justice do occur in the Family Court.[30] How many of these go unnoticed by the public because of parents feeling they have been gagged and don't know their rights – for example, their right to apply to the court for permission to talk to the media about the detail of the proceedings?

It is unclear whether such an application would be considered to fall within the scope of the legal aid certificate granted to the parents in the care proceedings. Many parents who have been through care proceedings and had their children removed do not have either the financial or the emotional resources to go back to court to seek permission to tell their story to a journalist. In terms of human rights, what is the difference between refusing a prisoner the right to speak to a journalist about an appeal against what he or she considers to be an unsafe conviction and refusing to allow parents to speak to a journalist in detail about the circumstances which give rise to the risk of their child being permanently removed from their care and placed for adoption? Hanna's answer is that there is no difference.

As Tickle put it to me:

> *"The parents are pulverised by the Family Court process and have nothing left to fight with".*

There is a strong case for increasing transparency in the Family Court. Any notion that achieving greater transparency in the Family Court is going to lead to a vast increase in the number of cases being reported in the media is, it seems to me, fanciful. As I noted earlier, both Hanna and Farmer make the point that, at regional level, resources – financial and human – have fallen dramatically over recent years and continue to fall. Even if it were easier for journalists to report on the work of the Family Court, they are never going to come into the Family Court in droves. Even the national me-

---

[30] I noted earlier that Sweeney has made five documentaries concerning the miscarriage of justice in the *Webster* case.

dia does not have the capacity to operate on anything other than a limited, targeted basis.

All of the five factors I identified earlier present a very significant hurdle for the media. These are the real reasons why the media have not taken up the opportunity to attend hearings in the Family Court on a regular basis. It is not because they are not interested.

The introduction of the rule permitting duly accredited representatives of news gathering and reporting organisations to attend hearings in the Family Court has not led to the hoped-for improvement in transparency or to any significant improvement in the standing of the Family Court in the eyes of the public. It was an important step forward, but a step that needed to be followed by other steps if it was to have any real impact on the level of transparency in the Family Court.

Judicial guidance
In 2011, the then President of the Family Division, Sir Nicholas Wall, and Bob Satchwell, then Executive Director of the Society of Editors, convened a group to try to find a way forward that would increase transparency (which the media and the public wanted) whilst at the same time protecting the privacy of children and families (which was a key concern of many professionals and academics working in this area). The result was the publication on 29 July 2011 of *Guidance issued by the President of the Family Division, Sir Nicholas Wall, the Judicial College and the Society of Editors*. The guidance reads:

> *"There is no more difficult issue in family justice than the reporting of cases. There is a tension between concerns about "secret justice" and legitimate expectations of privacy and confidentiality for the family. Both standpoints are valid, and the question is whether they are irreconcilable. Against this background, and under the wise tutelage of the Lord Chief Justice, a group of lawyers and journalists, including representatives from both the print and broadcast media, have got together to talk to each other. As part of these discussions, they commissioned a paper which would set out a statement of the current state of the law in this most complex area. The result is the document which follows this Preface. It has been drafted by two members of the bar, Adam Wolanski and Kate Wilson.*[31] *It is an analysis of where we are at the moment: what we can and what we cannot do. It is, in*

---

[31] Adam Wolanski and Kate Wilson are two very experienced media lawyers. Since the Guidance was published Adam Wolanski has taken silk and is now Adam Wolanski QC.

our view, a substantial and very important piece of work. Its publication is all the more timely as the debate on increased transparency and public confidence in the family courts moves forward. It will serve to inform future consideration of this difficult and sensitive area, including the questions of access to and reporting of proceedings by the media, whilst maintaining the privacy of the families involved."

The paper by Wolanski and Wilson was clear and comprehensive. Given that relatively little real progress has been made towards increasing transparency in the Family Court since their paper was written more than eight years ago it may be of some benefit, particularly to the judiciary, if an up-to-date version were to be published.

5: NEXT STEPS

> *"I need to repeat, and here I do not think I am a lone voice, that the senior judiciary is in favour of greater transparency. I do believe that the circle can be squared, and I remain of the view that a wider and more informed public appreciation of the work we do is both important and in our interests. I very much welcome the initiative, which is piloting the anonymisation and publication of judgments given by the professional bench and lay justices. I have long advocated the publication of judgments in anonymised form, and press releases in cases of complexity and controversy. I would welcome sensible discussion with the Press...".* (Lord Justice Wall)[1]

Chapter 3 dealt with the first two changes introduced with a view to increasing transparency in the Family Court – the amendment of the rule relating to the disclosure of information in family proceedings relating to children and the introduction of a new rule which gave duly accredited representatives of news gathering and reporting organisations the right to attend certain hearings in the Family Court. In this chapter I shall deal with the next two steps that were taken – the *Family Court Information Pilot* and the Children, Schools and Families Act 2010.

The Family Court Information Pilot
I noted in Chapter 3 that whereas the first consultation paper on transparency, published by the Government in 2006,[2] had proposed that transparency be achieved by permitting duly accredited representatives of news gathering and reporting organisations to attend hearings in the Family Court, the second consultation paper, published in June 2007, proposed that it would be preferable for steps to be taken to increase the amount and quality of information coming out of the family courts.

On 16 December 2008 the then Justice Secretary, Jack Straw, announced in the House of Commons that the Government had:

---

[1] *Justice for children: welfare or farewell?* – a keynote address by Lord Justice Wall for the National Conference of the Association of Lawyers for Children, Manchester, 20 November 2009, para. 66.
[2] *Confidence and confidentiality: Improving transparency and privacy in family courts* – Consultation Paper CP 11/06.

> "decided to pilot the provision of written judgments when a final order is made in certain family cases. The courts in the pilot areas – Leeds, Wolverhampton and Cardiff – will, for the first time, routinely produce a written record of the decision for the parties involved. In selected cases, where the court is making life-changing decisions for a child, it will publish an anonymised judgment on line so that it can be read by the wider public."[3]

And so it came about that the Family Court Information Pilot was born.

One of the key participants in the Advisory Board which planned this project was Mavis Maclean CBE. Maclean has carried out socio-legal research in Oxford since 1974. She served as an academic advisor to the Lord Chancellor's Department (now the Ministry of Justice) from 1990 to 2009. She continues to be actively involved in research.

Maclean took part in the preparatory work necessary to set up the pilot and in the evaluation of the pilot after it completed. In October 2006 she chaired a meeting organised by the Lord Chancellor's Department which took place under the title: 'Confidence and Confidentiality: Openness of Family Courts – A Day of Perspectives'. The meeting was held in the Bunker, the former World War II underground cabinet war rooms in St James' Park, London. The irony of the choice of venue was not lost on those who attended. Maclean notes that:

> "There was some amusement at the meeting about the DCA[4] sense of what is appropriate – in this case, to discuss openness and transparency for the courts in what has historically been the most restricted location in London."[5]

The meeting was attended by professionals from a variety of backgrounds including representatives from the judiciary, the Family Law Bar, child and adolescent psychiatry and Cafcass.[6] Representatives from the National Union of Journalists, the Newspaper Society, the Press Association and the Press Complaints Commission also attended, as did journalist John Sweeney (then BBC Current Affairs Reporter). Those present watched a

---

[3] Hansard, 16 December 2008, Column 981.
[4] Department for Constitutional Affairs.
[5] See *Opening up the Family Courts: The Media, the Ministry and the Children, Schools and Families Act 2010* chapter 5, page 81 in *Making Family Law: A Socio Legal Account of Legislative Process in England and Wales, 1985 to 2010* – Mavis Maclean with Jacek Kurczewski, (2011), Hart Publishing, London.
[6] Children and Family Court Advisory and Support Service.

DVD, prepared by Cafcass, of a group of young people discussing their feelings about media reporting of hearings in the Family Court. All the children involved in the making of the DVD had been involved as subject children in proceedings in the Family Court. They were clear that they didn't want anyone knowing their business. They were opposed to media reporting of family court hearings involving children. One of the young people made the point that the media don't care about "us", they just want to make money and sell more newspapers.

It was not only children who raised concerns about the publication of judgments. Those living and/or working in rural areas were also concerned. Welsh magistrates expressed concern about the risk of jigsaw identification[7] of children living in small rural communities where, it was believed, the process of anonymisation was likely to be ineffective. They made the point that you don't have to use names in order for people to be recognised. The Advisory Board agreed that anonymisation of judgments published on Bailii needed to be as watertight as possible.

Speaking to Maclean one gets some insight into the immense amount of work and the great commitment, dedication and care that went into setting up this pilot. Great care was taken to avoid any risk to the privacy of the families concerned, while at the same time attempting to increase the information in the public domain about these cases. The Advisory Board was well aware of the risks involved in the pilot and of the fact that the very idea of undertaking a pilot was not universally welcomed. There was a fear of proceeding too quickly, of doing too much and of opening up a Pandora's Box. The Advisory Board was determined to deliver a protocol that was well structured, well managed and rigorously evaluated.

The pilot was run in three (Magistrates') Family Proceedings Courts and two County Courts. The pilot contained three strands.

First, the pilot courts were to provide written judgments to all parties in certain types of serious Children Act cases. That meant no change so far as Family Proceedings Courts were concerned because they already provided written reasons to the parties in every case. However, the County Court did not routinely do so. Many judgments in the County Court were extempore judgments that were recorded but almost never transcribed. If the court was

---

[7] Jigsaw identification occurs when information from different sources (e.g. a published judgment and material posted on social media) is pieced together thereby enabling a particular child to be identified even though the judgment itself will have been anonymised. See the further discussion of jigsaw identification on pages 102, 182 and 185.

being invited to approve a final order agreed between the parties (whether in public law or private law proceedings) even an extempore judgment was rare. In the five pilot courts all cases were to be accompanied by written reasons (Family Proceedings Court) or a written judgment (County Court) to provide a record for the parties involved in these cases of the reasons that led to the court's decision.

Second, the pilot examined the possibility of retaining a written record of the court's decision which could be accessed by the child in later life.

Third, the pilot required that anonymised versions of all of the reasons and judgments in cases where there was a possibility that a child would be removed or contact with a parent might be ended should be published on the Bailii website.[8] This was the most controversial of the proposals.

By the time this pilot was completed, Sir Nicholas Wall had been appointed President of the Family Division of the High Court in succession to Sir Mark Potter. At the annual President's Conference in May 2010, Sir Nicholas presented a paper with the disarmingly simple title: *Transparency: A Discussion Paper*. With respect to the Family Courts Information Pilot he said this:

> "32. I am a member of the Project Board which is currently overseeing the pilots of anonymised judgments being placed on Bailii. Bailii itself is more than willing to create a special category for publishing family proceedings court reasons and county court judgments. In my view this publication is a partial answer [to the problem of transparency]. It puts our work into the public domain. It provides the answer to the tendentious litigant who would have the world believe that his or her version of events is the truth. In the pilots, anonymisation is being undertaken by the transcriber. Whilst this is resource intensive, it is sensible and immensely time-saving. In my view, the prospects of identification or recognition are minimal, leaving on one side the cases in which it is in the public interest to name individuals."

The pilot ran from November 2009 to December 2010. In August 2011 the Ministry of Justice published a review of the pilot. With respect to the reasons and judgments that had been published on Bailii, the review noted that there had been:

> "27. ...no increase in media interest...observed as a result of the pi-

---

[8] www.bailii.org.

> *lot. In general, there had been initial press interest on the first day following the April 2009 rule changes but none thereafter, an experience borne out by the January 2010 Ministry of Justice study into the impact of the changes to the media attendance rules...*
>
> *38. ...Only one member of the press found the site useful in describing both sides of the case.*
>
> *39. Others were disappointed with the level of detail and lack of identifiable information..."*

In 2012 Maclean contributed to a collection of essays published under the title: *Fifty Years in Family Law – Essays for Stephen Cretney*.[9] Maclean's essay was called *Openness and Transparency in the Family Courts: A Policy Journey 2005-2011*. In the final section of her essay, Maclean discusses the evaluation of the Family Courts Information Pilot. She says that the:

> *"Evaluation had been carefully planned by the Advisory Board to review the impact of the process on those working in the five courts, the benefits to the parties and the wider public of the availability of a wider range of judgments and the potential cost of rolling out the programme nationally...[A] user survey had been run by Bailii to report the views of those who had accessed the website. And finally local press comment on the pilot courts were checked for any comments but little was found... The press, who had pressed long and loudly for change were not satisfied with the process, as while it gave detail on 165 cases it did not provide the names and addresses they wanted..."*

Maclean ends by noting that a key reason why the pilot was not rolled out nationally was "because there was genuine non-negotiable conflict between the aims of increasing openness and protecting the privacy of the vulnerable". That conflict still exists.

Maclean recalls that there was a noticeable lack of response by the media to the reasons and judgments published during the pilot, largely because of the format in which they were published. This was assumed, wrongly in my opinion, to be an indication of a lack of interest by the media. The media had wanted more than the pilot proposed to deliver. In particular, the media wanted names. That was never going to happen. However, the real reason for lack of press interest was, in my opinion, because of the excessive extent to which the reasons and judgments had been anonymised. I give just one

---

[9] Published in 2012 by Intersentia Publishing Limited, Cambridge.

example. The reasons that follow are the full reasons given by lay magistrates at the final hearing of a local authority's application for a care order heard in December 2009.[10]

Neutral Citation Number: [2009] EWMC 8 (FPC)
In the Magistrates' Court
Family Proceedings Court

Before:
Magistrates

- - - - - - - - - - - - - -

Between:

X Local Authority	Applicant
and	
Miss P	1st Respondent
Mr D	2nd Respondent
Miss W	3rd Respondent
T (A child)	4th Respondent

- - - - - - - - - - - - - -

Miss G for the Applicant
Mrs B for the 1st Respondent
Miss McN for the 2nd Respondent
Miss W for the 3rd Respondent
Miss B for the 4th Respondent
Hearing date: 9 December 2009

- - - - - - - - - - - - - - - - - - - -

Justices' Reasons

(1) **Evidence received by the court**

We have read the bundle and heard representations.

(2) **Background to application**

This is the Local Authority's application for a care order in respect of T, date of birth [a date].

---

[10] [2009] EWMC 8 (FPC).

(3)   T's parents are Miss P and Mr D.

(4)   The local authority issued these proceedings in relation to T because of initial concerns of neglect and domestic violence as set out in the court documents.

(5)   The Local Authority's plan is that T should be cared for by maternal Great Aunt, Miss W. Both mother and father agree with this plan. Today we are asked to make a care order as there are some outstanding issues in relation to financial matters between the Local Authority and Ms W, which the Local Authority is optimistic of resolving. At that point consideration will be given to revoking the care order and making a Special Guardianship order in favour of Miss W. Threshold is conceded on the basis of the documents set out in the bundle on pages 13 – 15 dated 9.12.09. We accept the amended schedule in relation to the threshold Criteria that has been agreed between the parties.

(6)   **Findings of the court regarding statutory/threshold criteria – Section 31(2) Children Act 1989 (Care/Supervision Order)**

The court is satisfied that:

(a)   The child is suffering, or is likely to suffer, significant harm; and

(b)   That the harm, or likelihood of harm, is attributable to the care given to the child, or likely to be given to her if the order were not made, not being what it would be reasonable to expect a parent to give her.

(7)   **This is because**: of the matters indicated in the Local Authority's schedule in relation to threshold.

(8)   **Welfare Checklist (s1 (3) Children Act 1989**

The court adopts paragraphs 6-35 in the report of the Children's Guardian dated 1 December 2009 in relation to the checklist.

(9)   **Human rights considerations**

The court has had regard to Article 8 and has undertaken a balancing act of all the parties' rights under the Act. It is satisfied that the

(10) **Order(s) of the court**

We accept today that it is appropriate to make a Care Order in respect of T in favour of X Council.

(11) We leave the contact to be at the discretion of the Local authority as outlined in the care plan dated 8.12.09. Contact will be reviewed at the Looked After Child reviews which take place on a six monthly basis.

(12) We are optimistic that in the fulness of time the Care Order will be discharged and a Special Guardianship Order made in favour of Miss W.

(13) Before Magistrates.

(14) 9th December 2009.

The anonymisation in this case is almost total. We are not told the name of the court. That is unusual but not unheard of. We are not told the names of the magistrates. They are sitting in a judicial capacity. In my experience it is highly unusual for a published judgment not to state the name of the judge (or, in this case, the magistrates). In 2019, Sir James Munby underlined that point very clearly. He said:[11]

> *"I cannot leave these cases without drawing attention to the slapdash approach which, on top of everything else, featured in three of these cases: Campbell-Anderson v Anderson, Baron v Baron and Bird v Bird, the second and third of these being cases proceeding in a Regional Divorce Unit. On three occasions, as I have recorded, it is impossible to read the name of the Deputy District Judge or Assistant Justices' Clerk who gave the special procedure certificate: the scrawled name is illegible. This is not good enough. Litigants and others have the right to know who it is who makes an order, gives some direction or gives a statutory certificate. As Watkins LJ memorably observed in R v Felixstowe Justices ex parte Leigh [1987] QB 582 at 595, "There is ... no such person known to the law as the anonymous JP." And that applies equally to anyone, Judge, Justices' Clerk or Legal Adviser, who is exercising a judicial function. Moreover, as I have had to*

---

[11] *Baron & Ors (4 Defective Divorces)* [2019] EWFC 26 at paragraph 58.

record, on two occasions the Assistant Justices' Clerk was too hard pressed to make the appropriate deletions on the certificate he (or she) was signing. Again, this is simply not good enough. This is an important document which should be completed carefully and properly."

In the pilot judgment which I have just set out, the names of the child and the child's parents are not given. That is normal. The parents are described as Miss P and Mr D which tends to suggest that they are not married, though that is a presumption and not a fact. The child's age is not stated. It is normal not to state a child's date of birth but less usual for the order to be silent about the child's age – not even an indication of whether the child is pre or post school age. Initially the sex of the child is not stated. One wonders whether reference to 'her' in paragraph 6(b) was an intentional disclosure of the sex of the child or an accidental oversight. We are not told how old the parents are nor anything about their history. We are told that there has been neglect and domestic violence. Neglect and domestic violence cover a spectrum of seriousness. We do not know where this case falls on the spectrum.

Before the court is entitled to make any public law order in respect of this child it must first be satisfied that the threshold set by section 31(2) of the Children Act 1989 is met. Whether or not it is met is a matter for judicial determination. The burden of satisfying the court that the threshold is met rests upon the local authority. The standard of proof is the balance of probabilities standard. The decision that the threshold is met must be based on the evidence before the court. In this case we are not told what that evidence is save that it is to be found on pages 13 to 15 of the hearing bundle. Those pages have not been placed in the public domain.

If the court is satisfied that the threshold is met then it must go on to consider what order should be made. In other words, it must make a welfare determination. The approach to that part of the judicial task is set out in section 1 of the Children Act 1989. Section 1(1) of the 1989 Act requires that in deciding what order to make (if any): "the child's welfare shall be the court's paramount consideration". In deciding what is in a child's best welfare interests the court: "must have regard in particular" to the factors set out in section 1(3) – normally referred to as the welfare checklist. In this case, so far as concerns the welfare checklist, the magistrates' reasons simply say that: "The court adopts paragraphs 6-35 in the report of the Children's Guardian". That report is not in the public domain.

In this case the document setting out the magistrates' reasons has been so rigorously and comprehensively stripped of all meaningful information that it is hard to envisage how even the most imaginative and creative journalist could write up a report of the case, a human-interest news story, for publication in a newspaper. These particular magistrates' reasons are not atypical of the body of reasons and judgments published on Bailii during the pilot. It is, in my opinion, very clear indeed why the media paid so little attention to the reasons and judgments that were published on Bailii during the pilot. The media were not provided with any reportable information – nothing that would either interest or educate their readers.

In *In re Guardian News and Media Ltd*,[12] Lord Rodger memorably asked "What's in a name?" He answered his own question, at paragraph 63, in the following terms:

> *"'A lot', the press would answer. This is because stories about particular individuals are simply much more attractive to readers than stories about unidentified people. It is just human nature. And this is why, of course, even when reporting major disasters, journalists usually look for a story about how particular individuals are affected. Writing stories which capture the attention of readers is a matter of reporting technique…"*

Lord Rodger went on make the point that Article 10 of the ECHR protects not only the substance of ideas and information reported by the press but that it also protects the form in which the ideas and information are conveyed. He said that:

> *"This is not just a matter of deference to editorial independence. The judges are recognising that editors know best how to present material in a way that will interest the readers of their particular publication and so help them to absorb the information. A requirement to report it in some austere, abstract form, devoid of much of its human interest, could well mean that the report would not be read and the information would not be passed on. Ultimately, such an approach could threaten the viability of newspapers and magazines, which can only inform the public if they attract enough readers and make enough money to survive."*

In light of the points I have made, it seems to me to be almost inconceivable that the press would ever run a story based on the reasons and judgments published during the pilot. With respect to my description of the blandness of the reasons and judgments that were published, don't just

---

[12] [2010] UKSC 1.

take my word for it. You can read them yourselves. The reasons and judgments published during the pilot are available on the Bailii website. Go to: http://www.bailii.org/databases.html#ew. Halfway down the page is a sub-heading 'England and Wales Case Law'. Scroll down the list and click on the link to England and Wales Magistrates' Court (Family) to access all of the published reasons handed down in the three Family Proceedings Courts involved in the pilot. Immediately below that link there is a link to England and Wales County Court (Family) where you can find the published judgments handed down by District Judges in the two County Courts which took part in the pilot.

Maclean's view is that the pilot was a well-designed and well-executed project which did what was asked of it. I do not disagree with her. Maclean makes the point that the pilot was designed to test if it was possible to publish anonymised information about court decisions in serious child protection cases without risking the privacy of the families. The pilot demonstrated that that was possible. The information published on Bailii was found useful by lawyers and social workers for training purposes, though not, apparently, by the media and the public.

Although the pilot did what was asked of it, it did not lead to an acceptance that anonymised reasons and judgments in the Family Court should be routinely published. Reflecting on the impact of the pilot, in 2011 Maclean wrote:

> "At the end of the day a great deal of effort and stress had been required to run a small pilot scheme, which does not appear to be highly valued by those involved and very unlikely to have any impact on the parties or the general public...Despite extensive policy work in preparation and consultation, and pilot schemes to test feasibility, confidence and confidentiality remain hard to reconcile. The outcome is yet to be seen."[13]

The Children, Schools and Families Act 2010

The second development was the passing of the Children, Schools and Families Act 2010. This Bill was rushed through Parliament in the dying days of the last Labour Government. Part 2 of the Act dealt with the issue of transparency and sought to build on the rule change in 2009 which permitted duly accredited representatives of news gathering and reporting organisations to attend some hearings in the Family Court. Although the Bill was passed and the Act went onto the Statute Book, no date was set for

---

[13] *Making Family Law* ibid at page 95.

Part 2 to be brought into force. In 2013 Part 2 was repealed.[14] It would serve no useful purpose to outline the detail of the Act.

On 14 July 2011 the House of Commons Justice Committee published a report on the *Operation of the Family Courts*.[15] So far as concerns the Children, Schools and Families Act 2010, one paragraph of that report says all that needs to be said about this ill-fated piece of legislation:

> *"We recognise the need for transparency in the administration of family justice, and the equally important need to protect the interest of children and their privacy. However, our witnesses were united in opposing implementation of the scheme to increase media access to the family courts contained in Part 2 of the Children, Schools and Families Act 2010. While their reasons for doing so differed, and were sometimes contradictory, such universal condemnation compels us to recommend that the measures should not be implemented, and the Ministry of Justice begin afresh. We welcome the Government's acknowledgment that the way the legislation was passed was flawed, and urge Ministers to learn lessons from this outcome for the future."*

Neither the pilot nor the Act led to any improvement in transparency in the Family Court. In Maclean's opinion the heart of the difficulty was that the need for caution to safeguard privacy was necessarily of higher priority than increasing transparency. That was a widely held point of view. As Maclean puts it, the circle has not yet been squared. I agree. The criticisms of the 'secret' Family Court continued. They were not confined to one reporter or to one newspaper. Indeed, they were not confined to the media. They were widespread and getting louder. Could nothing be done that would restore public confidence in the Family Court? Could the circle ever be squared?

---

[14] See section 17(4) of the Crime and Courts Act 2013.
[15] *https://publications.parliament.uk/pa/cm201012/cmselect/cmjust/518/518i.pdf*, page 84, paragraph 281.

6: PRACTICE GUIDANCE ON TRANSPARENCY

> *"A common concern about many of these cases is that they are conducted in private, even though the decisions may have life-changing and lifelong consequences. It is the tension between doing justice in public and protecting the privacy of the vulnerable and those who reasonably expect their private affairs to remain private…In ancient Rome they achieved transparency by simply building their courts with no walls, but in our country both climate and concern for privacy are against that. However, the tension between transparency and privacy remains."* (Sir Mark Hedley)[1]

The Family Court Information Pilot was not rolled out nationally. Nothing came of it. Part 2 of the Children, Schools and Families Act 2010 was never brought into force. As I noted in Chapter 5, it was repealed in 2013. So, what next?

The period from 2010 to 2014 was a period of great change in the family justice system. In January 2010 the Government launched a Family Justice Review. The review was chaired by David (now Sir David) Norgrove. An interim report was published in March 2011. The final report was published in November 2011. The issue of transparency was not a significant aspect of the review. It occupied just four paragraphs of the interim report and one paragraph of the final report. In the latter the Review expressed its agreement with the decision which had by then been taken to repeal Part 2 of the Children, Schools and Families Act 2010. It may be helpful to set out the four paragraphs from the interim report in full. Under the heading 'Transparency and public confidence' the interim report stated that:

> *"3.16 Our terms of reference asked us to have regard to transparency. We are aware of concerns about the balance between a right to privacy and the need for public understanding on the one hand, and how that affects public confidence in the system on the other. Our own work has not led us to share concerns that arbitrary or ill-founded decisions are taken. In fact the reverse is the case. We have been im-*

---

[1] *The Modern Judge: Power, Responsibility and Society's Expectations*, Sir Mark Hedley, formerly the Honourable Mr Justice Hedley, (2016), LexisNexis, Bristol, pages 4 and 17.

> *pressed by the great care taken by the courts and all those involved in these difficult decisions. We recognise, of course, that the public are not granted the access that we have been afforded. However, we have not taken evidence on the controversial issue of public access and none of our recommendations affects, or needs to affect the openness or otherwise of the family courts. We can therefore only offer our own comments.*
>
> *3.17 The family courts deal with issues that are hugely sensitive to the people involved in them. This would not, in itself, be enough reason to restrict access and reporting of proceedings. But the involvement of children makes the difference and they are absolutely clear that they would not want any publicity about their cases. We can all imagine, from our own childhoods, how devastating it could be at school and with friends (and other children who are not friends) if our family circumstances were laid out in the local or national media.*
>
> *3.18 On the other hand, panel members who travelled to Australia were impressed by the way in which members of the public and those waiting for their own cases to be heard could sit at the back of the court while other proceedings were in progress. This had advantages in terms of parties – particularly people representing themselves – being able to see how their own cases would be handled, and no one we met identified any problems with it. The media in Australia are not permitted to report anything that identifies parties or expert witnesses.*
>
> *3.19 Legislation in this area has to cover a range of circumstances and the detail of which cases can be open and which not (for example final adoptions) matters. In our view, based on our limited consideration of the issue, the general principle should be that people – including the media – should be able to attend court hearings but not be allowed to do or say anything that might identify the parties in public.*

Commenting on the Review's final report, the then President of the Family Division, Sir Nicholas Wall, said that:

> *"The Family Justice Review Panel .... has taken great care to examine all aspects of cases involving children. I recognise the need for all agencies to work together to reduce delay and improve their practices to secure the best possible experience and outcomes for the families and children who become involved with the Family Justice System."*

There followed a period of intense activity implementing the reforms. Sir Nicholas Wall appointed Mr Justice (now Lord Justice) Ryder as the judge in charge of modernisation of family justice. The key legislative change was contained in The Crime and Courts Act 2013. Section 17 created a new, single Family Court in England and Wales. The single Family Court was launched on 22 April 2014.

All of this important work was carried out against a backdrop of continuing criticism of the Family Court as a 'secret' family court. Criticism mainly came from the media although one Member of Parliament, in particular, was also a very vocal critic. At that time John Hemming was the Liberal Democrat MP for Birmingham, Yardley. He used his blog to criticise many aspects of the family justice system including its alleged 'secrecy'.[2] On one occasion his over-zealous criticism of the Family Court led to him being severely criticised by the Court of Appeal.[3] Giving the leading judgment, Lord Justice Wall said:

> *"168. As to Mr. Hemming, my judgment is that his self-imposed role as a critic of the family justice system is gravely damaged, and speaking for myself I will not be persuaded to take seriously any criticism made by him in the future unless it is corroborated by reliable, independent evidence."*

Strong words, particularly given Mr Hemming's then status as a Member of Parliament. This judgment suggests that some of his advice to parents, if followed, could make their predicament worse rather than better.

An item on Family Law News on 13 January 2014 reported that:

> *"Liberal Democrat MP and chairman of the Justice for Families group, John Hemming, has told tonight's BBC's Panorama that he has been contacted by hundreds of parents who claim they have been treated unfairly by social services. Mr Hemming has commented that the legal system is heavily biased against the parent and in favour of*

---

[2] I cannot resist the temptation to note that on one occasion, in June 2010, Mr Hemming used his blog to laud one of my judgments – *Re X, Y and Z (Children)* [2010] EWHC B12 (Fam). The headline read "Clifford Bellamy – a good judgment". It was that same judgment that was strongly (and, as I accept, appropriately) criticised by the then President of the Family Division, Sir Nicholas Wall, in *X, Y, and Z & Anor v A Local Authority* [2011] EWHC 1157 (Fam) who said that I "should not, in the circumstances of this case, have made such swingeing criticisms" of a medical expert witness. The moral of this tale would seem to be that whatever utterance a judge may make there is always scope for a contrary view!

[3] *RP v Nottinghamshire County Council and the Official Solicitor* [2008] EWCA Civ 462.

> local authorities and thereby advises parents who are suspected of child abuse to go abroad if they can afford it.
>
> 'All the cards are held by the local authority. It has large resources to fight the cases, it does all the assessments,' he told BBC Panorama.
>
> 'My advice to people, if they can afford it, is just to go abroad. You can't rely on a fair trial here because you can't rely on the evidence being fair. It's best simply to go if you can, at the right time lawfully.'
>
> Mr Hemming also called for more transparency to report proceedings to journalists from the family courts...'[4]

That leads me to a more general point. A brief search of the internet discloses the existence of several organisations concerned with supporting parents who are involved in proceedings in the Family Court. Any parent who finds themselves involved in care proceedings is likely to be very distressed, anxious and keen to get some advice quickly. In today's internet age people look for advice from many different sources including, for example, the internet and social media. They don't necessarily turn to a professional for advice. Some of the advice they get from social media platforms may be sound. However, some will not. It may not be possible to distinguish between sound and unsound advice. Taking advice from the internet or social media can be as dangerous as self-diagnosing an illness based on the results of a search on Google. Following bad advice can lead to a catastrophic outcome both for parents and for their child.

On this issue of transparency, whilst still an MP Hemming did, to his credit, try to build on the limited progress that had been made during the previous decade. He introduced a private members Bill: 'The Transparency and Accountability Bill'. The Bill had its first reading on 2 July 2014. Clause 2(1) of the Bill proposed that:

> "Any party to proceedings in the Family Court...shall be permitted to have up to five observers present providing that no more than fifteen such observers shall be present at any one hearing."

The Bill had its second reading in the House of Commons on 17 October 2014. As a result of the general election called in 2015, Parliament was prorogued and the Bill was lost. It is, though, appropriate to consider some passages from the Hansard record of this debate which gives some insight

---

[4] https://www.familylaw.co.uk/news_and_comment/John-Hemming-130114-489.

into government thinking five years after journalists had first been allowed to attend hearings in the Family Court. At that time, the Minister of State at the Ministry of Justice was Simon Hughes MP.

Simon Hughes: "Let me summarise what we have done in response to these important issues. About 250,000 people go into our family courts every year in connection with care proceedings, children's proceedings, adoptions or family divorce and separation. We are not talking about insignificant numbers, and my hon. Friend the Member for Birmingham, Yardley reminded us that this was the context of the Ashya King case, the Rotherham scandal and many other issues. The Ministry of Justice is not the only Department involved; the Department for Education plays a lead role, and I know that my hon. Friend has talked to the Under-Secretary of State for Education, the hon. Member for Crewe and Nantwich (Mr Timpson), who is responsible for children's issues.

On family justice, we have introduced wide-ranging reform of the family justice system so that cases do not drag on for long periods. We have thus provided greater certainty for the children and families involved, which is positive and a plus. I pay tribute, as did my hon. Friend the Member for Birmingham, Yardley, to the president of the family division for how he has led on this and other issues. We have also reformed the way in which cases are managed before and during the court process so that children are placed firmly at the heart of the system. This very weekend, we are going to confirm that next week the law comes into operation that will mean that the presumption thereafter will be that children will benefit from both parents continuing to be involved in their lives. That is a hugely important principle. It may not always be possible, but that will be the legal presumption from next week onwards.

We have also taken steps to shine a light on the activities of the Family Court and the Court of Protection by encouraging the provision of more media access to hearings, and by publishing judgments to show how decisions are reached. That is still work in progress, and I spoke to the president of the family division only this week about the need for us to do better."

John Hemming: "As I have said on a number of occasions, the media cannot afford to have someone in every family court. Does the Minister accept that media access to hearings is not, in itself, that big a thing?"

Simon Hughes: "It is, in fact, quite a big thing. What has always been of concern is how to protect the confidentiality of the proceedings, which will involve all sorts of sensitive issues, and now that judgments are being made public, a delicate balance must be struck. In some cases in which publicity has been given only to the judgment, the identities of the parties have none the less been revealed, because in a small community it may be quite easy to put the pieces of the jigsaw together. The position is not as uncomplicated as my hon. Friend suggests. As he knows, there are tensions and difficulties, not because we do not want to be more transparent, but because the protection, safeguarding and interests of children and families must be weighed in the balance."

The Practice Guidance on Transparency

Sir James Munby was appointed President of the Family Division of the High Court and Head of Family Justice in January 2013. By then, the implementation of the Family Justice reforms was gathering pace. In April 2013 the President began to publish a monthly 'View from the President's Chambers'. This was a means of disseminating, particularly to family court judges, key information about the progress of the implementation of the reforms. It was also a means of encouraging family judges, especially Designated Family Judges,[5] to ensure that the reforms were fully and timeously implemented in their areas. In the fourth edition of his 'View'[6] the President set out his views and intentions concerning transparency in the Family Court. He said:

"Transparency: I am, as you will know, very concerned about this. I repeat what I said earlier this year, [2012] Fam Law 548:

---

[5] Some Circuit Judges are appointed to be a Designated Family Judge (DFJ). Every Designated Family Centre has a DFJ. The DFJ carries out significant leadership and management duties. The DFJ is responsible for that Family Centre and for all other family hearing centres in that area. The DFJ is also responsible for leading all levels of the family judiciary (including other Circuit Judges as well as the district bench, the magistrates and legal advisers) at the courts for which he or she has responsibility, and for ensuring the efficient and effective discharge of judicial family business at those courts. The work of the DFJ is carried out in addition to the judge's normal sitting requirements and without any additional remuneration. In four major cities – Manchester, Liverpool, Leeds and Birmingham – the DFJ is remunerated by being appointed a Senior Circuit Judge. At the time of writing (January 2020) it has just been announced that a further six DFJ posts are to be designated as Senior Circuit Judge posts: East London (East London Family Court); West London (West London Family Court); Central London (Central Family Court, First Avenue House); Lancaster (Lancaster County and Family Court); Cardiff (Cardiff Civil and Family Justice Centre); and Newcastle (Newcastle upon Tyne Combined Court Centre).

[6] https://www.judiciary.uk/wp-content/uploads/JCO/Documents/FJC/Publications/VIEW(4)+-publications.pdf.

> "I am determined to take steps to improve access to and reporting of family proceedings. I am determined that the new Family Court should not be saddled, as the family courts are at present, with the charge that we are a system of secret and unaccountable justice. Work, commenced by my predecessor, is well underway. I hope to be in a position to make important announcements in the near future."
>
> The law is highly technical and far too complex. The need for reform has been recognised for at least 20 years. Too little has been done. My views on the subject are no secret: see, for example, 'Access to and Reporting of Family Proceedings', [2005] Fam Law 945, and 'Lost opportunities: law reform and transparency in the family courts', [2010] CFLQ 273. I propose to adopt an incremental approach. I propose initially to issue Guidance on the Publication of Judgments. As a first step I have published a draft of the proposed Guidance for comment and discussion ... I shall welcome and value your views."

Sir James' determination that more Family Court judgments should be published was underpinned by a continuing concern – a concern held not only by Sir James but by other senior family judges, too – about public confidence in the work of the family courts, most of which was conducted in private. As I noted in the Introduction, this had given rise to the insistence by some that the family courts were, in truth, secret courts.

What was required was not a semantic debate concerning the difference in meaning between 'closed', 'private' and 'secret' but a determined effort to make the work of the Family Court more open, more transparent, to educate the public about what actually happens in the Family Court and thereby, it was hoped, to improve public confidence in the family courts.

As I described in Chapter 3, this was a process that had been ongoing for almost a decade by the time Sir James was appointed President of the Family Division. Every effort to make the Family Court more transparent had either failed or been of only limited success. The Family Court was still regarded (and invariably described) as a secret court. It was attacked as such by politicians, parents and the media. The concerns were widespread. They were not going away. Without change, they were unlikely to go away.

In the next chapter I shall discuss in detail the reaction to the President's Practice Guidance and the extent to which it has been complied with by judges. Before I do that, it is important that there is clarity about what the Guidance actually requires.

Following the consultation, the final version of the Guidance was issued on 16 January 2014. It came into effect on 3 February 2014. The *Daily Mail* claimed it as a victory – reminiscent of *The Times'* claim to victory in April 2009 when journalists became entitled to attend hearings in the family courts. An online article written by the *Daily Mail's* correspondent, Steve Doughty, began:

> ***"At last! Victory on secret courts: Rulings in family cases to be made public after Mail campaign***
>
> - *Family Court and Court of Protection judgements will now be made public*
>
> - *Expert witnesses, including social workers, are to be named*
>
> - *Councils applying to take children into care can no longer claim anonymity*
>
> - *New rules laid down by President of the Family Division Sir James Munby*
>
> - *Daily Mail has exposed a series of major scandals over the past year*
>
> - *These have resulted from justice being conducted behind closed doors."*

Like *The Times* in 2009, the *Daily Mail* had failed to read the small print. It significantly over-stated the reach of the Practice Guidance. Its statement that family court judgments 'will now be made public', that expert witnesses, including social workers, 'are to be named' and that councils 'can no longer claim anonymity' is not an accurate representation of what the Practice Guidance says.

Although the *Daily Mail* reported that there were to be 'new rules', that, too, is not accurate. What was being published was Practice *Guidance*; not a Practice *Direction* or a new rule. In an evaluation of the Practice Guidance,[7] Dr Julie Doughty (no relation to the *Daily Mail's* Steve Doughty), Alice Twaite and Paul Magrath say that they:

> "understand that the President is able to issue guidance to judg-

---

[7] *Transparency through publication of family court judgments: An evaluation of the responses to and effects of, judicial guidance on publishing family court judgments involving children and young people* published in March 2017 by Cardiff University.

es without first having to seek and obtain the approval of the Lord Chief Justice and the Master of the Rolls, as he would to issue a Practice Direction. Issuing a Practice Direction would be a lengthy process, whereas simple 'guidance' can be communicated to the judiciary very quickly. The latter, however, has the disadvantage of less formality and perhaps an appearance of lower status than a Practice Direction..."

The new Practice *Guidance* would not be binding on judges in the way that a Practice Direction or a rule is binding on them. Whilst Sir James strongly encouraged family court judges to comply with the Practice Guidance, judges were not compelled to follow it – and many have not done so. Although the Practice Guidance has undoubtedly led to an increase in the number of family court judgments being published it remains the case that the number of judgments published in the period from 3 February 2014 to 31 March 2019 is only a small proportion of the total number of judgments that have been handed down by family court judges in England and Wales during that period.

The Guidance distinguishes between two classes of judgment – those that *must* be published and those that *may* be published. Although the use of the word 'must' suggests a mandatory requirement, as I have already noted, that is not the case. It would be more accurate to substitute the word 'should' for the word 'must'.

As for the judgments which 'should' normally be published, the Guidance states that:

15. The following paragraphs of this Guidance distinguish between two classes of judgment:

(i) those that the judge must ordinarily allow to be published (paragraphs 16 and 17); and

(ii) those that may be published (paragraph 18).

16. Permission to publish a judgment should always be given whenever the judge concludes that publication would be in the public interest and whether or not a request has been made by a party or the media.

17. Where a judgment relates to matters set out in Schedule 1 or 2 below <u>and a written judgment already exists in a publishable form or the judge has already ordered that the judgment be transcribed</u>, [em-

> *phasis supplied] the starting point is that permission should be given for the judgment to be published unless there are compelling reasons why the judgment should not be published.*

The words that I have underlined in paragraph 17 of the Guidance are very important since they define the judgments that should be published. There is no requirement to publish any judgment that does not fit one or other of the alternative descriptions given in paragraph 17 – a written judgment that exists in publishable form or a recorded judgment which the judge has ordered should be transcribed.

At the end of a contested hearing in the Family Court, the judge is required to give judgment. Normally, the judgment will set out the relevant background history to the case, identify the issues which the court is being called upon to determine, set out the evidence that has been placed before the court by all of the parties, set out the relevant law which the judge must apply in arriving at a decision, make findings of fact based upon the evidence that has been presented and, finally, arrive at his or her ultimate conclusion on outcome giving reasons why he or she has arrived at that conclusion.

Although I am not aware of the existence of any statistical information on the point, I am in no doubt that the majority of judgments given in the Family Court are extempore judgments (given immediately, or very soon after, the judge has heard all of the evidence and submissions) and not written judgments. There is a duty on advocates to take a contemporaneous and detailed note of an extempore judgment given by the judge. After the hearing the advocates should co-operate with each other in producing an agreed note of the judgment and should submit that note to the judge for him or her to approve. In my opinion an agreed note of judgment, even if approved by the judge, is not "a written judgment that exists in publishable form" for the purpose of paragraphs 16 and 17 of the Guidance.

All judgments given in the Family Court are digitally recorded. When the judge gives an extempore judgment, any party can request a transcript of that judgment or the judge may take the initiative and order a transcript. When the judge agrees that an extempore judgment should be transcribed a digital copy of the recording is made available on CD and sent to an authorised firm of transcribers who will normally produce the transcript within two or three weeks (unless the court specifically directs that it must be provided sooner). Unless the judge orders that the judgment be transcribed 'at public expense' the burden of paying for the judgment to be transcribed falls on the party who applies for the transcript.

In any case where the judge has delivered an extempore judgment rather than a written judgment and where he or she has not ordered that the extempore judgment should be transcribed, there is no judgment 'in a publishable form' and therefore the judge does not have to be concerned about the provisions of the Practice Guidance.

If the judge prepares a written judgment and agrees that the judgment should be published, he or she must make sure that the judgment is properly anonymised so that it does not contain any information (e.g. the names of the children or their parents) which would enable the children to be identified. If the judge orders that an extempore judgment should be transcribed then, in the first instance, the transcriber should prepare the judgment in an anonymised format.

As for the schedules referred to in paragraph 17 of the Practice Guidance, Schedule 1 concerns children and Schedule 2 concerns incapacitated adults. I am only concerned with the former. Schedule 1 provides that:

> *"In the family courts (and in due course in the Family Court), including in proceedings under the inherent jurisdiction of the High Court relating to children), judgments arising from:*
>
> *(i) a substantial contested fact-finding hearing at which serious allegations, for example allegations of significant physical, emotional or sexual harm, have been determined;*
>
> *(ii) the making or refusal of a final care order or supervision order under Part 4 of the Children Act 1989, or any order for the discharge of any such order, except where the order is made with the consent of all participating parties;*
>
> *(iii) the making or refusal of a placement order or adoption order under the Adoption and Children Act 2002, or any order for the discharge of any such order, except where the order is made with the consent of all participating parties;*
>
> *(iv) (the making or refusal of any declaration or order authorising a deprivation of liberty, including an order for a secure accommodation order under section 25 of the Children Act 1989;*
>
> *(v) any application for an order involving the giving or withholding of serious medical treatment;*

(iv) any application for an order involving a restraint on publication of information relating to the proceedings."

At paragraph 18, the Practice Guidance goes on to state that:

"In all other cases, the starting point is that permission may be given for the judgment to be published whenever a party or an accredited member of the media applies for an order permitting publication, and the judge concludes that permission for the judgment to be published should be given."

The Practice Guidance gives a very clear steer in support of publishing Family Court judgments. However, contrary to the claim by the *Daily Mail*, it does not make publication mandatory. Neither does it remove or water down the requirement, in every case, for the judge to balance the rights of the child and his or her parents under Article 8 of the ECHR, to the protection of their private and family life, against the rights of the media, under Article 10, to freedom of expression.

Similarly, and again contrary to the *Daily Mail*, there is no absolute rule that local authorities and expert witnesses must be named. Paragraph 20(1) of the Guidance provides that they should be named 'unless there are compelling reasons why they should not be so named". The Guidance does not give an indication of what might amount to 'compelling reasons'. This is clearly a matter for the discretion of the judge in the particular circumstances of the case.

The *Daily Mail* states in clear terms that: "Expert witnesses, *including social workers*, are to be named" (my emphasis). This, too, is not accurate. Although, plainly, social workers are trained and experienced in the field of social work, and have on occasion been described by Sir James Munby as "experts with a small 'e'", so far as the Practice Guidance is concerned they are not 'expert witnesses'. That is made clear by section 13(8) of the Children and Families Act 2014. Section 13 is headed *Control of expert evidence, and of assessments, in children proceedings*. Section 13(8) states that the following categories of professionals are *not* experts for the purpose of this section (and therefore, in my opinion, are also *not* 'experts' for the purpose of the President's Practice Guidance). Section 13(8) provides that:

"References in this section to providing expert evidence, or to putting expert evidence before a court, do not include references to –

(a) the provision or giving of evidence –

> *(i) by a person who is a member of the staff of a local authority or of an authorised applicant,*
>
> *(ii) in proceedings to which the authority or authorised applicant is a party, and*
>
> *(iii) in the course of the person's work for the authority or authorised applicant…*
>
> *(c) the provision or giving of evidence by an officer of the Children and Family Court Advisory and Support Service when acting in that capacity…'*

The President's Practice Guidance has nothing explicit to say about whether social workers should or should not normally be named. Paragraph 20(iii) of the Guidance provides that:

> *"anonymity in the judgment as published should not normally extend beyond protecting the privacy of the children and adults who are the subject of the proceedings and other members of their families, unless there are compelling reasons to do so."*

Whilst it is arguable that this paragraph is wide enough to include social workers amongst the categories of witnesses who should be named, it remains the case that whether they are named is a matter for the discretion of the judge in the circumstances of the particular case. I shall deal with this issue in more detail in Chapter 8.

Judgments should be published on the 'Bailii' website: www.bailii.org. The public has free access to this website. I am informed that in November 2019 recent weekly usage (page requests) were 2,333,569 hits per week, recent weekly users were 104,857 per week and the domains currently referring to Bailii were 1,538.

Academics, lawyers and representatives of the media regularly visit the website. When a published judgment leads to a news story being published by the media, it is invariably the case that the judgment has been picked up from the Bailii website. How the media deal with information contained in published judgments is an issue to which I shall return in Chapter 10. Although a number of non-lawyers have said to me that they do not find the Bailii website easy to navigate it is a free and an invaluable resource. My experience of Bailii is that it is very efficient. Judgments sent to Bailii are normally uploaded onto their website the same day and quite often within a couple of hours. There are occasions when a judge who has placed a judgment on Bailii will need urgently to have it taken down, for example, because an error has been noticed in the anonymisation of the judgment. Again, my experience is that, when asked, Bailii removes judgments from their website very quickly indeed.

The President's Practice Guidance was not universally welcomed. Many judges were opposed to it. A number of organisations and practitioners representing the interests of children were also opposed to it. I shall deal with judges' objections in the next chapter. I shall discuss the objections of children's groups in Chapter 12.

The consultation on next steps
Sir James Munby was clear from the outset that he did not see the publication of judgments as being sufficient, by itself, to improve the level and quality of transparency in the Family Court. Six months after the Guidance came into force the President issued another consultation paper: *Transparency – The Next Steps: A Consultation Paper published by the President of the Family Division on 15 August 2014*. The Consultation Paper was silent as to the timescale for responses and as to the date when the outcome of the consultation would be published. Sir James Munby retired in July 2018. The results of the consultation have never been published. The reason for this, I believe, is because there was no consensus on what, if anything, should happen next. Views were polarised – as they have been since 2004 when political and media interest in the issue of transparency began.

Although the results of the consultation were never published and the proposed 'next steps' never taken, the consultation paper did raise some important issues (in particular the proposal that certain categories of documents on the court file should be disclosed to the media) which continue to be of concern and which should not be allowed to be swept under the proverbial carpet.

The Practice Guidance and the consultation on next steps clearly demonstrated Sir James Munby's intended direction of travel. The problem was that some of those dealing with children's cases in the Family Court were reluctant to travel with him.

7: THE IMPACT OF THE PRACTICE GUIDANCE

"I have yet to come across any function of the state that works better in secret. I'm guessing that's why council meetings, parliamentary debates, criminal trials and election counts are all held in public. The law that prevents reporting of what goes on in family courts is meant to protect individual children's interests, but it is clearly now working to hide bad, and even sometimes unlawful, social work practice." (Louise Tickle)[1]

The objective of the President's Guidance on Transparency is set out in its opening paragraph. It was *"intended to bring about an immediate and significant change in practice in relation to the publication of judgments in family courts"*. The reason for this change, according to the President, was that "there is a need for greater transparency in order to improve public understanding of the court process and confidence in the court system". It was another step intended to address continuing public concern about the 'secret' Family Court and to restore public confidence in the work of the Family Court. In this chapter I shall consider the extent to which that objective has been achieved.

In 2016/17 a research project, funded by the Nuffield Foundation, evaluated the responses to and effect of the Practice Guidance. The project team was led by Dr Julie Doughty of the School of Law and Politics at Cardiff University ('the Doughty research'). The aims of the Doughty research were to analyse the cases that were published in the first two years of the Guidance, to evaluate the effects of and responses to the Guidance by the courts, the media and other stakeholders and to evaluate the contribution the Guidance had made to increasing public legal education.

It is clear that the authors of this report were handicapped in the analysis they were able to undertake – and therefore, also, in the conclusions they were able to draw – as a result of the limitations (some might say the inadequacies) of the data collected by the Ministry of Justice (MoJ). The report states that:

---

[1] Freelance journalist writing for *The Guardian* on 3 August 2017.

> *"We had originally aimed to analyse the relationship between the number of judgments published on BAILII and the number of relevant cases heard in individual courts. We had hoped to be able to report on whether more reports are published by busier courts than by others. That has, however, not been possible because of the way court statistics are recorded. There is no publicly accessible data on the number of cases that come within the categories in para. 17 of the 2014 guidance. Nor is it possible to estimate this from the data that is published about the throughput of cases. The number of cases in the family courts is however known to be rising."*[2]

The report goes on to make further criticisms of the quality, intelligibility and usefulness of the MoJ's statistics. Such criticisms are not new. Throughout my judicial career judges have repeatedly expressed concern about this issue. Plus ça change.

One of the outcomes of the research was to highlight the fact that although initially, after the Guidance came into effect, there was a significant increase in the number of judgments published, by 2015 the rate of publication had begun to slow. This is well illustrated by the graph on page 95. The graph represents my own analysis of the evidence available on Bailii concerning the number of judgments published. The graph shows the total number of judgments published by Circuit Judges each quarter from March 2014 to March 2019.

Some Circuit Judges are authorised under section 9 of the Senior Courts Act 1981 to sit as a Deputy High Court Judge in the Family Court and also in the Family Division of the High Court. They do this on an ad hoc basis according to need. The graph includes all of the judgments published by individual Circuit Judges including judgments published when sitting as a Deputy High Court Judge.

Some judges told the researchers that at the time of the research they were submitting fewer rather than more judgments to Bailii. The analysis revealed that only 17 Circuit Judges had published ten or more judgments during the period of the study.

Another finding was that the application of the Guidance by judges was 'patchy'. This meant that the researchers were not able to make an accurate estimate of the proportion of cases that do and do not appear on Bailii, nor the reasons behind this.

---

[2] See paragraph 3.2.2 of the report.

The Impact Of The Practice Guidance

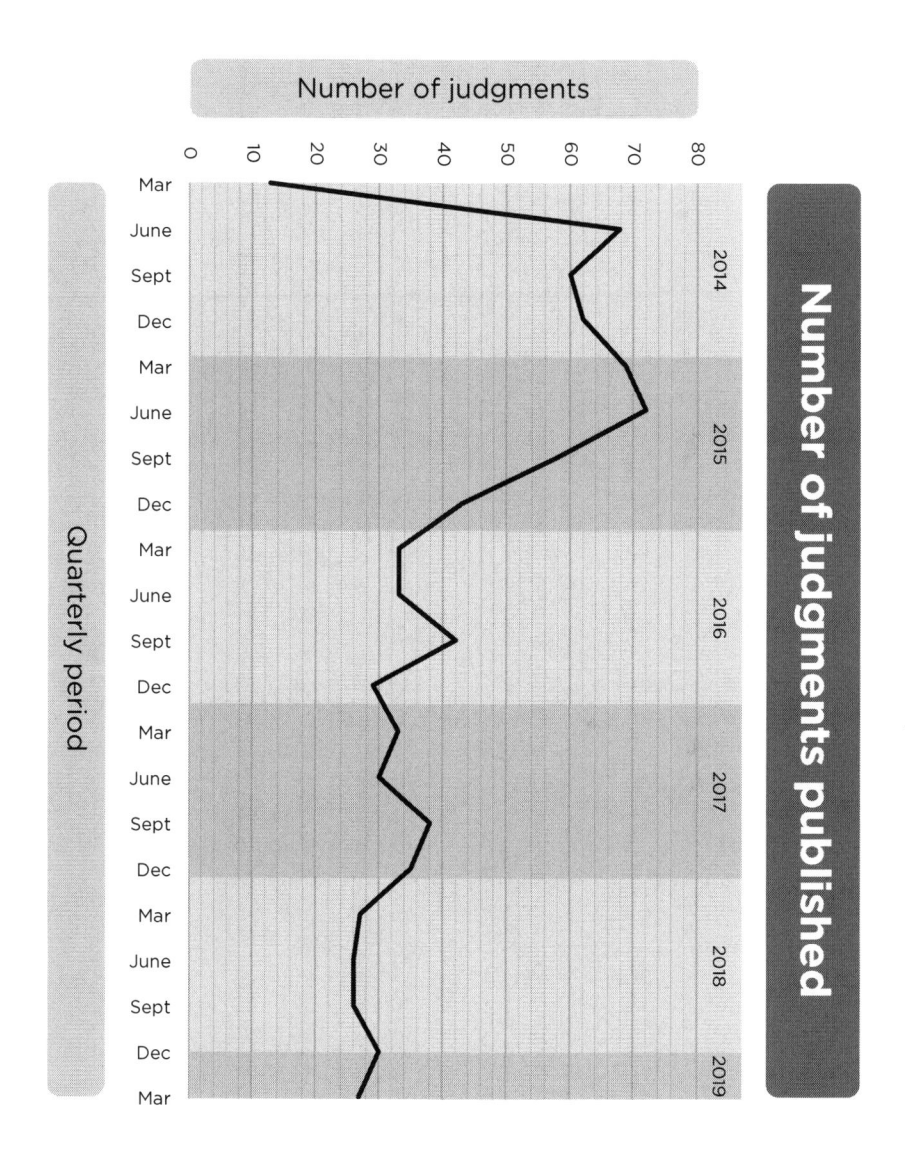

In addition to analysing the statistical evidence concerning the number of judgments published and by which judges, the research went on to consider a number of other key issues including the problem of effective anonymisation of judgments, the media's reporting of Family Court cases and the views and experiences of judges, journalists and other stakeholders.

The research team undertook a survey of judges. Unfortunately, despite the President's encouragement to all family judges, only 13 Circuit Judges responded to the survey. That inevitably raises an issue about whether the views of those who responded are genuinely representative of the total number of family Circuit Judges in England and Wales. Notwithstanding the very small response to the survey, the authors of the research report felt able to make the following point with a degree of force. They say that:

> *"There is however a clear message that the judiciary are very conscious of the necessity for effective anonymisation and the heavy burden this responsibility places on them and on lawyers and HMCTS staff. It seems reasonable to conclude from these views that lack of time, resources and training may well contribute to the low rate of publication across the country. Some judges had developed methods to help them overcome the challenges but it was generally recognised that the task was more difficult for circuit judges who do not have clerks to assist them."*[3]

The report notes that after the 2014 guidance was introduced, some social workers expressed concern about the personal impact on them of being named in a published judgment. I shall discuss issues relating to the naming of social workers and other professionals in Chapter 8.

In the final section of their report, under the heading 'Conclusions and recommendations' the authors reflect on the outcome of their research. They summarise both the positives and the negatives. They say:

> *"The 2014 guidance has led to a large number of family court judgments being available to the public and the media, that would not otherwise be in the public domain. These are potentially a valuable resource for public legal education. The guidance also seems to have achieved its aims to reduce (if not entirely negate) the level of allegations of secrecy in the court system made in the main stream media. Publishing on BAILII seems to work well at High Court level, where most cases of interest to the media will be heard.*

---

[3] See section 6.11 of the report.

However, patchy understanding of and adherence to the 2014 guidance over the country means that the aim of presenting a holistic picture of the system is not being achieved. The burden of preparing judgments for publication, with all the associated concerns about identification of children, families and practitioners is falling inequitably on some areas. The rate of publication on BAILII is falling and the demands of the publication process may make it unsustainable in the current resource-starved environment."

As for the guidance itself, the authors identify five options for the way forward: first, to continue as at present; second, to reverse the President's Practice Guidance; third to incorporate a version of the guidance in the Family Procedure Rules 2010 (i.e. to make compliance compulsory); fourth, to hold family court hearings in public; or fifth, to pilot a variation of the 2014 Guidance. The researchers discount the first four options, instead arguing in favour of their fifth and final option. They say:

"We do not think that the current situation is satisfactory, nor that it achieves the original aim of the guidance to make public the work of the Family Court throughout the jurisdiction. We suggest that the 2014 guidance could be modified to require every court and every circuit judge to provide a small and manageable representative sample of cases that fall within paras 16 and 17 of the guidance. Applications under para 18 should also be supported by making transcripts more easily obtainable."[4]

Their suggestion that a variation of the 2014 Practice Guidance should be piloted has not been acted upon. The position today, therefore, is that the Practice Guidance remains in force as originally published – but to what effect?

Judicial responses

With permission from the current President of the Family Division, Sir Andrew McFarlane, I have conducted my own survey of some of those Circuit Judges who are authorised to deal with cases concerning children brought under the Children Act 1989. I have been informed by the President's office that 196 Circuit Judges in England and Wales are authorised to deal with this area of work. In the period from 3 February 2014 (when the Practice Guidance came into effect) until 31 March 2019, 752 judgments were published by 114 family Circuit Judges. It follows, therefore, that during that five-year period 82 family Circuit Judges did not publish any judgments at

---

[4] See section 10 of the report.

all.[5] When the figures are analysed in detail it can be seen that only 20 judges published more than ten judgments, the rest were all in single figures. 11 judges published more than 20 judgments.

There is also regional variation. In Wales only two judges published judgments. 96% of those judgments were published by just one judge. In one major court centre (Birmingham) a total of five judgments were published by three judges. In some courts – Wolverhampton, Telford and Worcester, for example – no judgments were published at all.

There is no information available (because it is not a statistic that is recorded) concerning the total number of judgments given by family Circuit Judges in Children Act cases during the five-year period I am concerned with. Speculation would be both unhelpful and almost certainly wrong. Without that information it is impossible to state the percentage of Family Court judgments that were published during the relevant period. The furthest I am able to go – and for the reasons I have given it is inevitably no more than an educated guess – is to say that I am confident that the total number of judgments handed down by family Circuit Judges during the five-year period I am considering is likely to have been very substantially more than the 752 that have been published on Bailii.

The fact that Bailii names the 114 Circuit Judges who have published judgments has enabled me to approach some of them to invite them to respond to a questionnaire. I sent questionnaires to 55 Circuit Judges. 36 responded. That is a 65% return.

Identifying the 82 judges who have never published a judgment has been more challenging. I have only been partially successful.

There are 42 Designated Family Judges in England and Wales.[6] By considering both the judges listed on Bailii as having published a judgment and the list of the 42 DFJs in post, it can be seen that 18 DFJs in post when I undertook the survey have never published a judgment on Bailii.

That gave me a small pool to begin with. I have been able to identify another ten judges who have never published a judgment. That increased the size

---

[5] The survey I undertook by questionnaire provides only a snapshot at a particular moment in time. Since I carried out the survey in 2019 some judges will have retired and some new judges will have been appointed. My instinct tells me that the figure today may well be higher than it was when I carried out the survey, though that is pure speculation.

[6] See Chapter 6, page 84, footnote 5 for a description of the role of a Designated Family Judge.

of my pool to 28 judges. I sent each of them a questionnaire. 17 responded. That is a return of 61%.

For the purpose of my analysis of the responses I have received, I shall refer to the group of judges who have never published a judgment as Group A and the group of judges who have published at least one judgment as Group B. I want to look at some of the key issues that were raised in response to my survey.

The pressure of time
The views of family Circuit Judges about the merits of the Practice Guidance are varied covering a spectrum from unconditional support to outright hostility. In Group A there was some common ground between the 17 judges who responded. For the vast majority of this group the main reason advanced for not publishing was lack of time caused by pressure of workloads. It is striking that almost 43% of DFJs in England and Wales are part of Group A. The concern about time pressure caused by high workloads mirrors a finding made in the Doughty research. At section 6.4.1 of that report, under the heading 'Problems identified' the list which follows includes:

- Finding the time to write a publishable judgment.

- Three judges listed lack of resources as the main problem. Comments included: No time was allowed in the working day, with circuit judges under a great deal of pressure ... there is no time or support to edit judgments; already working at full capacity – until 8pm or 9pm most nights.

Having spent more than 14 years as a family Circuit Judge, the last 12 as a Designated Family Judge in three different court centres, I am sympathetic to those views. They accord with my own personal experience. Those views also resonate with the fact that in the last two years both the current President of the Family Division, Sir Andrew McFarlane, and his immediate predecessor, Sir James Munby, are on record as describing the Family Court as being in 'crisis'. The cause of this crisis is the exponential increase in the volume of both public and private law work in recent years, a rise that has not been matched by any increase in resources – judges, court clerks, social workers, Cafcass officers and so forth.

A 'View from the President's Chambers' published by Sir James Munby in the summer of 2016 was entitled 'Care Cases – the Looming Crisis'. It began:

> "In my last view (August 2016), I drew attention to the seemingly relentless rise in the number of new care cases. The fact is that we are approaching a crisis for which we are ill-prepared and where there is no clear strategy to manage the crisis. What is to be done?"

On 13 June 2018, shortly before he succeeded Sir James Munby as President, Sir Andrew McFarlane gave a speech at the *Care Crisis Review Launch*. In his speech, Sir Andrew said that:

> "'Crisis' maybe an overused word and some, outside the court system, may have questioned its deployment by Sir James Munby two years ago in relation to the rise in the number of care applications being received by the courts. For my part, I consider that Sir James was fully justified in calling this a crisis and, as the continuing figures have borne out since, Sir James was plainly right to blow the whistle when he did. The CAFCASS figures for last month, May 2018, record the second highest monthly figure for care applications received. I, too, am clear that this is a crisis and I am extremely concerned to see that it is by no means abating."

A similar point was made by Sir Andrew in his first 'View from the President's Chambers', published in January 2019.

In passing, it is interesting to note that the same problems exist in the criminal justice system. The unidentified author of *The Secret Barrister – Stories of the Law and How It's Broken*[7] (page 14) makes the point that:

> "On the day after a parliamentary report published in May 2016[8] began with those nine damning words – <u>the criminal justice system is close to breaking point</u> – not one single newspaper thought it more newsworthy than repetitive scare stories about migration or, in one case, a confected 'scandal' over Britain's Got Talent...If the criminal justice system were the NHS, it would never be off the front pages."

The author goes on to say (page 16):

> "A working criminal justice system, properly resourced and staffed by dedicated professionals each performing their invaluable civic functions, for the prosecution and the defence, serves to protect the inno-

---

[7] First published by Macmillan in 2018.
[8] House of Commons Public Accounts Committee, *Efficiency in the criminal justice system*, 23 May 2016.

> *cent, protect the public and protect the integrity, decency and humanity of our society. This should be a societal baseline. Not a luxury."*

There are many working in the family justice system who understand and share his or her pain and who would agree with the Doughty research report's reference to 'the current resource-starved environment' in which we work.

Returning to the concerns of the current President, it is also appropriate to note Sir Andrew's concern about the well-being of those working in the family justice system in light of the pressure caused by ever-increasing workloads. He said:

> *"I have, on every occasion that I have spoken about these issues, stressed my concern for the well-being of social workers, lawyers, judges and court staff who are conscientiously continuing to deliver a professional service in a timely manner despite the increase in workload... It is ... I believe right for me to say publicly in this 'View' something which I have said on some occasions to some gatherings in the past few weeks. In these highly pressured times, I think that it is neither necessary nor healthy for the courts and the professionals to attempt to undertake 'business as usual'. For the time being, some corners may have to be cut and some time-limits exceeded; to attempt to do otherwise in a situation where the pressure is sustained, remorseless and relentless, is to risk the burn-out of key and valued individuals in a system which is already sparsely manned in terms of lawyers, court staff and judges."*

Concern about the additional time pressures required to produce anonymised judgments suitable for publication was also a common theme in the responses from the judges in Group B. When this issue was explored further it became clear that some judges had begun publishing judgments with every intention of complying with the Practice Guidance but had quickly found that the task of producing an anonymised judgment that is fit for publication is an onerous task for which they simply did not have the time.

The Doughty research reports that one of the outcomes of their discussions with judges was that it was the process of anonymisation that was particularly problematic. This process is very time consuming. That problem is compounded by the responsibility on the judge to get the anonymisation right. The consequences for children and families of publishing a judgment that has not been adequately anonymised are obvious. And yet it does happen. It happens at every level. On one occasion I had to draw to the attention of a Court of Appeal judge an anonymisation error in a judgment he had just published.

The burden of responsibility
I have no doubt that it is not just the pressure of time but the combination of time and responsibility that presents such a significant stumbling block to the willingness of Circuit Judges to honour both the word and the spirit of the Practice Guidance. In a judgment delivered in 2016[9] Sir James Munby stated very clearly that:

> "... I stress the two cardinal points as they apply to judgments given in the Family Division or the Family Court:
>
> *(i) First, it is the responsibility of the judge, and of the judge alone, to decide whether to send a judgment to BAILII and to ensure (if a judgment is sent) that (a) the correct version is sent and (b) the version sent has been appropriately anonymised.*
>
> *(ii) Secondly, and following on from (i), it is for the judge, and the judge alone, to decide whether BAILII should be invited to take down a judgment which the judge has previously sent to BAILII. So any suggestion that such a judgment be taken down should be made to the judge (either directly or through the judge's clerk or through the Judicial Office) and not to either HMCTS or BAILII."*

Unlike High Court Judges, to each of whom is assigned a clerk who can help with administrative tasks, family Circuit Judges do not have a designated clerk nor any other clerical support in checking judgments before publication. When combined with the time required to produce an anonymised judgment suitable for publication, the additional pressure of making sure that the anonymisation is absolutely correct is, for many judges, a strong inhibiting factor and a step too far.

Jigsaw identification and the views of young people
With respect to the judges in Group A (those who have never published a judgment), one judge said that he considered it to be wrong to place information on the internet (i.e. on Bailii) without the consent of the child or young person concerned. He did not accept that the anonymisation of judgments necessarily overcame the problem of jigsaw identification. He was aware of a case where jigsaw identification had led to the child's birth family being identified and harassed. Another judge said that she did not

---

[9] *In the matter of X (A Child) (No 2)* [2016] EWHC 1668 (Fam) at paragraph 30.

The Impact Of The Practice Guidance

publish judgments because of her concern to protect the confidentiality of the proceedings and the privacy of the families involved. These points were raised by a number of other judges in Group A. Two judges in this group were of the opinion that publishing judgments contains an element of self-publicising or 'trumpet-blowing' and in the case of younger judges perhaps also an element of promotion-seeking.

Concern was expressed by one judge about the fact that once a judgment has been published by Bailii it is likely to be copied and posted on other websites. I am grateful to Paul Magrath of the Incorporated Council of Law Reporting[10] for commenting on that concern. It may be helpful to set out his views in full. He informs me that:

> *"until recently the risk of a judgment being copied and posted on other websites, while not negligible, was at any rate not high. BAILII's terms of use do not permit users to download and re-use their content in bulk, especially by some automated process. Moreover, their robots prevent Google searching the contents or displaying snippets in the result of a search. However, BAILII cannot prevent individuals downloading and reposting individual judgments. BAILII's contract requires them to publish what the judiciary send them, and if anyone reports something wrong with a judgment, they need to tell the judge, since…it is the judge's decision…to remove content.[11] However, BAILII usually remove it pretty quickly, possibly in anticipation (pending confirmation or re-supply). If it has in the meantime been copied and published elsewhere, it is unlikely that BAILII could do much about it…What is clear from all this is that it would be better if there were resources available to really check and vet judgments before there is any risk of a wrong version getting out. In the face of technical innovation I doubt BAILII will be able to maintain even the level of protection it currently imposes."*

It follows from the above that once a judgment is posted on Bailii there is a very high risk that the information will remain on the internet for ever, even if the judgment was taken down by Bailii.

With respect to the judges in Group B (those who have published at least

---

[10] Paul Magrath is Head of Product Development and Online Content at the ICLR. I reproduce his advice to me with his permission.

[11] This point was made very clear in the judgment of Sir James Munby in *In the Matter of X (A Child) (No 2)* [2016] EWHC 1668 (Fam) at paragraph 30. A request for a judgment to be taken down should be sent to the judge either directly or through the judge's clerk or through the Judicial Office.

one judgment), three judges said that in their opinion the risk of jigsaw identification has been overstated. However, other judges acknowledged the validity of the concerns about jigsaw identification,[12] one making the point that the price is high if children are identified as having been the subjects of public law proceedings. Another judge expressed concern that however carefully a judgment is anonymised there will always remain a risk of the family being identified. None of the judges in Group B expressed concern about the need to have the consent of the child or young person when deciding whether to publish a judgment on Bailii.

The issues of jigsaw identification and the views and wishes of children have been the subject of extensive academic research. I shall address these issues in Chapter 12.

The role of the media
The former President of the United States of America, Lyndon B Johnson, once famously said: "If one morning I walked on top of the water across the Potomac River, the headline that afternoon would read: 'President Can't Swim.'" It is that kind of cynicism that underlies the views of some judges towards the media's reporting of the work of the Family Court.

By far the greatest concern of judges in Group B related to the way information is handled by the media. There is a strong feeling that the media cannot be relied upon to present the facts accurately and in the right context and that some newspapers are unable to resist the temptation to sensationalise a story. Save for one judge (who gave permission to be named) I have anonymised the judges who raised concerns about this issue.

Judge A described a judgment which had been the subject of a 30-minute report on national radio. In his opinion, most of the discussion was ill-informed. More generally, Judge A expressed concern that the press appears to pick up on minor points in the case and make them appear as if they were central to the case, thereby creating a misleading impression. This point was also made by other judges.

Judge B spoke about a newspaper report in which, although the judgment had been reported accurately, the emphasis had been misplaced 'to make an attractive headline'.

Judge C referred to an article which had appeared in a national newspaper concerning one of his cases in which the journalist had incorrectly reported

---

[12] See the discussion in Chapter 12 on pages 182 and 185.

remarks about 'social engineering'. It appeared that the journalist had either not read or not understood the judgment.

Judge D expressed concern about an item published in a Sunday newspaper concerning secrecy in the Family Court. The journalist had stated that Judge D had made an order without the knowledge of the parents. Not for the first time so far as this particular journalist is concerned, he had accepted the story from the parents without question and without checking. The President's Office had published a transcript of the decision which showed clearly that the parents had been represented at that hearing and therefore had knowledge of the order.

Judge E expressed concern about a judgment she had published which related to the making of care and placement orders in respect of a toddler. The news story repeatedly stated that these orders had been made because the parents smoked, a wholly distorted account of the judge's reasons for making the orders. Judge E described the consequences as being 'widespread and significant.' The family was identified locally and door-stepped by the Press. Judge E is not alone in saying that at times she has found Press reporting of her judgments to be 'extremely stressful'.

Another judge, Judge F, said that, in her experience, media reporting is never completely accurate. The context is never understood and, therefore, assumptions are made that are wrong. She goes on to say that she is 'media savvy enough' only to put on Bailii cases which will get sympathetic treatment in the media.

The present practice of some judges is coloured by their experience of publishing judgments in the past. Judge G, for example, says that media reporting of his judgments has been 'wildly inaccurate' causing him 'widespread vilification' in the media. He is not the only judge to report personal attacks in the media.

Judge H has had experience of a judgment being the subject of a report on national radio and on the BBC news website. She describes the reporting of that case as 'entirely inaccurate'. The headlines had distorted the issues. Her impression was that the journalists concerned had either not read or had not understood her judgment. In her opinion, it is vital that journalists reporting family cases 'have a full and clear understanding of the issues'. Judge H says that since that experience she has 'rarely published anything'. In her opinion, some journalists are simply looking for a headline.

Judge J, too, is concerned about misleading headlines. That is not her only

105

concern. She is aware that some doctors feel very vulnerable as a result of the publication of Family Court judgments. Some have told her that if a case is reported in the Press it puts a doctor's decision under scrutiny. There is some evidence that that encourages (and thereby increases) the number of complaints against doctors and boosts online 'anti-doctor' forums.

Judge K was a little more sympathetic to the Press. In his opinion, the Press do want to report cases accurately. Inaccuracy creeps in when journalists try to explain the working of the Family Court without having any real understanding of how the Family Court actually works. He points to occasions when journalists have given the impression that judges decide cases on a whim without reference to principle.

Judge L was particularly annoyed that a news headline had wrongly stated that he had made an unlawful order locking up a teenage girl against her will. In fact, not only was the order he made a lawful order, it was also an order that was made with the consent of the young person concerned. The Judicial Office made a complaint to the broadcaster. The amended report published by the broadcaster was, says the judge, even worse.

Interestingly, notwithstanding that unsatisfactory experience, Judge L said that he remained of the view that the move towards greater transparency is necessary in order 'to slay many of the myths that exist'. He says that he is disappointed that the Practice Guidance has not been 'enforced' – if for no other reason than that unless all judges comply with the Guidance, the limited publication of judgments which actually takes place gives but a partial picture of what is going on in the Family Court.

I set out in some detail an experience reported by Her Honour Judge Eleanor Owens. I refer to her by name with her permission. In my opinion, one of the experiences she describes gives some understanding of why lack of trust continues to be a problem in the relationship between judges and the media.

Judge Owens refers to a case in which she was criticised by the media[13] for not stating her name in a published judgment. The judgment was published on Bailii.[14] I set out the following account with the full permission of the judge.

---

[13] *https://www.telegraph.co.uk/news/uknews/law-and-order/11341063/Secret-family-court-case-leaves-even-judge-anonymous.html.*
[14] *RBC v J-M* [2014] EWFC B174.

The case related to three children referred to in the judgment as *R (aged 9), K (aged 6) and O (aged 2)*. Care proceedings relating to these three children were heard in the Family Court sitting at Reading in December 2014. As can sometimes be the case, because of the number of people referred to in the judgment, anonymisation makes the facts difficult to follow. In addition to R, K and O the judgment also refers to JM (the mother of R, K and O), TR (JM's mother), JJ (JM's partner), DD (R's father), EJ (paternal grandmother of K and O) and SCJ (JM's former partner).

Although it is normal for the names of some of those involved in a case to be anonymised in order to try to prevent the children and their parents from being identified, it is highly unusual for a published judgment either to omit or anonymise the name of the judge. In this case, it appeared that the judge had not been named. *The Telegraph* assumed this to be a deliberate omission. The headline read:

> **"Judge left anonymous in family court case is named**
>
> *Judicial Office names judge in Reading case as Eleanor Owens after identities of everyone involved kept secret in highly-unusual move."*

The article that followed said:

> *"Judicial officials have revealed the identity of a judge whose name was missing from a written family court ruling she had made. The identities of everyone involved in the case had been kept secret in a highly unusual move. Parties were listed as "RBC", "R" & "J-M", lawyers were not named and there was no indication of the identity of the judge. An MP who campaigns for improvements in family justice said he presumed that there had been a mistake which would be put right. A spokesman for the Judicial Office later named the judge as Eleanor Owens."*

The article went on to set out a comment by the then Liberal Democrat MP, John Hemming, who said: "I understand the need to protect children in family court cases, but not identifying the judge is taking anonymisation a step too far, I think."

The apparent error was explained by The Transparency Project in its weekly email update. It said that:

> *"In fact there was nothing to put right. A quick check with BAILII confirmed that the name never had been suppressed. It had simply*

been left off the HTML version of the judgment (the one you see first on the website). It was and always had been on the original transcript in RTF format which the judge had sent and which you can download with a simple click of the mouse and print out. Something neither the Press Association nor the Telegraph thought of bothering to do."

A blog post on the website of The Transparency Project made the point that:

"There is an assumption in some parts of the media that the Family Courts are deliberately operating in a secretive manner in order to cover up the sinister conduct of social workers, doctors, and local authorities, and that is why hearings are held in private (i.e. in "secret") and judgments are not released or only in heavily redacted form. The recent transparency agenda promoted by Sir James Munby, President of the Family Division, has done something to address this. Old habits die hard, however, and the idea that there is some sort of conspiracy remains the default position for some journalists. They seem reluctant to believe that missing information has not merely been accidentally omitted but must have been intentionally suppressed."[15]

The reality is that this was a non-story. What was the purpose of running this story? Then, as now, the media (and in particular the print media) regularly referred to the Family Court as a 'secret' Family Court. Although that description was not given in this instance the clear inference is that the court was being excessively and inappropriately economical with the information put into the public domain. In short, that it was being secretive. That would seem to be the point *The Telegraph* was making – a point it has made on many other occasions.

I have dealt at length with the experience judges have had of the way their judgments have been treated by the media. If the Practice Guidance is to continue, it is in my opinion very important indeed that there is a measure of trust between judges and journalists. That is not a new point. It is a point that has been made repeatedly by the senior judiciary for more than a decade. In a lecture given in 2006, Lord Justice Wall said that:

"There should be an ongoing dialogue with the press and the media

---

[15] The curious incident of the judge with no name, The Transparency Project, 15 January 2015, available at *http://www.transparencyproject.org.uk/the-curious-case-of-the-judge-with-no-name/*.

The Impact Of The Practice Guidance

generally about family justice and how it is administered. We, the judiciary and the practitioners, have nothing to fear from public scrutiny: indeed, we should welcome it."[16]

We really do need to work with the media to build trust and confidence and to encourage the highest quality of media reporting. There needs to be a close working relationship not only between the President of the Family Division and the Society of Editors but at local level too. That could be achieved by Designated Family Judges seeking to build relationships with local media (local radio, regional television and the editor of the local newspaper). I am aware that this is already happening in some areas. It would be helpful for there to be some guidance from the President on this issue.

Another media issue raised by several of the judges who responded to the questionnaire was the almost total absence of accredited representatives of the media from hearings in the Family Court. Some judges interpreted this as a lack of interest on the part of the Press. As I argued in Chapter 4, I don't accept that to be the case. There are other, more significant, reasons why the media have not taken advantage of their right to attend hearings in the Family Court.

What judgments should be published?
One of the purposes of the Practice Guidance is that the publication of anonymised judgments published on Bailii should give the public an accurate picture of what goes on in the Family Court. The cases that come before the Family Court cover a wide spectrum. They include:

- the very serious, for example, children who have suffered life-threatening injuries;

- the complex, for example, injuries to a baby which may have been inflicted by being shaken by a parent but which could conceivably be birth-related;

- those with a sexual context, for example, involving children who have been the victims of very serious sexual abuse by a family member; and, more frequently,

- cases involving parents with addictions to drugs and/or alcohol, or who

---

[16] *Opening up the Family courts: a personal view* – the Association of Lawyers for Children annual lecture in memory of Allan Levy QC and David Hershman given in Birmingham on 29 June 2008 at page 20.

suffer from significant mental health difficulties, or between whom there is domestic violence, any one or more of which may render them incapable of providing safe care for their child.

It is clear from the responses to the questionnaires that some judges are under the mistaken belief that only those judgments handed down in cases that are serious, complex or which have some remarkable feature should be published and that the more routine cases are of no interest. One judge responded: "I cannot imagine that any of my judgments would be of the slightest interest to anyone". Several other judges made similar self-deprecating comments. My interpretation of the Practice Guidance is different. In my opinion, one of the objectives of the guidance is to give the public an insight into the full range of the work conducted in the Family Court and not just a snapshot of the sensational, the tragic and the salacious. Far more cases fall into the 'routine' category than into any of the other three categories.

Risk

In a lecture given in 2013 under the title *Being a judge today*[17] the former Lord Chief Justice, Lord Judge, made a very telling point. He said:

> "...judges have to make decisions that are profoundly unpleasant and have serious consequences. But they have to make them. To send someone to prison when his spouse believes that he is innocent; to take children away from one or other, or even both, parents because it is no longer safe for them to be living with that parent; to tell the government of the day, or all the many authorities that have power over us, that they are acting unlawfully is a difficult responsibility. This is not a fun job. And you have to do it. The parties and the public are entitled to a decision from you. And you must give it to the best of your abilities".

It would be wrong to leave this chapter without referring to one other issue raised in some of the responses to the questionnaire. That issue is the personal safety of judges and the personal risks they face. I do not intend to identify any of the judges who have raised this point either by name, gender or location. I do not want to add to their stress and distress. However, the public should know that there are judges who have received death threats, who have been vilified in the media, who have experienced online criticism both on the online news feed of the media and on social networking sites,

---

[17] *The Safest Shield: Lectures, Speeches and Essays*, Hart Publishing, 2015, pages 283 to 293 at page 290.

who have had to have security systems installed at home and who have had to take special measures to protect their children.

With the judge's permission, I refer in detail to only one of the incidents judges have described to me. The judge was the subject of an ongoing publicity campaign taking place outside the court buildings. The campaign was organised by a pressure group which used social media to mobilise people to parade outside the court using loud hailers and banners to draw attention to grievances relating to public law proceedings. At the end of the day the judge walked to the station unaware that he was being followed. At the station he was approached by a woman who informed him of threats being made against him on social media. The judge reported the matter promptly. The police were involved. A risk assessment was undertaken. Appropriate safety systems were put in place. The person responsible for making the threats was arrested, remanded in custody and eventually convicted and sentenced to a term of imprisonment.

Other, even more serious examples, could be given.

The business of family law can be highly emotive especially in cases relating to children both in public law and in private law cases. I suspect that most family Circuit Judges accept that an element of risk comes with the job. It is something judges live with. Whilst there is no reason to believe that the publication of judgments does, of itself, heighten that risk, the way the judgment is dealt with by the media most certainly can.

Conclusion
In my judgement, though a laudable and valuable attempt to improve transparency in the Family Court, the President's Practice Guidance on Transparency has only been of limited success. If the Family Court is to become more transparent, more – much more – needs to be done.

8: WHO SHOULD BE NAMED IN JUDGMENTS?

> *"There is likely to be an increasing reluctance on the part of professional and expert witnesses to participate in court proceedings if they are to be subjected to the scrutiny of the media. This could lead to increasing delay in dealing with some family cases."*[1]

I noted in Chapter 6 that the *Daily Mail* hailed the President's Practice Guidance on Transparency as a victory for the *Mail*'s campaign against secret family courts. The journalist who wrote that article, Steve Doughty, went on to inform the *Mail*'s readers that this breakthrough meant that in future: "Expert witnesses, including social workers, are to be named". I pointed out in Chapter 6 that that statement was not accurate. However, I have no doubt that Steve Doughty accurately represents the media's position in suggesting that local authorities, social workers and expert witnesses should normally be named.

The media would argue that the need for the court to name the local authority, social workers and expert witnesses is an important part of open justice. When the court publishes a judgment in which it is critical of a local authority, not to name that local authority is to shield it from public scrutiny, from public comment and from being held to account. It gives the impression of the court allowing that local authority to sweep its failings under the carpet, out of sight. That criticism, if well-founded, would be consistent with the ongoing concern that the Family Court is a 'secret' Family Court.

Paragraph 20 of the President's Practice Guidance provides that:

> *"In all cases where a judge gives permission for a judgment to be published:*
>
> *(i) public authorities and expert witnesses should be named in the judgment approved for publication, unless there are compelling reasons why they should not be so named;*

---

[1] From the response of the Family Justice Council in November 2006 to the Government's Consultation Paper on Transparency in the Family Courts.

...

> *(iii) anonymity in the judgment as published should not normally extend beyond protecting the privacy of the children and adults who are the subject of the proceedings and other members of their families, unless there are compelling reasons to do so."*

In every case in which the judge intends to publish his or her judgment the judge must ask himself or herself, should the local authority be named? Should the social workers be named? Should the expert witnesses be named? A search through published judgments shows that the answers given are 'yes' to some questions and 'no' to others, though it may not always be clear why the judge has decided 'yes' in one case and 'no' in another!

So, what are the key principles the judge should have in mind in deciding whether the local authority, the social worker and any expert witness should be named? In the discussion that follows it is important to keep in mind that although there are established principles to guide the judge in coming to a decision on these questions, ultimately, the decision is a matter for the exercise of judicial discretion. Every decision is fact-specific.

Naming the local authority
In 2004 Sir James Munby published a judgment[2] concerning three brothers who were aged 15, 10 and 4 at the time care proceedings were issued in January 2003. The local authority applied for emergency protection orders.[3] Those orders were made even though the parents had not been given notice of the hearing. The children were removed from their home that day and placed in foster care. The local authority then began care proceedings and obtained interim care orders. The children were eventually returned to the care of their parents in October 2003. In his judgment, Sir James was highly critical of the local authority's conduct in applying for emergency protection orders without giving notice to the parents. He gave guidance on the approach that should be taken in future by a local authority seeking the urgent removal of a child. Notwithstanding his criticism of that local

---

[2] *In the Matter of the B children, X Council v B and others* [2004] EWHC 2015 (Fam).
[3] An emergency protection order (EPO) is an order which can be made by the court urgently with only short notice (and in exceptional circumstances no notice) being given to the parents, where it is considered that the risk to the child is so great that immediate action needs to be taken either to remove the child from the care of her parents or to prevent a parent from removing her from hospital or any place in which she was being accommodated immediately prior to the order. An order lasts for up to eight days. The order can be extended for up to a further seven days. Only one extension may be granted (see sections 44 and 45 of the Children Act 1989).

Who Should Be Named In Judgments?

authority, he did not name the local authority.

Some while later, the boys' mother wrote to Sir James in terms which will strike a chord with many parents whose children are taken from them and placed in local authority care. The mother said:

> *"I know that the judgement is being used in other cases and that it is helping other families in many ways ... but Justice Munby where does it help us[?] ... We cannot name and shame our local authority which is what we would want to do more than anything. Could you please explain to us what we can do with this damning judgement you handed down, because it seems of little use to us. Could you please explain to us why our local authority are protected from publicity ..."*

In 2007, having given the other parties the opportunity to respond to the mother's letter, Sir James published a second judgment.[4] In responding to the mother's letter, Sir James set out his views very clearly. He said:

> *"14. There will, of course, be cases where a local authority is not identified, even where it has been the subject of stringent judicial criticism. A recent example is Re X (Emergency Protection Orders) [2006] EWHC 510 (Fam)...But current practice shows that local authorities involved in care cases are increasingly being identified...*
>
> *15. I propose to adopt the same approach here as that which I set out in Re B. Is there some proper basis for continuing the local authority's anonymity? In my judgment there is not.*
>
> *16. In the first place, as the local authority very frankly accepts, whatever anonymity it enjoys is somewhat precarious, given the fact that the solicitors in the case have all been publicly identified. More importantly, however, I cannot see that there is any need to preserve the local authority's anonymity in order to protect the children's privacy and identities. Disclosure of the name of the local authority is not of itself going to lead to the identification of the children. In this respect the case is no different from Re B and Re X.*
>
> *17. The real reason why the local authority seeks to perpetuate its anonymity is more to do with the interests of the local authority itself (and, no doubt, the important interests of its employees) than with*

---

[4] *Re B, X Council v B* [2007] EWHC 1622 (Fam).

115

the interests of the children. That is not a criticism of the local authority's stance. It is simply a statement of the realities.

18. I can understand the local authority's concern that if anonymity is lifted the local authority (or its employees) may be exposed to ill-informed criticism based, it may be, on misunderstanding or misrepresentation of the facts. But if such criticism exceeds what is lawful there are other remedies available to the local authority. The fear of such criticism, however justified that fear may be, and however unjustified the criticism, is not of itself a justification for affording a local authority anonymity. On the contrary, the powers exercisable by local authorities under Parts IV and V of the Children Act 1989 are potentially so drastic in their possible consequences that there is a powerful public interest in those who exercise such powers being publicly identified so that they can be held publicly accountable. The arguments in favour of publicity – in favour of openness, public scrutiny and public accountability – are particularly compelling in the context of public law care proceedings: see Re X, Barnet LBC v Y and X [2006] 2 FLR 998 at para [166].

19. Moreover, and as Lord Steyn pointed out in R v Secretary of State for the Home Department ex p Simms [2000] 2 AC 115 at page 126, freedom of expression is instrumentally important inasmuch as it "facilitates the exposure of errors in the governance and administration of justice of the country." How can such errors be exposed, how can public authorities be held accountable, if allowed to shelter behind a judicially sanctioned anonymity? This is particularly so where, as in the present case, a public authority has been exposed to criticism. I accept, as the local authority correctly points out, that many – indeed most – of the matters in dispute in this case were never the subject of any final judicial determination, but the fact remains that in certain respects I was, as my judgment shows, critical of the local authority. And that is a factor which must weigh significantly in the balance: see Re X, Barnet LBC v Y and X [2006] 2 FLR 998 at para [174].

20. In my judgment the balance here comes down clearly in favour of the local authority being identified."

Though undertaking the balancing exercise in any particular case may be difficult, the approach to deciding whether a local authority should be identified is clear and straightforward. The court must balance the risks that naming the local authority may lead to the identification of the child and the possible consequences for the child if that risk materialises, against the media's right to freedom of expression – in other words balancing the child's Article 8 rights against the media's Article 10 rights.

The ultimate decision will be fact-specific and will require the judge to have regard to all relevant facts. For example, a child living in the area of a small local authority (e.g. Rutland, the smallest county in the country) may be more easily identifiable than a child living in the much larger area of neighbouring Leicestershire County Council. It could be argued that in such a situation identifying the local authority is a piece of the jigsaw which could potentially lead to or increase the risk of so-called 'jigsaw identification'. However, even if the court is persuaded that there is some risk that by naming the local authority the child may be identified, there may nonetheless be other factors, for example findings by the court of significant malpractice by the local authority, which the public has the right to know about, which tip the balance in favour of naming the local authority.

I have undertaken a brief review of the judgments reported on Bailii in 2018 – those published by High Court Judges, Circuit Judges and Recorders. In 2018 the local authority is identified in just under 50% of the relevant judgments reported. Other researchers may find it interesting to undertake a more in-depth study analysing not only the frequency of naming local authorities but also the frequency of naming social workers and expert witnesses. It is possible – and I put it no higher than that – that such a study would reveal an inconsistency of approach.

Naming social workers
As with identifying a local authority so, too, when considering whether to identify a social worker, the court must undertake a balancing exercise, balancing the social worker's rights under Article 8 of the ECHR and the media's rights under Article 10. The starting point is that social workers do not have an automatic right to anonymity either under the general law or as a result of section 12 of the Administration of Justice Act 1960. To achieve anonymity social workers must persuade the court that their Article 8 rights outweigh the media's Article 10 rights.

There have been a number of cases in which this issue has been considered.[5] The key points which emerge from the case law would appear to be that social workers are public servants responsible for making life-changing decisions in the context of judicial proceedings. They cannot generally expect

---

[5] See, for example, *BBC v Rochdale Metropolitan Borough Council and X and Y* [2005] EWHC 2862 (Fam); *Dr A v Ward* [2010] EWHC 16 (Fam).

anonymity. If they seek anonymity they must produce compelling evidence to justify their application. That evidence must be specific and not merely anecdotal. Evidence of actual harassment, threats of physical or other harm or compelling evidence of the social worker being at risk of such behaviour, is likely to be required before the court will order that the identity of the social worker should not to be included in a published judgment.

These points have been underlined in two judgments given by Sir James Munby. In the first,[6] Sir James said:

> *"44. [referring to his earlier decision in Re J (Reporting Restriction: Internet: Video) [2013] EWHC 2694 (Fam)] ...the "fear of ... criticism, however justified that fear may be, and however unjustified the criticism, is, however, not of itself a justification for prior restraint by injunction ... even if the criticism is expressed in vigorous, trenchant or outspoken terms ... or even in language which is crude, insulting and vulgar...a much more robust view must be taken today than previously of what ought rightly to be allowed to pass as permissible criticism.*
>
> *45. But there is a fundamental difference between ideas, views, opinions, comments or criticisms, however strongly or even offensively expressed, and harassment, intimidation, threats or menaces. The one is and must be jealously safeguarded; the other can legitimately be prevented.*
>
> *46. The freedom of speech of those who criticise public officials or those exercising public functions, their right to criticise, is fundamental to any democratic society governed by the rule of law. Public officials and those exercising public functions must, in the public interest, endure criticism, however strongly expressed, unfair and unjustified that criticism may be. But there is no reason why public officials and those exercising public functions should have to endure harassment, intimidation, threats or menaces.*
>
> *47. ...Freedom of speech no more embraces the right to use words to harass, intimidate or threaten, than it does to permit the uttering of words of menace by a blackmailer or extortionist. Harassment by words is harassment and is no more entitled to protection than harassment by actions, gestures or other non-verbal means. On the contrary,*

---

[6] *In the matter of an application by Gloucestershire County Council for the committal to prison of Matthew John Newman* [2014] EWHC 3136 (Fam).

it is the victim of harassment, whether the harassment is by words, actions or gestures, who is entitled to demand, and to whom this court will whenever necessary extend, the protection of the law.

48. I do not wish there to be any room for doubts or misunderstanding. The family courts – the Family Court and the Family Division – will always protect freedom of speech...But the family courts cannot and will not tolerate harassment, intimidation, threats or menaces, whether targeted at parties to the proceedings before the court, at witnesses or at professionals – judges, lawyers, social workers or others – involved in the proceedings. For such behaviour, whatever else it may constitute, is, at root, an attack on the rule of law...

50. I do not want anyone to be left in any doubt as to the very serious view that the court takes of such behaviour. In appropriate cases immediate custodial sentences may be appropriate. And deterrent sentences may be justified. The court must do what it can to protect the proper administration of justice and to ensure that those taking part in the court process can do so without fear."

In the second case,[7] on this occasion concluding that the social workers should not be named, Sir James said that:

"102. It will be noticed that I have, quite deliberately, not identified either SW1 or SW2 or TM, though their employer has, equally deliberately, been named. There is, in principle, every reason why public authorities and their employees should be named, not least when there have been failings as serious as those chronicled here. But in the case of local authorities there is a problem which has to be acknowledged.

103. Ultimate responsibility for such failings often lies much higher up the hierarchy, with those who, if experience is anything to go by, are almost invariably completely invisible in court. The present case is a good example. Only SW1, SW2 and TM were exposed to the forensic process, although much of the responsibility for what I have had to catalogue undoubtedly lies with other, more senior, figures. Why, to take her as an example, should the hapless SW1 be exposed to public criticism and run the risk of being scapegoated when, as it might be thought, anonymous and unidentified senior management should never have put someone so inexperienced in charge of such a demanding case. And why should the social workers SW1, SW2 and TM be

---

[7] *In the matter of A (A Child)* [2015] EWFC 11.

> *pilloried when the legal department, which reviewed and presumably passed the exceedingly unsatisfactory assessments, remains, like senior management, anonymous beneath the radar? It is Darlington Borough Council and its senior management that are to blame, not only SW1, SW2 and TM. It would be unjust to SW1, SW2 and TM to name and shame them when others are not similarly exposed."*

The point made by Sir James concerning anonymous and unidentified senior management is a point raised in my discussions with journalists. One made the point that, as a matter of fairness, it is invariably the case that it is the local authority that should be named and shamed and not the social worker.

Being caught in a media firestorm

In some cases, naming social workers in published judgments can put them at risk from service users and their families. Social workers also face the risk of being caught up in a media firestorm. The dangers of this happening as a result of very serious criticisms of a particular social worker and his or her employing local authority are well illustrated in the case of Peter Connelly.

On 3 August 2007 Peter Connelly died. He was just 17 months old. At the time news of his death came into the public domain, he was known to the public as 'Baby P'. His mother, her boyfriend and her boyfriend's brother were all convicted of 'causing or allowing' Peter's death. Baby P was the latest in a growing list of young children who have lost their lives as a result of gross ill-treatment by their carers.

When news of the circumstances of Peter's death became public there was a media firestorm. Sharon Shoesmith, the Director of Education and Children's Social Care Services for the relevant local authority, Haringey London Borough Council, quickly found herself at the centre of this media firestorm. She was held to have overall responsibility for this tragedy. She was dismissed from her post. She began proceedings for judicial review. Though unsuccessful at trial,[8] she was partially successful on appeal.[9]

Shoesmith later wrote a book, *Learning from Baby P*.[10] In it she describes the way the media treated both her and some of her social workers. She refers

---

[8] *Shoesmith v Ofsted, Secretary of State for Children, Schools and Families* [2010] EWHC 852 (Admin).
[9] *Shoesmith v Ofsted and Others* [2011] EWCA Civ 642. With respect to her claims against the Secretary of State for Children, School and Families her appeals were allowed. With respect to her claim against Ofsted her appeal was dismissed.
[10] See Chapter 3, page 50 footnote 11.

(page 16) to a review of child deaths which:

> *"described the intensity, volatility and hostility of the public's attitude to social workers in the media coverage that followed news of Peter's death as reaching 'entirely new levels of irrationality'".*

She goes on to say (page 70) that:

> *"For social workers, the fear of either wrongly identifying or failing to prevent a case of child abuse has embedded a 'fear of failure' in the social work profession and a level of unavoidable anxiety which disrupts their work...the social work profession lives with a high degree of uncertainty and insecurity."*

So far as concerns the case of Baby P, Shoesmith says (page 179) that:

> *"In effect, the realities of familial child homicide are denied and blame is projected onto social workers...The death of Baby P was portrayed erroneously as the result of incompetent social workers, a rogue director and a hopeless local authority, in an otherwise sound system."*

Shoesmith draws the conclusion that (page 195):

> *"...blaming social workers for harm to children has become a habitual process of denying the realities of familial child abuse and homicide. That social workers are to blame has been forged and embedded as a belief, a reality, a truism or 'trope'. A 'trope' in literature is a word or expression used in a figurative or symbolic sense. It refers to a theme that is important and recurrent. The theme becomes overused such that it becomes a motif or cliché. A trope, in effect, is devoid of thought or reason. Referring to the blaming of social workers as a trope draws attention to the recurring nature of the blame which has become habitual and devoid of reason."*

Shoesmith was not the only person to be in the media's firing line. Sylvia Henry, a social worker employed by the London Borough of Haringey, was falsely accused of being partly responsible for Peter Connelly's death. On 2 December 2009 *The Sun* newspaper published an article headed: "Baby P social workers are still drawing full pay while on suspension." The article included an allegation that Ms Henry had behaved negligently and that her negligence had contributed to Peter Connelly's death. Ms Henry brought proceedings for damages for libel. The allegations against Ms Henry were said to have been published in about 80 articles. *The Sun* organised an online petition calling for the dismissal of Ms Henry. The campaign went on for around four months. *The Sun* admitted that the allegations were untrue. *The Sun* apologised and agreed to pay damages.[11]

Although the names of Sharon Shoesmith and Sylvia Henry did not come into the public domain as the result of the publication of a court judgment, the media's behaviour towards them should, in my opinion, give rise to a degree of caution about naming social workers in published judgments. There may be occasions when the egregious nature of a social worker's behaviour is such that the court really has no alternative but to name that social worker. However, in light of the experience of the media reporting of the case of Peter Connelly, judges should be aware of the potential media consequences, for the social worker and for his or her family, of naming the social worker in a published judgment.

A point made by Professor Judith Masson QC in 2016 concerning the naming of social workers is, in my opinion, a valid point. She says:

> *"The effect on local authorities is chilling. It is already very difficult to recruit and retain good social workers, and this adds to the pressure. Being named and shamed does not stop with the law report but is carried on in social media, impacting on social workers' families, their other clients and their work. The most egregious example of this occurred following the death of Baby Peter. The public's view of social work is diminished, making those in need less likely to seek or accept social work support. Overall, this approach to transparency makes it more difficult to protect children."*[12]

Judges can only come to a decision about whether a social worker should be named in a published judgment based on the evidence before the court and the findings made. However, when making the decision whether to name a social worker, I am concerned that there is a real danger of the court setting the bar too low. Clearly, if a social worker seeks anonymity on the basis that he or she has been abused by a service user then the social worker must adduce detailed, cogent evidence to prove the facts alleged. However, in my opinion, in deciding whether to name a social worker the court should

---

[11] Ms Henry also successfully sued Haringey LBC for posting on its website a statement alleging that she had been negligent. The local authority admitted that that allegation was untrue. Ms Henry received an apology and damages.

[12] *Reforming Care Proceedings in England and Wales: Speeding Up Justice and Welfare?* in J.Eekelaar (Ed.), Family Law in Britain and America in the New Century, Essays in Honor of Sanford N Katz (pp 187-206). [12] Netherlands: Brill Academic Publishers.

be prepared to take account of other factors that are matters of general knowledge such as, for example, the known risk of violence towards social workers from service users[13] and the risks that can flow from significant media criticism.

Naming other professionals
In care proceedings it is often the case that in addition to hearing evidence from the social worker and expert witnesses the court also hears evidence from other professionals involved with the family. This could include, for example, the family's GP, a health visitor, a midwife, a hospital doctor, nurses and teachers. Paragraph 20(iii) of the Practice Guidance on Transparency is wide enough to include all of these professionals and more. The position of such witnesses is similar to that of social workers. They have no automatic right to anonymity either under the general law or under section 12 of the Administration of Justice Act 1960. All such professionals have the right to apply to the court for an order that their identity should remain anonymous and should be given adequate opportunity to make an application. Such an application would need to be supported by relevant and cogent evidence of harm actually suffered or of the risk of future harm. The logic of naming all such professionals is impeccable. The wisdom of doing so must be open to some doubt.

As I noted in Chapter 7, one of the judges who responded to my questionnaire made the point that she has become aware that some doctors feel very vulnerable as a result of the publication of Family Court judgments. Some have told her that if a case is reported in the Press it puts a doctor's decision under scrutiny. There is some evidence that that encourages complaints and boosts online 'anti-doctor' forums. Though no evidence on the point has been drawn to my attention, it is reasonable to suppose that other professionals may well have similar concerns.

With respect to this category, which I have described as "other professionals", I noted earlier the views of Sir James Munby about whether they should be named. In a recent judgment[14] another High Court Judge, Mrs Justice Lieven, took a different view. The context was an application by

---

[13] See, for example, the article by Rachel Shraer in the *Community Care* journal in September 2014: *https://www.communitycare.co.uk/2014/09/16/violence-social-workers-just-part-job-70-incidents-investigated/* and the report published by the British Association of Social Workers Northern Ireland in June 2018: *Insult and Injury: Exploring the impacts of intimidation, threats and violence against social workers*: *https://www.basw.co.uk/resources/insult-and-injury-exploring-impacts-intimidation-threats-and-violence-against-social*.

[14] *Manchester University NHS Foundation Trust v Midrar Namiq, Karwan Mohammed Ali and Shokhan Namiq* [2020] EWHC 181 (Fam).

Manchester University NHS Foundation Trust for a declaration that it was lawful to: *"make arrangements for…mechanical ventilation treatment to be withdrawn to allow [a child] a kind and dignified death."*

All parties were agreed that the NHS Trust, the child and the parents should be named in the published judgment. The only issue concerned the naming of the healthcare professionals who were involved in treating the child. The parents wanted them to be named. The judge decided that they should not be named. Although, as with all such cases, this decision was fact-specific, in my opinion the judge's approach is of some relevance to the approach that should be taken in care proceedings with respect to the naming of professionals such as, for example, teachers, health visitors and midwives. The judge said:

> *"16. These cases are necessarily fact specific and I do not purport to set down general guidance. I do however somewhat differ from the views expressed by the President in A v Ward as set out above. This may be because the facts of the case differ. In my view there is an important distinction between professionals who attend court as experts (or judges and lawyers), and as such have a free choice as to whether they become involved in litigation, and treating clinicians. The latter's primary job is to treat the patient, not to give evidence. They come to court not out of any choice, but because they have been carrying out the treatment and the court needs to hear their evidence. This means they have not in any sense waived their right to all aspects of their private life remaining private. In my view there is a strong public interest in allowing them to get on with their jobs without being publicly named. I do not agree with the President that such clinicians simply have to accept whatever the internet and social media may choose to throw at them. I note that the President's comments were made before the well publicised cases of Gard and Evans, and perhaps at a time where the risks from hostile social media comment were somewhat less, or at least perceived to be less. There may well be cases where the factual matrix makes it appropriate not to grant anonymity and each case will obviously turn on its own facts. But in my view the balance in this case falls on the side of granting the order."*

The decision was appealed. The appeal was dismissed. So far as concerns the naming of professionals who are not giving evidence as expert witnesses, the observations made by the President, Sir Andrew McFarlane, are important. He said:[15]

---

[15] *Re M (Declaration of Death of Child)* [2020] EWCA Civ 164.

> *"102. ...In short terms, in the decade since Sir James Munby considered this matter the world has changed. The manner in which social media may now be deployed to name and pillory an individual is well established and the experience of the clinicians treating child patients in cases which achieve publicity, such as those of Charlie Gard and Alfie Evans, demonstrate the highly adverse impact becoming the focus of a media storm may have on treating clinicians. The need for openness and transparency in these difficult, important and, often, controversial cases is critical but can, in the judgment of the court, be more than adequately met through the court's judgments without the need for identifying those who have cared for [this child] with devotion since September 2019.*
>
> *103. Moving from the general to the specific, here the judge had evidence from Dr G of six specific untrue allegations that the father had made with respect to the hospital's care of his child. Parents no doubt say and do all manner of things in the tragic and difficult circumstances in which they find themselves in such cases. But the judge was entitled to be satisfied that there was a basis for this application being made in this particular case...*
>
> *104. ...the Respondent Trust has taken the view that it is likely that the potential for any adverse publicity will have significantly diminished once the ventilator has been disconnected and a short time has passed. They therefore would agree to a time limit being placed upon the RRO so that it would expire, subject to any further application, twenty eight days after the date upon which the ventilator is disconnected..."*

It is important to make the point that this was not a case proceeding under the Children Act 1989. Could there be a place for time-limited reporting restriction orders in Children Act cases? I can see no reason, in principle, why not.

Naming expert witnesses

In a judgment given in 2007[16] Sir James Munby dealt with the issue of naming expert witnesses in published judgments. As with social workers, expert witnesses have no automatic right to anonymity either under the general law or under section 12 of the Administration of Justice Act 1960. In this

---

[16] *British Broadcasting Corporation v Cafcass Legal and others* [2007] EWHC 616 (Fam) (the first *Ward* case) – see, in particular paragraphs 33-37. Sir James quoted those paragraphs in full in his judgment in the second *Ward* case to which I referred earlier.

judgment Sir James set out what he described as four "powerful arguments, founded in the public interest, for denying expert witnesses' anonymity". These included, firstly, "a general public interest in knowing the identity of an expert witness"; secondly, "a particular and powerful public interest in knowing who the experts are whose theories and evidence underpin judicial decisions in relation to children which are increasingly coming under critical and sceptical scrutiny"; thirdly, "the equally important public interest, especially pressing in a jurisdiction where scientific error can have such devastating effects on parents and children... not only of exposing what [was]... once called 'junk science' but also of exposing other less egregious shortcomings or limitations in medical science"; and, fourthly, "a powerful public interest in knowing whether or not someone putting himself forward as an expert has been criticised by another judge or other judges in the past".

Sir James went on to say that:

> "35. On the other hand, there is an important public interest which, it might be said, justifies preserving the anonymity of expert witnesses involved in care proceedings. This work, though very important, is voluntary. The concern is that if expert witnesses in care cases are publicly identified this will be likely to lead to a further drain on the already diminishing pool of doctors and other experts willing to do child protection work. Doctors and experts in other disciplines may be yet further disinclined to do such work if they see that the evidence they give to the court on the understanding that it (and their own identities) will remain confidential may become public knowledge and be the subject of public criticism. The already inadequate number of experts willing to assist the courts in vitally important child protection cases may, it is feared, be even further reduced."

Sir James repeated these comments in a judgment given in 2010.[17] When writing that judgment he had the benefit of expert evidence from three expert medical witnesses including Professor Sir Alan Craft, then the Immediate Past President of the Royal College of Paediatrics and Child Health. In his witness statement Sir Alan said that:

> "The real concern is that if the confidentiality which normally attaches to child protection is lifted, and professionals are identified in the media, then they may be subjected to reprisals or campaigns of harassment. It is well known by paediatricians that there is what

---

[17] *Dr A v Ward* [2010] EWHC 16 (Fam).

> *appears to be an orchestrated campaign against doctors involved in child protection. Much of this has been concerned with those acting as experts but not exclusively. This has been a campaign both in the media and on the internet."*

In response to that evidence, Sir James said:

> *"151. ... if the anonymity of expert witnesses such as Dr A and Dr B is to be justified it can only be...on the basis of the various concerns identified in particular by Professor Sir Alan Craft, by Dr Hamilton and by Dr Samuels; concerns which, I accept, engage both the private interests of the expert witnesses themselves, insofar as they fear that if identified they will be subjected to targeting, harassment and vilification, and also the public interest, insofar as the consequence of such fears may be, as I said in [the first Ward judgment] at para [35], a further drain on the already diminishing pool of experts prepared to do child protection work."*

Sir James decided that the medical experts should be identified in the published judgment.

The difficulty in finding doctors willing to act as expert witnesses in the Family Court is now even more acute than it was at the time when Sir James gave his judgments in the two *Ward* cases, the first of them more than a decade ago. The difficulties are greater in some disciplines than in others. Speaking to former colleagues I am told that there are today real problems in finding paediatricians, paediatric radiologists, neonatologists, paediatric neurosurgeons, neuroradiologists and histopathologists who are willing and able to accept instructions to act as an expert witness in the Family Court.[18] Despite this, I do not sense that the balance carried out by Sir James in the second *Ward* case would lead to a different outcome if carried out again today. That is a view that is shared by former colleagues.

When addressing the issue of whether an expert witness should be named, the court must take a balanced approach, balancing the Article 8 rights of the expert witness against the Article 10 rights of the media. As I said

---

[18] At the time of writing this chapter (December 2019) the President of the Family Division has just published for consultation (November 2019) the draft report of the Working Group on Medical Experts in the Family Courts. The draft report identified four main factors as barriers or disincentives to medical experts accepting instructions to provide evidence in cases to be heard in the Family Court. The fourth of those factors was 'Perceived criticism by lawyers, Judiciary and Press'. The Working Group is expected to present its final report to the President in the Spring of 2020.

earlier, it is not difficult to set out the relevant law. The difficulty comes in applying it to the particular circumstances of individual cases.

In 2011, I was criticised, entirely appropriately, by the then President of the Family Division, Sir Nicholas Wall, for publishing a judgment in which I was highly critical of an expert witness without giving the expert opportunity to respond to the criticisms.[19] I did not name the expert. An investigative journalist made an application to the court for the expert to be named. In his judgment Sir Nicholas made some general points which bear repetition. He said:

> *"76. It is, in my judgment, of the utmost importance that the Family Justice System should be as transparent as possible, consistent always with the need to protect the identities of the children who are involved in it. A number of myths about expert witnesses need to be exploded. The first is that they are "hired guns" supporting invariably the side which pays them. In my experience, nothing could be further from the truth. The FJS depends upon the integrity of the expert witness, and the duties of the expert witness to the child and to the court are spelled out in case law, in the Rules and in the Practice Direction.*
>
> *77. Judges do not decide cases on the words of expert alone. Expert witnesses are just that. They have an expertise which the rest of us do not share, but which the judge analyses and debates in the context of all the evidence in the case. It is by reference to the latter that the judge decides the case, not simply the evidence of the expert.*
>
> *78. Although they do the work voluntarily, experts are nonetheless paid to advise. Their advice is normally given within the proceedings themselves: normally, the judge reads the report and hears the witness. The expert's view is then tested in cross-examination in the overall context of the case and other expert evidence. That is how the system operates in practise.*
>
> *79. Where this occurs, the judge fully explains the conclusions he or she has reached and where such a judgment is either written or transcribed, I see no reason why it should not be published, and many reasons why it should. Indeed, I have long been of the view that it is highly desirable for judges to publish their judgments in disputed care and family cases. Unfortunately, particularly in the county court, where the pressure is greatest, there are rarely either the resources or*

---

[19] *X, Y, and Z & Anor v A Local Authority* [2011] EWHC 1157 (Fam).

the time for this to be done. But that there needs to be a debate about the quality and content of expert evidence I have no doubt.

80. It is, in my judgment, equally important that it is an informed debate. In the same way that the Court of Appeal is rightly critical of a judge who lacks impartiality or whose work is not properly informed, we are and should be similarly critical of any media source which proceeds from a tendentious, biased or ill-informed standpoint, or which has a particular agenda."

Although I have set out the general approach to the determination of the question whether an expert witness should be named, the reality is that the ultimate decision is a matter for the discretion of the judge. Although the judge's decision must be a principled decision, having in mind the relevant case law to which I have referred, it has to be accepted that on the same set of facts different judges may come to different views both on the primary question of whether the judgment should be published and on the secondary question of who should be named in the judgment. If the decision is to publish the judgment but not name the local authority or the experts, the reasons for that decision should be set out in the judgment.

Some conclusions

Although it has been said that there is a trend towards naming local authorities more frequently than in the past, it is arguable that they are still not named as frequently as they should be. Whilst this must remain an issue for the exercise of the judge's discretion in every case, and in every case requires a careful balancing of rights under Article 8 and Article 10, in my opinion the approach should be for the judge to begin by asking himself or herself 'why shouldn't the local authority be named?' rather than 'why should the local authority be named?'

In light of the comments made by Sir James Munby and Sir Nicholas Wall, to which I have just referred, I would suggest that a similar approach should be taken to naming expert witnesses.

In contrast, in my opinion, the reverse is the case so far as concerns the naming of other professionals and, in particular, social workers. Even if the social worker has not been the target of abuse in the particular case before the court it is very clear that naming social workers in published judgments may well lead to them being targeted. Should that be regarded as being simply part of the territory of being a social worker? In my judgment it should not. Naming the social worker needs to be justified by following the balancing exercise set out above.

The whole of this discussion proceeds on the premise that judgments in the Family Court should be published in accordance with the Practice Guidance which came into effect on 14 February 2014. However, there is undoubtedly a strong body of opinion that judgments should not be published as frequently as that Guidance requires, if published at all. Those who take that position argue that the risks of identification of the child concerned and of that child suffering harm as a result are simply too great.

9: THE MEDIA – THE FACTS OF LIFE

"A newspaper has two sides to it. It is a business, like any other, and has to pay in the material sense in order to live. But it is much more than a business; it is an institution; it reflects and it influences the life of a whole community; it may affect even wider destinies. It is, in its way, an instrument of government. It plays on the minds and consciences of men. It may educate, stimulate, assist, or it may do the opposite. It has, therefore, a moral as well as a material existence, and its character and influence are in the main determined by the balance of these two forces." (C P Scott)[1]

It is now a little over a decade since the rules were changed to permit duly accredited media representatives to attend some hearings in the Family Court. Although there was an initial flurry of activity in response to this much fought-for change in the rules, the reality has been that the right to attend has been relatively little used. I discussed the reasons for that in Chapter 4.

As we have seen, the whole issue of openness in the Family Court remains hotly contentious. Journalists still do not come into the Family Court in large numbers. Some of those working within the family justice system have hopes (others have fears) about how that might change if, for example, steps were taken to address the reasons for non-attendance described earlier including, perhaps, by taking at least some of the 'next steps' suggested by Sir James Munby in the consultation paper he issued in August 2014. I have come to the very clear conclusion that even if those obstacles were removed, journalists would still not come into the Family Court in great numbers. What is the reason for that?

The current state of the media
It is a fact that over the last 20 years there has been a significant decline in the financial and journalistic resources available to the media. In 2010 the

---

[1] From a leading article written in May 1921 by the then editor of the *Manchester Guardian*, C P Scott, to mark the centenary of the paper. The essay was published under the headline "A Hundred Years". It is still recognised around the world as the blueprint for independent journalism.

outcome of a survey[2] reported that:

> *"There is some evidence to suggest that the cuts in the regional press have been deeper than in the national press. At the Daily Mail and General Trust, for example, losses at its regional division, Northcliffe Media, over the past few years have typically been more than double those at Associated Newspapers, the national division, and this is reflected in the redundancy plans...*
>
> *While the print news sector may be the hardest hit, the reports suggest that no media sector has emerged unscathed, including television. In September 2008, for example, ITV announced 1,000 jobs cuts, including 430 newsroom positions, accounting for almost 20% of its total workforce. And jobs cuts have not only been ordered at advertising-supported media companies. For example, in October 2007 the BBC announced that 2,500 jobs would be axed as part of wide-ranging reforms driven, in part, by budget shortfalls."*[3]

More recently, the *Cairncross Review: A sustainable future for journalism*, published in February 2019, noted with concern that:

> *"The most striking aspects of the change [in journalism] that is occurring are its speed and its extent. A majority of people - in the case of young people, a huge majority - now reads the news entirely or mostly online. In 2018, the Reuters Institute for the Study of Journalism reported that 74% of UK adults used some online method each week to find news, and 91% of 18-24 year olds. Most online news is available for free and much of it is carried by aggregators such as Google News or Apple News, posted on Facebook's news feed, or sent from one person to another at the tap of a finger. This vastly expanded availability of news, and the speed with which it can be found, is clearly something that people value.*
>
> *At the same time, sales of both national and local printed papers have plunged: they fell by roughly half between 2007 and 2017, and are still dropping. In addition, print advertising revenues, which used to carry much of the cost of producing news, have fallen even faster, declining in a decade by 69%. Small wonder so many news groups*

---

[2] *Laid off. What do journalists do next?* - An exploratory study by François Nel, Director of the Journalism Leaders Programme at the University of Central Lancashire, Preston, UK, in collaboration with Journalism.co.uk.

[3] Even as I was putting the finishing touches to this book, on 29 January 2020 BBC News announced that by 2022 it intended to cut 450 jobs to save £80 million.

are struggling, including digital-only groups like HuffPost and Buzzfeed, as well as many local newspaper publishers. To cut costs, there have been mergers, as well as heavy cuts in staffing: the number of full-time frontline journalists in the UK industry has dropped from an estimated 23,000 in 2007, to 17,000 today, and the numbers are still swiftly declining. Moreover, the switch to online has changed the way people find news and the way they absorb it. They are much less likely to see the mixed bundle of politics, finance, entertainment and sport that constitutes many papers, and more likely to see an individual story, chosen by a computer program and not necessarily clearly labelled with the name of a particular publisher. This "unbundled" experience has implications for the visibility of public-interest news and for trust in news."[4]

As I read the responses from judges to the questionnaire I sent out and listened to the journalists who agreed to be interviewed, it became clear to me that judges and other professionals working in the family justice system may have some unrealistic expectations of what the media can deliver. Journalists will only come to court when they know *in advance* that the court is dealing with a case that is newsworthy and which has a strong public interest value. They will not come – editors cannot afford for them to come – on a speculative 'just in case' basis – i.e. just in case there happens to be something of interest in the court list that day. In my interviews with Mike Dodd, legal editor of PA Media, and *Daily Mail* journalist, Josh White, they made the same point that other journalists have made to me. Dodd said: "We very rarely find out what cases are coming up." White made the point that court lists are uninformative. Compared with the Crown Court, there is a lack of ability to flag up interesting – newsworthy – cases.

There are, of course, a variety of reasons why a case might be considered newsworthy. It may be because, for example, there is concern about a miscarriage of justice. The *Webster* case I referred to in Chapter 3 is a case in point. A case may be newsworthy because it relies on controversial expert medical evidence, for example a case of alleged shaken baby syndrome or of fabricated or induced illness (previously referred to as Munchausen's Syndrome by Proxy). It may be because there are concerns about the conduct of a local authority. A lot of publicity was attracted by a case heard in 2012/13 involving a pregnant Italian woman who came to England for a short visit and, whilst here, became seriously mentally unwell and was detained in hospital under section 3 of the Mental Health Act 1983. On

---

[4] *https://assets.publishing.service.gov.uk/government/uploads/system/uploads/attachment_data/file/779882/021919_DCMS_Cairncross_Review_.pdf.*

the application of the NHS Trust, the Court of Protection gave permission for the baby to be delivered by Caesarean section. The next day the Family Court made the baby the subject of an interim care order. Ultimately, final care and placement orders were made and the child was placed for adoption.[5] A national newspaper headline read: 'EXPLAIN WHY YOU SNATCHED BABY AT BIRTH'.

These are all the kind of stories that carry high public interest value and are therefore considered by the media to be newsworthy. The vast majority of children's cases heard in the Family Court, though of the utmost significance and perhaps of life-changing importance so far as the children and families involved are concerned, are likely to be of little, if any, media interest.

Journalist Louise Tickle makes the point that the media does not, as standard, tell 'good news' stories; the media reports on what is remarkable or shocking. We should not, therefore, expect that the media will report on those unremarkable cases which achieve good outcomes for children. However, it does then become very important to know whether the media is presenting the 'remarkable' and the 'shocking' as being the norm (which I would strongly dispute) or whether it acknowledges that they are, in fact, outliers that are not representative of the vast majority of cases that are dealt with by the Family Court (which I would contend).

With respect to the media's interest in the case involving the Italian mother and her baby, Sir James Munby, hearing an application for a reporting restrictions order, said:

> "35. The public has an interest in knowing and discussing what has been done in this case, both in the Court of Protection and in the Chelmsford County Court. Given the circumstances of the case and the extreme gravity of the issues which here confronted the courts – whether to order an involuntary caesarean section and whether to place a child for adoption despite the protests of the mother – it is hard to imagine a case which more obviously and compellingly requires that public debate be free and unrestricted.
>
> 36. The mother has an equally obvious and compelling claim to be allowed to tell her story to the world. I repeat what I have [said] on previous occasions (see most recently Re J, para 36) about the importance in a free society of parents who feel aggrieved at their expe-

---

[5] *Re P (A Child)* [2013] EWHC 4048 (Fam).

riences of the family justice system being able to express their views publicly about what they conceive to be failings on the part of individual judges or failings in the judicial system and likewise being able to criticise local authorities and others. I repeat what I said last week (Re P [2013] EWHC 4037 (Fam), para 4):

> *"The mother wishes to complain publicly about the way in which the courts in this country have handled her and her daughter. The court should be very slow indeed before preventing a parent doing what the mother wishes to do in the present case."*

If ever there was a case in which that right should not be curtailed it is surely this case. To deny this mother in the circumstances of this case the right to speak out – and, I emphasise, to speak out, if this is her wish, using her own name and displaying her own image – would be [an] affront not merely to the law but also, surely, to any remotely acceptable concept of human dignity and, indeed, humanity itself."

A second, equally important, point arose in that case. Some of the media reporting was inaccurate. Rather than being a point for criticism, Sir James Munby was sympathetic about the difficulties the media had faced. He said:

> *"43. Before parting from the case there are two points that require to be addressed with honesty and candour. Both relate to the fact that, when this story first 'broke' on 1 December 2013, none of the relevant information was in the public domain in this country.*
>
> *44. The first point is this: How can the family justice system blame the media for inaccuracy in the reporting of family cases if for whatever reason none of the relevant information has been put before the public?*
>
> *45. The second point is, if anything, even more important. This case must surely stand as final, stark and irrefutable demonstration of the pressing need for radical changes in the way in which both the family courts and the Court of Protection approach what for shorthand I will refer to as transparency. We simply cannot go on as hitherto. Many more judgments must be published. And, as this case so very clearly demonstrates, that applies not merely to the judgments of High Court Judges; it applies also to the judgments of Circuit Judges".*

There are some cases – and this was one – where the public interest in being properly informed doesn't simply merit publicity; such cases demand publicity. In light of the point made by the journalists I interviewed, how confident can we be that the media will be aware that those cases are taking place?

Equipping journalists
Journalists need to have a means of knowing in advance what cases the court will be dealing with. Additionally, if they are properly to fulfil the role expected of them of speaking truth to power, of reporting cases accurately, fairly and responsibly and of educating the public, it is essential that they know enough about the cases they are reporting on to enable them to discharge those responsibilities. In a lecture given in 2006,[6] Lord Justice Wall said that:

> *"press reporting must, in my view, be responsible. Once again, I see this as an issue which the family judiciary need to discuss with the press, so that a modus vivendi is achieved. The sensationalism of which the judiciary frequently complains seems to me at least in part to derive from the absence of full and proper information..."*

What does 'full and proper information' include? In a judgment I published in 2010[7] I was critical of an expert medical witness though I did not name him. An investigative journalist subsequently made an application for the expert to be named. That application was heard by the then President, Sir Nicholas Wall.[8] He ordered that the expert should be named. He went on to make the point that, in that case:

> *"88. ...the simple identification of Dr M does not meet the exigencies of this case. Indeed, as I have already indicated, it leaves us in my view in the worst of all worlds. The nature of the advice, and the terms in which it was given will not be known, nor will the doctor's justification for what he said. If there is to be a debate it must be a real debate, and a real debate requires the material for the debate to be available. In my judgment, this can only be achieved by the disclosure of Dr M's report."*

He then went on to make a very important general point concerning future practice. He said:

---

[6] *Opening up the Family Courts: a personal view* – Association of Lawyers for Children annual lecture given in memory of Allan Levy QC and David Hershman.
[7] *Re X, Y and Z (Children)* [2010] EWHC B12 (Fam).
[8] *X, Y, and Z & Anor v A Local Authority* [2011] EWHC 1157 (Fam). See, too, the discussion of this case on page 128.

> *"91. My decision to order disclosure of Dr M's report, albeit in a redacted form, leads me to consider what, in the future, the practice should be on the questions of the anonymity of experts and the publication of their reports.*
>
> *92. Mr Morgan's argument, and the arguments of the media generally would, I think be based on the proposition that without knowledge there can be no true investigation and no true debate. Where an expert's name and nothing else is disclosed, it seems to me that no-one is any the wiser. It will be known that Dr X advised in the case. The result of the case will also be known. What scope does this leave for debate?*
>
> *93. The anonymity of the child and the real risk that if the expert is identified the child will refuse to engage in the forensic process seem to me two good reasons against the disclosure of reports. But if they can be addressed, I can see little reason for a refusal to disclose the report of an expert to the world at large, either at the close of proceedings or if the facts warrant it, as the case progresses.*
>
> *94. I would therefore like to see a practice develop, in which expert reports would be routinely disclosed, and the media able to comment both on the report and on the use to which they were put in the proceedings. This would mean that the views of the judge on the expert evidence would also be disclosed."*

Those comments were plainly intended to assist journalists, in future, to have a better understanding of the issues in the cases they report on and thereby to enable them to report in more detail and with greater accuracy. Contrary to Sir Nicholas Wall's direction, the report prepared by Dr M was never published. His encouragement of the development of a practice whereby experts' reports are routinely disclosed, suitably anonymised, fell on deaf ears.

The question whether certain case papers might be disclosed to the media was an issue that was raised again in the consultation paper issued by Sir James Munby in August 2014. As I noted earlier, the results of the consultation were never published.

The journalists I spoke to were almost unanimous in saying that the disclosure of some of the case papers would be invaluable in enabling them to understand what the case is about and in deciding whether to attend. Claire Hayhurst made the point that:

> "reporters in the Crown Court are provided with details of defendant, the charges, pleas and any reporting restrictions that apply. Cases are usually explained by way of a prosecution opening or a judge's summary in sentencing remarks. This is not the case in family courts where reporters can feel blind and with no idea of what is going on."

Another journalist made the point that it is very difficult for journalists in court when advocates or the judge refer to documents in the hearing bundle, documents which the journalist has not had sight of. Tickle said that: "reading the papers before going into court would be really helpful to know what on earth is going on. What would be useful would be to have a case summary so you know what, specifically, is in dispute and what the parties are asking for." She also made the point that if journalists were allowed to see, for example, medical reports, they would be able to seek the court's permission to publish certain aspects of them. John Sweeney thought Sir Nicholas Wall had been right to advocate the publication of medical reports. He said that:

> "any system where there is a bias against information openness and scrutiny...they are not good systems...In a system which is now more in the shade than in the light there should be an onus on the publication of medical reports, suitably anonymised, because that gives people like me more chance of scrutiny and more chance of light."

However, Mark Hanna took a different approach. He said he couldn't see much point in allowing journalists to read material if they were then only to be allowed to print whatever was included in the judge's published judgment.

The issue of permitting journalists to read witness statements and experts' reports is controversial. As a matter of practicality, it could be difficult to achieve. In some cases the judge may take the view that the documents need to be anonymised and/or redacted. Where the judge is persuaded that there is such a need, who is to undertake that process? Who is to pay for it? Are journalists to be allowed to take the anonymised and/or redacted documents away from the court building? Even if the judge publishes his or her judgment at the conclusion of the case, is the reporter to be allowed to quote from a statement or expert's report that he or she has been allowed to see even if that quote is not mentioned in the judgment? Is the reporter to be allowed to discuss the documents with the parents? Should the journalist be allowed access to these documents even if he or she does not attend court in person? There are other questions that would also need to be answered. This is not a straightforward issue.

What would be more straightforward would be to provide journalists with an anonymised copy of the case summary. In care proceedings the local authority prepares a case summary for every case management hearing and for the final hearing. It would not be a difficult task for case summaries to be prepared in anonymised format at the outset. They would provide the journalist with a thumbnail sketch of the case. They would enable the journalist to know whether, for example, there are any experts' reports in existence and thus enable the journalist to consider whether it is appropriate to make an application to the judge for disclosure of such documents.

The real point, however, is that if journalists are required to go into court blind we can hardly complain if, on occasions, in their reporting they get some of the detail wrong. Giving journalists the right to go into the Family Court is a start – but only a start. Without equipping them to do their job the expectation that some had that journalists in court would shed a light on the working of the Family Court will remain a mere illusion.

Unreasonable expectations
It was clear from the responses to my questionnaire that some judges are irked by the approach taken by journalists when reporting a case based on a published judgment. When reading the headline and the journalist's story, the judge may wonder whether the journalist has read the full judgment. In fact, the journalist may well not have read it at all. It is common practice for media organisations to rely on agency copy circulated by the Press Association (now PA Media). That will be no more than a condensed version of aspects of the judgment. A newspaper using that copy is not obliged to reproduce it verbatim – and for reasons of space may not be able to do so. The end result is that whereas a judgment may run to 10,000 words or more the Press Association copy may be condensed to around 500 words. That may be further condensed to, say, 200 words for publication in a newspaper.

As a judge, I know that it can be irritating to find that a journalist has homed in on a part of the judgment which the judge regards as of least importance. The judge may feel that in concentrating on that part of the judgment the journalist has missed the whole point of the case. It needs to be remembered, however, that the journalist is not writing a law report. The journalist is writing a human-interest story that will engage the attention of the readers of that particular newspaper. What will engage the attention of the readers is for the journalist to discern and not for the judge to dictate. As Tickle puts it:

> *"The reporter's job is to be fair and accurate in their descriptions but also to identify stories that are sufficiently unusual or newsworthy or*

> *interesting or remarkable and in the public interest to be worthy of space in a very highly crowded media environment."*

In the case I referred to earlier involving the Italian mother and her baby, Sir James Munby repeated a point he had made in the past. He said:

> *"26. So far as concerns the relationship between the media and the court I can only repeat what I said earlier this year in a judgment that was widely reported at the time: Re J (A Child) [2013] EWHC 2694 (Fam). I forbear from extensive citation, merely repeating at this point, so as to emphasise, three key principles (Re J, paras 37-39). First, that "It is not the role of the judge to seek to exercise any kind of editorial control over the manner in which the media reports information which it is entitled to publish". Second, that "Comment and criticism may be ill-informed and based, it may be, on misunderstanding or misrepresentation of the facts [but the] fear of such criticism, however justified that fear may be, and however unjustified the criticism, is ... not of itself a justification for prior restraint by injunction of the kind being sought here, even if the criticism is expressed in vigorous, trenchant or outspoken terms ... or even in language which is crude, insulting and vulgar". Third, that "It is no part of the function of the court exercising the jurisdiction I am being asked to apply to prevent the dissemination of material because it is defamatory ... If what is published is defamatory, the remedy is an action for defamation, not an application in the Family Division for an injunction."*

Not every case that comes before the Family Court has a degree of public interest as high as that case. However, given the fact that, unlike in the criminal courts, journalists:

- get no advance notice of cases to be heard in the Family Court;

- are unable to determine from the anonymised court list what types of cases are being dealt with;

- currently don't have access to any of the court papers;

- are not allowed to approach parents at court to discuss information relating to the proceedings; and

- may never hear the outcome of a case because the judge's judgment is not published, one has to wonder whether there may be cases involving a point of significant public interest which never come across the media's radar; whether there are miscarriages of justice that take place which never see daylight; and all because the scrutiny of an independent media, supposedly one of the hallmarks of our free society, is effectively denied.

On 3 July 2019 the BBC Radio 4 programme, The Moral Maze, considered the issue of *The morality of anonymity*. Louise Tickle was one of the witnesses. In answer to one of the questions put to her, Tickle said:

> *"There are understandable reasons why children's privacy is protected in the Family Court, that's for sure. My argument is that there are serious human rights breaches that are going on in private family hearings which only very rarely make the light of day."*

Against that background, it is perhaps not surprising that some of the journalists I spoke to asked who benefits from this lack of media scrutiny? Is it the child, whose identity and privacy are protected with absolute certainty? Or is it the system?

Northern Ireland has recently gone through a Family Justice Review similar to the review in England and Wales which reported in November 2011. The Northern Ireland Review Group's report was published in September 2017. In acknowledging the tension between publicity and privacy in the Family Court, the review group made a valuable point with which I am in complete agreement:

> *"18.6 In recent years, there has been an emerging and growing consensus that the law should be reformed to ensure greater transparency in proceedings concerning the welfare of children. We must not underestimate the role that public debate, and the jealous vigilance of an informed media, has to play in exposing past miscarriages of justice and in preventing possible future miscarriages of justice. There is a compelling and irrefutable public interest in the effective operation of family justice courts, which deal with matters of the greatest importance."* (emphasis supplied).

The problems I have described are real and significant. They are the facts of life so far as the media is concerned. They are obstacles blocking the media's ability properly to fulfil its role as scrutineer-in-chief of what goes on in the Family Court. If that brief review indicates, as I intend, a degree of understanding and sympathy on my part in respect of the difficulties the media have to contend with, I am equally concerned about the difficulties the media create for others by the way they behave. I am concerned that there is a real issue relating to trust and truth. It is to that issue that I turn next.

10: THE MEDIA – TRUST AND TRUTH

"Here is the fact of the age: People believe nothing. They think everything is spin and lies. The minute a government says A is true, half the people on Earth know A is a lie. And when people believe nothing, as we know, they will believe anything."
(Peggy Noonan)[1]

The role the media should be allowed to play in the Family Court is an issue about which views are polarised. Mistrust of the media persists. Sometimes that mistrust is based on bad experiences in the past. If the media is to be allowed to play a greater role in reporting on the work of the Family Court then reassurance will be needed that the media can be trusted.

Trust and truth – the print and broadcast media

Giving the Huw Wheldon Memorial Lecture in 1997, journalist Fergal Keane said that: "The fundamental obligation of the reporter is to the truth".[2] The point he was making seems, at first blush, to be blindingly obvious. Surely no one would dissent from that proposition? What is remarkable is the fact that Keane felt the need to make the point at all. Having made the point it does, though, raise an interesting question: "What is truth?" That question, asked by Pontius Pilate[3] two thousand years ago, remains as relevant today as it did then.

Baggini recently said that:

"Somehow, however, the truth has ceased to be plain or simple. Indeed, it is not uncommon to hear people deny that there is any such thing as the truth at all only opinions, what is 'true-for-you' or 'true-for-me'...To rebuild belief in the power and value of truth, we can't dodge its complexity. Truths can be and often are difficult to understand, discover, explain, verify. They are also disturbingly easy to hide, distort, abuse or twist. Often we cannot claim with any certainty to know the truth. We need to take stock of the various kinds

---
[1] Author and journalist, writing in the Wall Street Journal on 11 May 2011.
[2] Referred to by Mick Temple in *The British Press*, McGraw Hill, 2008, page 124.
[3] St John's Gospel, chapter 18 v. 38.

of real and supposed truths out there and understand how to test their authenticity."[4]

The Leveson report[5] acknowledged that there are many versions of the truth:

> *"Newspaper readership is remarkably loyal. We want the news in the press to be true and accurate; we do not want to be misled or lied to. But we want, or are content for, it to be presented in a partisan way. We want a measure of balance and context, but we also want a perspective. We want the truth, but we understand that there are many versions of the truth, and incompleteness in all versions. Notwithstanding the emphasis put by both the industry and its critics on the difference between 'fact' and 'comment' these are by no means distinct and watertight categories. The very act of describing a fact is to comment on it. All forms of recording are selective."*[6]

There is also an issue as to whose truth we are talking about.

Keane's point is well made – the fundamental obligation of the reporter is to the truth. In this chapter I propose to take a simplistic approach to the idea of truth. I shall proceed on the basis that 'truth' is best understood by reference to its opposite. The opposite of 'truth' is 'falsity'. Again, I turn to the Leveson report:[7]

> *"The 'argument from truth', which identifies free speech as an important condition for the attainment of truth, is also not straightforward when applied to the press. Mill's argument that society will benefit from "the clearer perception and livelier impression of truth, produced by its collision with error" may hold in relation to the battle between truth and falsity expressed by individuals (but even then, only in the sort of discourse which aims at the truth). However, it is less certain that truth will prevail in the encounter between individual and institutional speech, or between different forms of institutional speech."*

Some would argue that in modern times the expression "never let the truth

---

[4] *A Short History of Truth*, Julian Baggini (2017) published by Quercus Editions Ltd.
[5] *Leveson Inquiry - Report into the culture, practices and ethics of the press* published 29 November 2012.
[6] *An inquiry into the culture, practices and ethics of the press*, November 2012, Volume 1, page 79, paragraph 3.5.
[7] Ibid at page 63, paragraph 3.6.

get in the way of a good story"⁸ has become the maxim of the British press.

The phone hacking scandal, which led to the appointment of the Leveson Inquiry, brought into very sharp focus the widespread concerns that existed about the low regard print journalists appeared to have for truth and about the ethical decline of, in particular, the national print media.

Accredited media representatives have the right to attend some hearings in the Family Court. The media would like greater rights. Journalists would like to have access to some court papers to enable them to understand the case the court is dealing with. They would like to be allowed to have direct access to parents to discuss the detail of the case and the evidence against them and to be able to publish the stories that parents want to tell. In their ideal world they would be able to name and publish images of parents. Anonymity is complete anathema to them. John Sweeney, freelance writer and broadcaster, made the point to me that:

> *"the moment you anonymise somebody it weakens the story...Because you cannot, most of the time, report the names and faces of the parents who are seeking to keep their children, it doesn't work in terms of journalism...You have got to give us some ability to tell the story that we pick up".*

Mike Dodd, legal editor of PA Media, said that the media does understand the need for anonymity in children's cases. However, if you get a story that is of some considerable public importance it is almost impossible to write the story in any meaningful way while ensuring there is no risk to the individual's anonymity.

That point is well illustrated by a story published by the media on 9 December 2019. One headline read: "Boy, 4, forced to sleep on floor because hospital had no beds".⁹ The story beneath the headline began: "A little boy is seen lying on the floor of a hospital on a pile of coats after he was rushed in by ambulance fearing he had pneumonia." The boy was named. His mother was named. The hospital was identified. Even if the media had been forbidden to publish images and identify the child, there would still have been a story. However, the power of the story was in the picture. Many other examples could be given. Although I would not for one moment contemplate or recommend that degree of freedom in publishing stories about cases heard in the Family Court, that story does illustrate the wide gulf that

---

⁸ Attributed to Mark Twain.
⁹ The *Metro*, 9 December 2019.

exists between what the media would like (and why) and what the state currently allows.

The media want to be in a position to describe what happens in the Family Court in order to be able to hold public authorities and the judiciary to account.[10] Tickle makes the point that, as a journalist, she is only interested in families' stories in so far as they illuminate the process the families have undergone. Sweeney expresses concern that there is 'no scrutiny or very little scrutiny' of what goes on in the Family Court. He has a point. Josh White, journalist with the *Daily Mail*, made the point that the expression 'secret' Family Court is a way of expressing the difference between the Family Court and other courts. He suggested that it may be that "the Family Court is one of the bastions of the legal system that has no concern about its PR – no-one is concerned about communication and how things should be presented."

The role of the media is not only to inform the public about what goes on in the Family Court but also to reassure the public that what goes on is fair or, if there is evidence in any case that it is not fair, to express their concerns publicly. To enable this to happen the media would like to see a relaxation of the current reporting restrictions imposed by section 12 of the Administration of Justice Act 1960 and section 97(2) of the Children Act 1989.[11]

It is the media's job to hold the judiciary and the local authority to account. Their role of scrutinising the work that goes on in the Family Court is very important. The media must be free to report not only on the substance of the cases they observe but also on the way families are treated by local authority social workers out of court and by the forensic process in court. That includes being able to comment on the behaviour of the judge, the lawyers and other professionals involved in the hearing. But their reporting must be accurate and fair. To give the media additional freedom, for example, freedom to read court papers such as witness statements and expert medical reports, would inevitably bring with it a degree of risk. Reporting which is neither accurate or fair can cause distress to those families whose cases are reported and could also, potentially, damage the public's confidence and trust in the family justice system itself.

Over the course of the last 20 years, several polls have suggested that the level of public trust in journalists in the UK, especially print journalists,

---

[10] On this point of holding judges to account see the decision of Russell J in *JH v MF* [2020] EWHC 86 (Fam) which I discuss in Chapter 15.
[11] See Chapter 4 for a discussion of these two sections.

is low. A Eurobarometer survey, cited in *The Guardian* on 24 April 2002, found that 75% of those who responded to the survey in the UK "tended not to trust the printed press – a much higher proportion than in any other country in the European Union".[12]

In that same year (2002) the Reith Lectures were given by the philosopher, Baroness Onora O'Neill. The title of her series of five lectures was "A Question of Trust". In her first lecture she noted that polls:

> *"repeatedly show that no profession is less trusted in the UK than journalism...Journalists – at least newspaper journalists – are typically less trusted than scientists and civil servants, and dramatically less trusted than judges, or ministers of religion or doctors."*[13]

The problem has not gone away. On 5 December 2016, an IMPRESS News headline proclaimed: "Trust in journalism sinks to all time low".[14] In an article published in 2017, Professor Brian Cathcart expressed the opinion that:

> *"... there are good grounds for saying that in recent years trust in national newspaper journalists to tell the truth has been consistently low or even very low, relative to trust in other journalists, in people in most other walks of life and in newspaper journalists in other countries. There is also strong evidence of a hierarchy of trust, with journalists at red-top newspapers trusted least. The article finds that the strongest explanation consistent with the data is the most obvious: that many people do not trust these newspaper journalists to tell the truth because many journalists have been seen not to do so. This should be a matter for concern for journalists in a changing market."*[15]

If it really is the case that journalists cannot be relied upon to tell the truth then that is a highly relevant factor when deciding whether, for example, to allow journalists routinely to have access to witness statements, expert

---

[12] See *Power without Responsibility*, James Curran and Jean Seaton, Routledge, London, seventh edition, published in 2010, pages 98, 336 and 337. In the eighth edition, published in 2018, the authors state that: 'In 2016, only 18 per cent of British adults said that they trusted national newspapers to tell the truth.'

[13] Lecture 1, *Spreading Suspicion*.

[14] This was based on a YouGov poll. According to the IMPRESS website (*http://impress.press*) IMPRESS "is a regulator designed for the future of media, building on the core principles of the past, protecting journalism, while innovating to deal with the challenges of a digital age."

[15] *Trust, Newspapers and Journalists: A Review of Evidence*, written by Professor Brian Cathcart and published in the journal *Radical Statistics* (No 118).

medical reports and other sensitive documents in cases relating to children. The journalists I have spoken to were agreed that it would be unacceptable for such material to be made available only to particular (trusted) journalists from particular (trusted) newspapers but denied to other journalists (for example, those working for the red-tops). If the court agrees to disclosure of such material to one accredited journalist then every accredited journalist should expect to be treated similarly. It is difficult to see any principled basis for taking a different view. That raises an issue about the adequacy of the present accreditation arrangements.

'Duly accredited' representatives of news gathering and reporting organisations have the right to attend some hearings in the Family Court. The Family Procedure Rules 2010 provide that "'duly accredited' refers to accreditation in accordance with any administrative scheme for the time being approved for the purposes of this rule by the Lord Chancellor".[16] The rules go on to state that the Lord Chancellor:

> *"has decided that the scheme operated by the UK Press Card Authority provides sufficient accreditation".*[17]

In my discussions with journalists I asked them whether there ought to be separate (additional) accreditation for those journalists who wish to work in the Family Court. I expected opposition to the suggestion. I was not to be disappointed. However, interestingly, a range of views were expressed. One said that the only thing that made her think it might be a good idea worth pushing forward is the poor take up by journalists of the right to attend hearings in the Family Court. Training which leads to separate accreditation would give journalists confidence, and reduce their present anxiety about publishing something they are not entitled to publish and finding themselves in contempt of court. She also made the point that these days a lot of young journalists are not very well edited or supervised so additional training could be beneficial in that respect too.

Another journalist said that whilst it may be helpful to provide a training course for journalists interested in working in the Family Court she did not think this should be made mandatory. To make it mandatory would be likely to exclude journalists currently entitled to work in the Family Court relying upon their UK Press Card. Polly Curtis (Tortoise Media) said she did not favour any additional qualifications being required. That would be likely to limit the number of journalists doing Family Court work. Josh

---

[16] Rule 27.11(7).
[17] Rule 27 Practice Direction 27B at paragraph 4.2.

White (the *Daily Mail*) thought that most of his colleagues would be hostile to the idea. He said: "It is a non-starter, in my opinion." Mark Hanna was the most positive of all the journalists I met with. He said that the Family Court needs to be reported on by journalists who have been well-trained. Although he appreciated that some would object to this on the basis that it smacks of state licensing of journalists (which he would not approve of), "at the moment things are so bad, there is so little being reported from the Family Court, that something has to be done about it". He suggested that perhaps some concession might have to be made by journalists in the kind of freedoms they normally expect as journalists.

Tickle did not consider that additional accreditation would be appropriate. However, she did agree that more training opportunities would be helpful. So, too, would be the opportunity for journalists working in (or wanting to work in) the Family Court to be able to meet with Family Court judges.

The Reith Lectures given by Baroness O'Neill predated the Leveson Inquiry report by a decade and yet her lectures resonate clearly with some of the issues the Leveson Inquiry had to deal with. In her final lecture, *Licence to Deceive*, O'Neill said:

> "*Outstanding reporting and accurate writing mingle with editing and reporting that smears, sneers and jeers, names, shames and blames. Some reporting 'covers' (or should I say 'uncovers'?) dementing amounts of trivia, some misrepresents, some denigrates, some teeters on the brink of defamation. In this curious world, commitments to trustworthy reporting are erratic: there is no shame in writing on matters beyond a reporter's competence, in coining misleading headlines, in omitting matters of public interest or importance, or in recirculating others' speculation as supposed 'news'. Above all there is no requirement to make evidence accessible to readers.*'

Some of the journalists I spoke to agreed that there are concerns about the behaviour of certain sections of the press. Tickle, for example, said: 'There is no point in dressing it up. It feels to me as if sections of the press have zero morality'. Claire Hayhurst said: 'I like to think the media is trustworthy but then there are instances where I just despair because things are published that arguably shouldn't be'.

In deciding what 'next steps' should be taken in the move to increase transparency in the Family Court – indeed, in deciding whether there should be any next steps at all – it is imperative that we keep well in mind the concerns that have been expressed about trust and truth. If journalists are to be entrusted with sensitive case papers to assist them in reporting more accurately on the work of the Family Court, there needs to be a high level of confidence that all journalists, print and broadcast, can be relied upon to be meticulous in ensuring that that material is used appropriately.

One outcome of the Leveson Inquiry was the setting up on 8 September 2014 of the Independent Press Standards Organisation (IPSO). Most mainstream press publications in the UK have subscribed to IPSO though some (e.g. *The Guardian* and the *Financial Times*) have not. Another outcome was the strengthening of the Editors' Code of Practice. The Code sets out the rules that newspapers and magazines regulated by IPSO have agreed to follow. The latest version of the Code came into effect on 1 July 2019. The preamble provides that:

> *"The Code – including this preamble and the public interest exceptions below – sets the framework for the highest professional standards that members of the press subscribing to the Independent Press Standards Organisation have undertaken to maintain. It is the cornerstone of the system of voluntary self-regulation to which they have made a binding contractual commitment. It balances both the rights of the individual and the public's right to know.*
>
> *To achieve that balance, it is essential that an agreed Code be honoured not only to the letter, but in the full spirit. It should be interpreted neither so narrowly as to compromise its commitment to respect the rights of the individual, nor so broadly that it infringes the fundamental right to freedom of expression – such as to inform, to be partisan, to challenge, shock, be satirical and to entertain – or prevents publication in the public interest.*
>
> *It is the responsibility of editors and publishers to apply the Code to editorial material in both printed and online versions of their publications. They should take care to ensure it is observed rigorously by all editorial staff and external contributors, including non-journalists.*
>
> *Editors must maintain in-house procedures to resolve complaints swiftly and, where required to do so, co- operate with IPSO. A publication subject to an adverse adjudication must publish it in full and with due prominence, as required by IPSO."*

Whilst there are several parts of the Code that are relevant to the issues with which I am concerned, it is sufficient for me to refer to Article 1, 'Accuracy'. Article 1(i) provides that:

> *"The Press must take care not to publish inaccurate, misleading or distorted information or images, including headlines not supported by the text."*

Whatever may be the merits of the Code, the provisions of the Code are nowhere near sufficient to address the risk of reporting which breaches or is likely to breach a child's right to privacy. Making a complaint to IPSO would be an inadequate response to the deliberate or careless reporting of a case in a way which led to a child being identified. A complaint to IPSO does not have the same deterrent effect as the prospect of an order for committal to prison for contempt of court.

Some journalists sought to persuade me that section 12 of the Administration of Justice Act 1960 should be repealed and should not be replaced. Their point is that journalists are fully aware of the need to protect the identities of children, including taking appropriate steps to guard against jigsaw identification. They are already well-used to doing this in criminal cases involving child victims and child witnesses. In the Family Court, too, stringent measures are taken to ensure anonymisation is successfully achieved. The power to commit to prison for contempt of court for breach of section 12 is not required.

Tickle expressed concern that the power to commit "chills almost all reporting." However, she also conceded that making a complaint to IPSO would make "not a scrap of difference". Notwithstanding Tickle's concerns, in my discussions with her she expressed the opinion that:

> *"journalists should be held to very rigorous account on the accuracy and fairness of their reporting. That is so important. If family courts are to be held to account for the decisions they make that affect people's lives and we are going to report on it then we have to be held to really serious account on the level of responsibility, trust, fairness and balance about the way we do it. We can't do the whole truth but we can do a fair truth."*

Curtis and Hayhurst assured me that 'the press is your friend'. I have no doubt that there are some judges who would not easily be convinced by that assurance. Dugan said that the judiciary 'need to trust us more'. I am sure she is right. Yet I have the words of Onora O'Neill ringing in my ears: "Trust, it is constantly observed, is hard earned and easily dissipated. It is valuable social capital and not to be squandered." It is a sad fact that there are still some journalists who are prepared to squander that capital – not just to their own detriment but to the detriment of the many committed, conscientious, hardworking journalists who genuinely seek to publish the truth and to hold truth to power. For those few – and I am prepared to accept that it is only a few – they would do well to remember the well-known words of C P Scott: 'Comment is free, but facts are sacred'.[18]

The standing of the broadcast media appears to be higher than that of the print media. For example, Curran and Seaton say that:

> *"The BBC is an engine of the mind. It has become a national treasure and world resource because it has been given the creative freedom and political responsibility to attract audiences, tell the truth and be playful...[It] has become a world by-word for reliability. Moreover, it has, over time, got it more right (and worried about getting it right) than most other organisations – and the public understand this. Indeed, the BBC is possibly more famous than Britain, more accepted all over the world, and as vulnerable as it has ever been."*[19]

Trust and truth – the internet and social media

The world wide web was publicly launched almost 30 years ago in 1991. In 2017 an estimated 49.7% of the world's population were internet users. Facebook, the first social networking platform, was launched in 2004 and has been followed by several others. In the report of the Leveson inquiry the point was made that:

> *"Although there is limited news provision in the terms that are relevant to this Inquiry on pure social networking sites, all social networks provide opportunities for individuals to disseminate and discuss news, information and comment. Indeed, everyday use of the Internet is increasingly characterised by the use of social networking sites and other social media. Their growth has been little short of phenomenal. Ten years ago there were no social networks; now the largest social networking site, Facebook, has over 800m users worldwide (although Facebook has recently suggested that as many of 100m of these accounts may be either dormant, fake or used for questionable purposes). The rise of Twitter has been similarly rapid. Founded in 2006, it now counts over 100 million active users each month, sending a billion tweets every four days. Perhaps most astonishingly (and for this Inquiry of concern to those who may be the subject either of Tweets that breach privacy or indeed the criminal or civil law), is*

---

[18] See Chapter 9, footnote 1.
[19] *Power Without Responsibility: Press, Broadcasting and the Internet in Britain*, James Curran and Jean Seaton, 8th edition, 2018, Routledge, London, at page 342.

the speed with which a message might be propagated. Colin Crowell, Head of Global Public Policy for Twitter Inc, noted that during the 2012 Superbowl, Twitter processed 12,000 tweets per second."[20]

The internet has also led to an explosion in the production of data. Richard Sambrook notes that:[21]

"News providers are no longer managers of a scarce resource, they are struggling to sustain a business and a role in an environment of information overload. The professional methods that developed a hundred years ago may seem less relevant in this new environment.

Eric Schmidt, chairman of Google, has estimated that every two days the world produces more data and information than had been produced from the dawn of civilisation until 2003.[22] *In these circumstances, many people question the relevance or practicality of a self-imposed or regulated standard of impartiality or objectivity on professional media producers. For many people, social media or citizen journalism is increasingly a source of news and information. But there can be no professional code or effective regulation of the live conversation underway on multiple sites on the internet – with no geographical or legal boundaries recognised."*

Sambrook goes on to raise a very serious question concerning the issue with which I am concerned, the issue of trust and truth. He says:

"As print and broadcast increasingly compete on the internet, and as the internet starts to feed video and text into our homes, indistinguishable from traditional media distribution, the regulators themselves are struggling to see how the dyke can hold. In these circumstances, what can be done to help the consumer identify what to believe and what not to believe? And what happens when information providers no longer care about truth or accuracy?"[23]

Curran and Seaton make the point that "The press at its best holds power to account". However, they immediately go on to talk about the "moral decline of the press" which they say:

---

[20] *https://www.gov.uk/government/publications/leveson-inquiry-report-into-the-culture-practices-and-ethics-of-the-press* Part 1, section 5 'Social networking sites', page 173 at paragraph 5.2.
[21] *Delivering trust: impartiality and objectivity in a digital age*, Richard Sambrook, Reuters Institute for the Study of Journalism, July 2012, page 10.
[22] *http://techcrunch.com/2010/08/04/schmidt-data*.
[23] Ibid pages 10/11.

> *"was caused by a new generation of cynical controllers, managerial bullying, a corporate culture of impunity and above all falling revenue. This led to the use of the 'dark arts' on an unprecedented scale, culminating in the phone hacking scandal. It also gave rise to increasing disregard for the damage that newspapers could inflict on innocent people in the public eye. And it resulted in sustained distortion… and fake news".*[24]

And yet it is the advent of social media, not the print or broadcast media, that has increased the scope for the dissemination of fake news and the manipulation of the general public. Curran and Seaton say that:

> *"Trump's victory, and the Brexit vote in the UK the same year, raised a new problem that mature democracies have not yet addressed. Both campaigns spent millions – in Trump's case, tens of millions of dollars – in tailoring political messages for individual voters on Facebook. These were received without the voters knowing the source of the message…The huge spend on Facebook posts was worth it. Surveys of the 2016 US election showed that the most popular fake news stories were spread more widely than the most popular mainstream (i.e. fact-checked) new stories."*[25]

The position today is that the mainstream media can be controlled and regulated. They can also be the subject of proceedings before the court, for example, for claims for damages for libel.[26] In contrast, social media and other sites on the internet cannot be so easily controlled. Information offered on social media is inherently more untrustworthy than that offered in the mainstream media since the source and reliability of its output cannot always be known. Sweeney said that he has "become afraid of the lack of policing of what is put online" and that he was "more worried about that than about what might be published" in a red-top. The lack of policing of what is posted online is "a major, major problem". It is the elephant in the room. It is not possible to control how people say things, the language they use. It is also impossible to pull back material posted online.

During the course of the Leveson inquiry, Lord Justice Leveson likened communication on Facebook to 'pub chatter' compared with the mainstream media in which the state 'has an interest in seeing is conducted on a

---

[24] Ibid at page 187.
[25] Ibid pages 396/7.
[26] In Chapter 8, I referred to a libel action brought by a social worker, Sylvia Henry against *The Sun* for wrongly accusing her of negligence in her dealings with Baby P thereby contributing to his suffering and to his death.

level playing field.' That is an interesting comparison though in the context of opening up the Family Court it seems to me that children and families have as much to be concerned about from the 'pub chatter' of Facebook, Instagram, Twitter and all the other social media platforms as they do from the mainstream media.

Professor Jo Delahunty recently made the point that:

> *"Social media has ripped through previously impregnable barriers by the public to information, news and view on our family justice system. There is now a climate of open challenge to the rightness of a judicial decision, whether through headlines such as 'Enemies of the people' or through social media campaigning conducted by enraged groups such as 'Alfie's Army'.*[27] *When a parent gets involved in the child protection system they don't have to rely on their trained lawyers for guidance, they have millions of voices they can listen to at the click of a button on their mobiles: and those voices are not singing the praises of the family justice system in harmony.'*[28]

The print media is sometimes considered to present an unacceptable risk of invading personal privacy – a key point for some of those who object to any increase in transparency in the Family Court. However, the reality is that the use of social media raises even more concerns about lack of respect for people's privacy. The Leveson report makes the following important point concerning privacy. It says that:

> *"It is right to acknowledge however that the nature of the public interest in privacy and our understanding of the implications of choices made by individuals about their privacy are matters which lie at the heart of a number of fast-moving contemporary social changes, about which a clear and stable consensus may not yet have been reached. The explosion in use of social media, particularly by the young, has not yet been matched by a settled understanding of the implications of the choices that people make in placing private material online; many do so unwisely or naively with disproportionate exposure to exploitation of such material and the compromising of their privacy."*[29]

---

[27] The reference to the public support for the parents of Alfie Evans is to the proceedings in which Alder Hey Children's NHS Foundation Trust applied for a declaration that it was in Alfie's best interests for intrusive, invasive treatment to be withdrawn.

[28] *Transparency in the Family Court: What Goes on Behind Closed Doors?*, Gresham College, 24 May 2018.

[29] https://www.gov.uk/government/publications/leveson-inquiry-report-into-the-culture-practices-and-ethics-of-the-press, Part 1, page 74 at paragraph 3.10.

Today, newspapers are not only published in print format; they are also published online. Whereas today's edition of a printed newspaper cannot be updated until the next edition is published tomorrow, the online version can be constantly updated 24 hours a day, seven days a week. News is now available instantly, on demand. Invariably, in the online version of newspapers there is a facility for members of the public to post a response to some news stories. With respect to reports of cases heard in the Family Court, online responses may be unsympathetic towards and/or harshly and unfairly critical of one or other of the parents or of the professionals involved in the case. Uninformed or ill-informed criticism of professionals, even from an unknown source, can damage reputations and destroy careers. Even knowledge of the risk of committal to prison for contempt of court does not always deter some from venting their spleen indiscriminately.

The online news story and the comments made in response are likely to remain online for a very long time. That is a problem. Even if a hearing in the Family Court relates to a baby, if the judgment in that case is published and reported on online by the media the likelihood is that there will still be online references to that case – to that child – even when he or she reaches adulthood.

A case in point
In January 2010 the Court of Appeal refused an application by a mother for permission to appeal against an order I had made transferring the care of her son to the boy's father.[30] My judgment was given in private. The Court of Appeal's decision was given in public. Following the Court of Appeal's judgment, the case was reported in some newspapers. The headline given to the story in the *MailOnline* was: "Judge orders boy, 11, to live with father he hates and hasn't seen for four years."

The story was published on a Sunday. Within a matter of hours 177 members of the public, from all around the world, had posted online responses. It is now almost ten years since that story was published. The story and the responses are still online today. The boy will, by now, be an adult.

The content of the 177 responses was very mixed. One said: "Good sensible decision". Another said: "Which Asylum do they wheel these judges out from?" Some of the language was intemperate. Many of the responses highlighted an underlying ignorance of the family justice system. With a degree of commendable perception, one person wrote: 'This isn't the whole story...without knowing this, no-one can fully support or disagree

---

[30] *Re S (A Child)* [2010] EWCA Civ 219.

the judge's decision."

The last point highlights a serious issue. After publication of the Court of Appeal's judgment, with the agreement of the parties I published an anonymised version of my own judgment. As a result, both my judgment and the Court of Appeal's judgment were available on the internet on the Bailii website. It would have been very simple indeed for the *MailOnline* to have included a link to the full judgments. That would have given their readers the opportunity to get a much fuller picture of the case. Even if the judgments had been made more easily accessible to the public, those who disagreed with my decision may well still have disagreed. However, they would have been better informed, would have had some insight into the complexities of the case and would have gained some understanding of the challenging cases Family Court judges have to deal with. This is an issue I discussed with journalists. The response was positive.

There is one further point. It is an obvious point but one that is nonetheless worth making. Publication of a judgment is not to a section of the media or to a section of the public. As a result of the internet, publication is to the world. As Mr Justice Hedley observed in 2008:[31]

> *"once disclosure is allowed it is disclosure to all the world and not every organ of the media may be as scrupulous or indeed as concerned [as ITV Wales] to protect the identity of [this child]."*

Once disclosed to all the world neither the court nor the publisher can exercise any real control over what happens to that story. Once the story is out it stays out. Or, as Dodd put it to me: "you must remember that publicity is a two-edged sword. You might like it but you can't control it once it is out of the box."

Standards, accuracy and responsibility
Since the rule change in 2009 which allowed journalists into the Family Court the media has continued to publish negative stories about the Family Court. Not only *The Times* but other newspapers such as the *Daily Mail*, the *Daily Express*, *The Sun* and *The Daily Telegraph* have all published negative stories. Camilla Cavendish is not the only journalist to have aimed her fire at the Family Court. For example, the late Christopher Booker, writing for *The Daily Telegraph*, was another regular critic of the Family Court. All of his pieces have been highly damning, both of the Family Court and of social workers. A small sample of his headlines illustrates the point: *"It's time*

---

[31] *Z County Council v TS & Ors* [2008] EWHC 1773 (Fam), paragraph 10.

to bring family law to book: Families are being torn apart by a system veiled in secrecy" (17 July 2010); *"Parents denied a voice in court against the child-snatchers"* (5 March 2011); *"My 'victory' over secrecy in the family courts has a nasty twist – High Court judgments are not always what they seem – I've still been silenced."*

Negative stories have not been confined to the print media. In Chapter 1, I referred to a story about the 'secret' Family Court which appeared on the Victoria Derbyshire show on BBC 2 in May 2019.

Is this something that the Family Court just has to accept? As I noted in Chapter 9, journalists have considerable latitude in the way they report cases heard in the Family Court. It is not the role of the judge to seek to exercise any kind of editorial control over the manner in which the media reports information which it is entitled to publish. In 2001 the European Court of Human Rights summarised its position on this issue:

> *"The Court further recalls the essential function the press fulfils in a democratic society. Although the press must not overstep certain bounds, particularly as regards the reputation and rights of others and the need to prevent the disclosure of confidential information, its duty is nevertheless to impart – in a manner consistent with its obligations and responsibilities – information and ideas on all matters of public interest. In addition, the Court is mindful of the fact that journalistic freedom also covers recourse to a degree of exaggeration, or even provocation..."*[32]

In a judgment given by Sir James Munby in 2003[33] he went further. He said:

> *"89. It is not the function of the judges to legitimise "responsible" reporting whilst censoring what some are pleased to call "irresponsible" reporting...[T]he freedom of expression secured by Article 10 is applicable not only to information or ideas that are favourably received, or regarded as inoffensive, but also to those that offend, shock or disturb the State or any section of the community. Article 10 protects not only the substance of the ideas and information expressed, but also the form in which they are conveyed. It is not for the court to substitute its own views for those of the press as to what technique of reporting should be adopted by journalists. Article 10 entitles journalists to adopt a particular form of presentation intended to ensure a particularly telling effect on the average reader. As Neill LJ recognised, a*

---

[32] *Bergens Tidende v Norway* (2001) 31 EHRR 16 at paragraph 49.
[33] *Re Roddy* [2003] EWHC 2927 (Fam).

> *tabloid newspaper is entitled to tell the story in a manner which will engage the interest of its readers and the general public. If there is no basis for injuncting a story expressed in the temperate or scholarly language of a legal periodical or the broadsheet press there can be no basis for injuncting the same story simply because it is expressed in the more robust, colourful or intemperate language of the tabloid press."*

In an interview with *The Times*, reported on 26 December 2019, Sir Alan Moses, the retiring Chair of the Independent Press Standards Organisation, made the point that:

> *"If you're the victim of something that is deeply offensive, it is the most unpleasant, uncomfortable thing that you can imagine. But what we have to acknowledge is that, in striking the right balance in this country, there is no right not to be offended."*

The next day, another headline in *The Times* read: "Judges must accept press hostility, says Lady Hale". The article which followed reported that Baroness Hale, who was about to retire as President of the Supreme Court, had said that judges must learn to live with criticism from the press. She said:

> *"We have a free press and if the press wants to attack us, that's fine. But we have to do the job according to our judicial oaths."*

Does all of this mean that there are no limits to how the press may report? Is this a charter for irresponsibility? In my opinion, it is not. Responsible reporting is a concept discussed by the House of Lords in an appeal heard in 1999.[34] Lord Hobhouse said:

> *"This case is concerned with the problems which arise from the publication of factual statements which are not correct--i.e. do not conform to the truth. This case is not concerned with freedom of expression and opinion. The citizen is at liberty to comment and take part in free discussion. It is of fundamental importance to a free society that this liberty be recognised and protected by the law.*
>
> *The liberty to communicate (and receive) information has a similar place in a free society but it is important always to remember that it is the communication of information not misinformation which is the subject of this liberty. There is no human right to disseminate information that is not true. No public interest is served by publishing*

---

[34] *Reynolds v Times Newspapers Ltd* [1999] UKHL 45.

or communicating misinformation. The working of a democratic society depends on the members of that society being informed not misinformed. Misleading people and the purveying as facts statements which are not true is destructive of the democratic society and should form no part of such a society. There is no duty to publish what is not true: there is no interest in being misinformed. These are general propositions going far beyond the mere protection of reputations."

In that same case, Lord Nicholls listed ten factors that were indicative of a matter of public interest being reported in a way that constituted a possible defence to libel. These included the efforts to which the journalist had gone to in order to verify the facts alleged within the relevant timescale. The '*Reynolds* Defence', as it became known, was replaced by section 4 of the Defamation Act 2013 which includes an objective test as to whether the author reasonably believed in all the circumstances that publication was in the public interest. When considering all the circumstances, the court is to make appropriate allowance for editorial judgment. Is any of this of relevance to reporting of the work of the Family Court?

I noted earlier that the preamble to the Editors' Code of Practice refers expressly to setting a framework 'for the highest professional standards and that in the standards that follow, top of the list is accuracy.'

The highest professional standards and accuracy are, together, the centrepiece of the Code. Even taking account of the considerable latitude the media have in deciding what to report and how to report it, it is still expected that they must act responsibly. So far as concerns the print media, that is the clear implication of the Code. The concept of responsible reporting discussed in *Reynolds* lives on in the Code.

A case in point
In 2011, I conducted a finding of fact hearing to determine the cause of a number of fractures sustained by a six-week old baby. The mother took advice from someone who is not a lawyer but who has developed a special interest in helping parents who are at risk of having their children removed. On his advice, arrangements were made for the baby to be taken by his grandmother to Ireland. An order was made in the Irish court that the baby should be returned to England. He was placed in foster care pending the final hearing. The mother disclosed that she had discussed the case with a journalist, the late Christopher Booker. Newspaper reports published before the court had heard any evidence in the case suggested there had been a miscarriage of justice. I asked the mother to inform Mr Booker that I would be very pleased if he attended the finding of fact hearing. He would then

have heard the entirety of the evidence which I heard. He did not attend. I asked the mother to tell Mr Booker the date when I would be handing down judgment and to invite Mr Booker to attend. He would then have heard not only my decision but also my analysis of the evidence and the reasons which led to my decision. Again, he did not. In my judgment I said this:

> "However, we should not lose sight of the fact that journalistic freedom brings with it responsibility, not least the responsibility to ensure fair, balanced and accurate reporting. So far as concerns the reporting of issues relating to family justice, the public needs to have the confidence that what it reads in the press is indeed fair, balanced and accurate...In my experience, parents involved in court proceedings cannot always be relied upon to be unbiased and dispassionate. More often, as Sir Nicholas Wall has said, they are partisan and tendentious. It is not only judges that need to recognise that but journalists too. As this case has shown, to rely uncritically upon what a parent says can lead to reporting that is unbalanced, inaccurate and just plain wrong."[35]

In care proceedings where allegations are made that a child has suffered significant harm at the hands of one or other of his parents, is it an example of the 'highest professional standards' to publish a story based only on information provided by one parent and to spurn an invitation from the judge to come to court to hear all of the evidence in the case? Is that responsible reporting?

Sensationalism and vilification
Sensationalism and vilification are journalistic techniques which journalists would argue are justifiable in some cases. In a book published in 2005[36] the authors say that:

> "Claims of sensationalism, which is the use and presentation of content designed to cause interest or excitement, have been levelled at journalists since at least the 1880s during which decade W.T. Stead distinguished it from untrue or exaggerated journalism and described it as 'justifiable up to the point that it is necessary to arrest the eye of the public and compel them to admit the necessity of action'...Closely linked to the dumbing down debate, sensationalism has increasingly been associated almost exclusively with the tabloid press...National newspapers came under sustained criticism during the 1980s and

---

[35] *Re L (A Child: Media Reporting)* [2011] EWHC B8 (Fam) at paragraph 193.
[36] *Key Concepts in Journalism Studies*, Bob Franklin, Martin Hamer, Mark Hanna, Marie Kinsey and John E Richardson, 2005, Sage Publications Ltd, London.

> *1990s for various things, including its sensationalism...It showed how this type of coverage can alienate sections of the public and prompt investigations like Calcutt[37] into press intrusions into privacy."*

In the research to which I refer in Chapter 12, children and young people expressed a significant anxiety about reporting that is sensationalist in tone or given a sensationalist headline. Whilst the desire of the press (and, it might also be said from a commercial perspective, the needs of the press) to grab hold of the attention of its readers is understandable, responsible journalism will understand that the child and his or her parents may become aware of the way in which the story has been told and may find it offensive, distressing and humiliating. In my opinion, the sensationalising of stories relating to children's cases heard in the Family Court is rarely justified and rarely, if ever, in the best welfare interests of that child.

This point was made in the Leveson report:

> *"Concerns at the damage that can be done by sensationalised reporting were also raised by Professionals Against Child Abuse (PACA), an organisation that represents the professionals who work in child care and social services. In its submission to the Inquiry, PACA set out its belief that sensationalised and sometimes inaccurate reporting of failings in social services were putting at risk the lives of vulnerable young people. PACA suggests that sensationalist reporting is damaging the profession through the popular vilification of individuals, and is impacting on retention and recruitment across the children's care sector."*

The report of the Leveson Inquiry notes that in his autobiography the former Prime Minister Sir John Major said:

> *"Across Fleet Street, sensational and exclusive stories sold extra copies– straight reporting did not. Accuracy suffered, squandered for something, anything, 'new'. Quotes were reconstructed, leaks and splashes abounded, confidentiality was not respected and reputations sacrificed for a few days' hysterical splash."*[38]

In June 2007, Sir John's successor as Prime Minister, Tony Blair, expressed similar concerns though in even more trenchant terms. He said:

---

[37] *The Calcutt Report: Review of Press Self-Regulation* (1993).
[38] *Report of the Inquiry into the Culture, Practices and Ethics of the Press* (the Leveson Report) Volume 2, Page 471.

"The reality is that as a result of the changing context in which 21st Century communications operates, the media are facing a hugely more intense form of competition than anything they have ever experienced before. They are not the masters of this change but its victims.

The result is a media that increasingly and to a dangerous degree is driven by "impact". Impact is what matters. It is all that can distinguish, can rise above the clamour, can get noticed. Impact gives competitive edge. Of course the accuracy of a story counts. But it is secondary to impact...

The audience needs to be arrested, held and their emotions engaged. Something that is interesting is less powerful than something that makes you angry or shocked...

...the fear of missing out means today's media, more than ever before, hunts in a pack. In these modes it is like a feral beast, just tearing people and reputations to bits. But no-one dares miss out...

...it is rare today to find balance in the media. Things, people, issues, stories, are all black and white. Life's usual grey is almost entirely absent. "Some good, some bad"; "some things going right, some going wrong": these are concepts alien to today's reporting. It's a triumph or a disaster. A problem is "a crisis". A setback is a policy "in tatters". A criticism, "a savage attack".

As I said earlier, I fully accept that it is not the role of the judge to seek to exercise editorial control over the manner in which the media reports information which it is entitled to publish, even if that reporting is unnecessarily and inappropriately sensationalist. However, it seems to me that if there were to be increased transparency by, for example, allowing the media to see documents such as psychiatric reports, it is reasonable to expect that in return the media will act responsibly in the way it uses that information. Over the course of my judicial career I have had occasion to read a great many expert medical reports concerning children and parents. It is not difficult to imagine how easy it would be for a journalist to sensationalise something contained in such a report. Judges, and the families who (invariably not through choice) find themselves appearing before the Family Court, need to be confident that, if the media is entrusted with sensitive personal information, that kind of irresponsible behaviour would not happen.

As in so many other issues we have considered, there are different views on the use of sensationalist reporting as a journalistic technique. In an article published in 2012,[39] journalist and lecturer, Mark Hanna, said that:

> *"What critics describe as a tendency to sensationalism in the media is not necessarily bad. The media storm of adverse publicity regarding child protection failures in the Baby P case is considered to have been a factor in the sharp increase in the number of children being taken into care since 2008/9, in that local authorities have responded to 'a rise in public and practitioner interest in, and sensitivity towards, child protection issues'12. Cafcass data show that the number of care applications in 2008/9 was 6,488 but in 2011/12 it was 10,299 – an increase of 59 percent. The Government concedes that this increase suggests that more children needed protecting, so it would seem that the media focus on how Baby P died has helped to safeguard thousands of children. But it continues to be asserted that media vilification of social workers for perceived failures in high profile cases has led to low morale and diminished recruitment in that profession."*

At first blush, Hanna appears to be suggesting that the ends justify the means; that sensationalism is justifiable if it leads to improved safeguarding for children who are at risk of harm. He also appears to suggest, for the same reason, that there may be occasions when vilification is justifiable. He told me that in the context in which he was writing, 'sensationalism' "means accurate journalism emotively expressed (and therefore crafted to stir up an emotional response in the reader)" and that 'vilification' "means fierce, denigrating criticism of an individual which is accurate factually (even if it contains vituperative expressions)". Hanna accepts that although his definitions may once have held good, the term 'sensationalist journalism' now tends to carry the implication that the journalism is inaccurate. There are similar difficulties in the use of 'vilification'. Hanna said that in his article he had in mind that 'vilification':

> *"is an expression of opinion harshly expressed based on what the social workers did or did not do. I was not seeking to defend inaccurate journalism but to say that harsh criticism of social work in the Baby P case seems to have led to greater protection for other children."*

Hanna accepted that vilification which is based on inaccurate reporting or misunderstanding of events is not beneficial and is not ethical journalism.

Although I understand Hanna's clarification of the use of 'sensationalism'

---

[39] *Irreconcilable Differences: The Attempts to Increase Media Coverage of Family Courts in England and Wales*, Mark Hanna, (2012) 4(2) Journal of Media Law 274-301.

and 'vilification' it seems to me that any journalist who chooses to use those journalistic techniques must be absolutely certain of the facts which it is contended justify their use. That is the moral to be learned from the Baby P case. It is said that "truth is the first casualty of war".[40] It might equally be said that truth is the first casualty of a media frenzy.

Conclusions

This chapter has been concerned with trust and truth. So, can the media be trusted? I do not think it is possible to give a straight 'yes' or 'no' answer. I noted earlier the cautionary words of Onora O'Neill: "Trust, it is constantly observed, is hard earned and easily dissipated. It is valuable social capital and not to be squandered." The journalists I have spoken to have been of the opinion that the number of journalists who are prepared to squander that capital is very small. Most journalists are responsible, committed and hard-working. They are journalists who genuinely seek to publish stories that are fair, balanced and accurate. The conclusion I come to, on balance, is that attempts to make further progress towards achieving greater transparency in the Family Court should not be derailed by the behaviour of the few. However, when they transgress, the few should be dealt with robustly by the court.

---

[40] It is said that a Republican Senator, Hiram W Johnson coined the phrase in 1917.

11: LEGAL BLOGGING

"If there be time to expose through discussion the falsehood and fallacies, to avert the evil by the processes of education, the remedy to be applied is more speech, not enforced silence." (Brandeis)[1]

On 1 October 2018 a pilot scheme was introduced to permit legal blogging in the Family Court.[2] The purpose of the pilot scheme was stated to be:

"to assess the use of new practices and procedures to allow for attendance at hearings in private by certain lawyers with a view to their being able to report on proceedings (as "legal bloggers") in addition to duly accredited representatives of news gathering and reporting organisations."

The rights of legal bloggers, and the restrictions imposed upon them, are identical to those which apply to journalists. Only "authorised lawyers" may attend such hearings under the pilot. To be an "authorised lawyer" a lawyer must either be authorised by a practice certificate to conduct litigation or exercise a right of audience in the family court, be a lawyer working for the Law School, Faculty or Department of a Higher Education Institution designated as a recognised body pursuant to section 216 of the Education Reform Act 1988 or be a lawyer attending on behalf of a registered educational charity. "Registered" means registered with the President's Office.

The Practice Direction does not restrict where a publication arising from the pilot should be published. The Transparency Project formally proposed this pilot to the Family Procedure Rules Committee who adopted a version of it following consideration.[3] The Transparency Project has published such blog posts produced by its own bloggers on its own website, and of-

---

[1] Point made by Brandeis J, Supreme Court Justice, in *Whitney v California* (1927) 274 US 357 at page 77.
[2] See Family Procedure Rules 2010, Practice Direction 36J – Pilot Scheme: Transparency (Attendance at hearings in private).
[3] For its work in developing and implementing the proposal for a pilot scheme permitting legal blogging, in November 2019 the Transparency Project received the Pro Bono Innovation of the Year award by the Bar Pro Bono Unit.

fers a platform to other legal bloggers to host theirs in future (subject to satisfying itself as publisher that the blog post does not offend against any reporting restrictions). Many solicitors publish blog posts on their firm's or chambers' website or blog, whilst others run their own individual blogs. At the time of writing none is thought to have attended court under the pilot or published a post on such sites (apart from a solitary post by a solicitor on the day the pilot began).

The Transparency Project argues that legal blogging has the potential to enable the public to gain a better understanding of what happens at private hearings in the Family Court. Bloggers are not constrained by the strict word counts imposed on journalists by their editors. They will, therefore, be able to write longer, more detailed and more informative pieces than space allows to journalists.[4] Moreover they are better equipped through familiarity to be able to pick up what is going on in any given hearing even without access to documents or prior knowledge of a case, and to be able to parse information and interpret and summarise the process accurately for a lay audience. Finally, legal bloggers are volunteers. Whilst there are economic disincentives for them to attend at all (they attend on a voluntary basis), legal bloggers are able, when they do attend, to sit in on and report cases that a journalist would not sit through, because they weren't 'interesting enough'. Legal blogging has the potential therefore to represent publicly the more run of the mill or typical cases that are rarely the subject of published judgments and that the mainstream media will never be interested in covering, thus minimising the endemic distortion that results from the combined effect of a highly selective publication of judgments, and a media focus on miscarriage of justice, failure or tragedy.

The pilot was originally intended to last until 30 June 2019. That deadline has been extended to 30 June 2020.

The take-up of the opportunities provided by the pilot has been very modest. Although a number of lawyers have recently expressed an interest in legal blogging, so far, almost without exception, bloggers have been supporters of The Transparency Project. Lucy Reed, Chair of The Transparency Project told me that in her opinion:

> *"The scheme so far has been a success. We are not surprised it is a slow take up – there was never any reason to think that the courts would suddenly be swamped with lawyers spending a rare day off*

---

[4] See, for example, *A day in the life of a district judge* by Lucy Reed, Chair of The Transparency Project: *http://www.transparencyproject.org.uk/a-day-in-the-life-of-a-district-judge/*.

back in court with a bloggers hat on! But there is a growing awareness of it, and we are getting more and more enquiries from lawyers thinking about giving it a try – and I think that over time the numbers will creep up. We are building a body of knowledge about how to do legal blogging well and with minimum disruption / stress to the main participants in a case. So far we think we've done it well and responsibly, and whilst the posts we've published are never going to make front page news, we hope those who read them will see a different aspect to family court work than is otherwise visible."

As Reed says, the fact that the take-up has been slow is not surprising. This is a relatively recent innovation in the Family Court though there are some similarities between this pilot and the Court of Protection transparency pilot which began in 2016. With respect to both pilots, their success or failure is not to be measured by the number of journalists (in the Court of Protection pilot) or bloggers (in the Family Court pilot) going into court but by making the hearings accessible to journalists and bloggers and through them helping to educate the public about the work that goes on in those courts. The development of legal blogging is potentially an important further step towards increasing transparency in the Family Court.

It is not yet clear whether, at the end of the pilot, there is to be an evaluation and, if there is, who is to undertake that evaluation and what the evaluation criteria will be. What is clear, as Reed says, is that those who are involved in legal blogging are determined to do it well and to develop principles of good practice that can be shared. The minutes of the Family Procedure Rule Committee show the pilot as a regular item on its agenda and insofar as any feedback has been received and recorded by the Committee all that feedback is positive.[5]

---

[5] Information concerning the Family Procedure Rule Committee can be found at: *https://www.gov.uk/government/organisations/family-procedure-rule-committee*.

12: RESEARCH AND THE VOICE OF THE CHILD

> *"There are few more difficult issues in family justice than the matter of open justice and the reporting of cases. There is a tension between concerns about 'secret justice' and legitimate expectations of privacy and confidentiality for the family. Both standpoints are valid and the question is whether they are irreconcilable".*[1]

On 28 June 2012, Sir Nicholas Wall, then President of the Family Division of the High Court, gave a lecture at Gresham College, London. He took as his title *Privacy and Publicity in Family Law – Their Eternal Tension*. He noted that the House of Commons Justice Committee's Sixth Report of Session 2010-12, *Operation of the Family Courts*, had said that the Committee:

> *"recognise the need for transparency in the administration of family justice, and the equally important need to protect the interests of children and their privacy."*

He went on to note that the Government had responded by saying that:

> *"whilst there are divergent views how to increase the transparency and accountability of the family courts, there is a general consensus that the status quo is unsatisfactory."*

Sir Nicholas suggested that:

> *"the general view is that greater transparency is required. What is equally clear, however, it seems to me, is that nobody knows quite how to achieve it."*

I agree there is "a general consensus that the status quo is unsatisfactory". I find it more difficult to accept Sir Nicholas' point that 'the general view is that greater transparency is required'. The Practice Guidance, *Transparency in the Family Courts: Publication of Judgments*, which came into effect on 3 February 2014, and the subsequent consultation paper, *Transparency – The*

---

[1] *Review of Civil and Family Justice in Northern Ireland*, Review Group's Report on Family Justice, September 2017 at paragraph 18.1.

Next Steps, issued on 15 August 2014, have highlighted a very deep fault line between supporters and opponents of greater transparency in the Family Court. On one side of the divide there are those who believe that the transparency agenda has not gone far enough and that more needs to be done to open up the Family Court. On the other side of the divide there are those who believe that the transparency agenda has already been pushed too far. If there is any common ground then, as it seems to me, it is only that there is a general acceptance of the importance of trying to protect the child's right to privacy – though even there, there is disagreement about whether or not the need to protect the child's right to privacy should be considered to be of overriding and paramount importance.

In this chapter I shall explore this polarisation of views by considering the research that has taken place during the last decade.

Research

The Children, Schools and Families Act 2010 received Royal Assent on 8 April 2010. As I noted in Chapter 5, Part 2 of that Act was controversial. As Dr Julie Doughty said at the time:[2]

> *"The implications of the Act are far-reaching, and have caused consternation amongst a range of practitioners already under pressure in family court work. In particular, the functions of clinicians and social workers who work with children and vulnerable families, are called into question."*

That 'consternation' prompted the publication of a number of articles hostile to implementation of the Act. For example, in February 2010 the Family Law Journal published an article by Alistair MacDonald,[3] then a barrister specialising in child law, in which he noted that:

> *"Article 12 of the United Nations convention on the Rights of the Child, and Arts 6 and 8 of the European Convention enshrine the right of children to participate in proceedings which are determinative of their futures…A child has his or her own right to a private life as distinct from his or her parents and a reasonable expectation of privacy…[Measures] which manifestly interfere with the psychological*

---

[2] Doughty J, 2013, *Confidentiality in the Family Courts: Ethical Dilemmas for Health and Social Work Practice* In: Priaulx, Nicolette Michelle and Wrigley, Anthony eds. *Ethics, Law and Society*, Vol 5. Farnham: Ashgate, pp 313-328.

[3] Now the Honourable Mr Justice MacDonald. The article was called *Bringing Rights Home for Children: Transparency and the Child's Right to Respect for Private Life*, and was published at [2010] Fam Law 180.

and physical integrity, the personal development, the development of social relationships and the physical and social identity that comprise cardinal elements of a child's 'private life' will constitute a breach of the right to respect for private life."

He set out his conclusions in very clear terms:

"Ultimately, applying the balancing test of proportionality, it is submitted that the child's Art 8 right to respect for private life should prevail over the Art 10 right to freedom of expression in the context of family proceedings by reason of the patent and disproportionate risk of serious and sustained damage caused to the fundamental elements of the child's private life by publication as outlined above."

It was concerns such as those which led the Children's Commissioner for England to identify an urgent need for research.

Dr Julia Brophy is the leading British academic to have undertaken research in this area. She was the lead researcher in three research studies whose reports were published in 2010, 2014 and 2015. Dr Brophy is a principal researcher in Family Justice. She was senior research fellow at the Oxford Centre for Family Law and Policy for many years and previously a principal investigator at the Thomas Coram Research Unit. She has sat on several advisory committees on family justice and has undertaken a range of studies about public law proceedings commissioned by the Ministry of Justice, the Department of Health, the Nuffield Foundation, the Office of the Children's Commissioner and other charities and NHS Trusts. Dr Brophy is highly respected across all parts of the Family Justice System, not least by the judiciary. It is essential that I should engage carefully with her work in this difficult area.

The 2010 report

At the request of the then Children's Commissioner for England, Dr Maggie Atkinson, Dr Brophy undertook an independent study of 51 children and young people with experience of proceedings in the family court, seeking their views concerning press access to and reporting of family proceedings.

Brophy's report, *The views of children and young people regarding media access to family courts*, was published in March 2010. To set that report in its historical context, by the time the report was published the rule change which allowed accredited media representatives to attend hearings in the family court had been in force for almost a year; the Family Court Information Pilot (see Chapter 5) was ongoing (it was completed in December 2010 and the evaluation was published in August 2011); and the Children, Schools and Families Bill was to receive Royal assent on 8 April 2010, the month after Brophy's report was published.

In a foreword to the report, Dr Atkinson said:

> *"For our research, we spoke to more than 50 children and young people, and what they said raises a number of serious concerns. The overwhelming view was that reporters should not be allowed into family court proceedings because the hearings address matters that are intensely private. The events discussed are painful, embarrassing and humiliating and the children and young people said their deeply personal details were the business of neither newspapers, nor the general public.*
>
> *They did not trust the press to get the facts right and felt strongly that articles would be sensationalised. They were worried about being identified and feared being bullied as a result.*
>
> *It is of great concern that the children and young people said that if a reporter was in court to hear the evidence they would not speak freely to professionals charged with undertaking assessments. This could seriously impact on a judge's ability to make difficult and often life changing decisions in the child's best interests...*
>
> *Article 12 of the United Nations Convention on the Rights of the Child states that children should have a say on decisions that affect their lives and article [16] says the law should protect children's private and home life. It is critical that these rights are adhered to so that children's rights are not breached when a decision is reached on the rules surrounding media access to family court proceedings."*

That passage succinctly summarises the essence of the conclusions arrived at by Brophy and her team. I don't propose to quote extensively from her report but it is appropriate to highlight some of the points she makes.

In the executive summary the report says that the cohort of children and young people interviewed for the purpose of this study,

> *"are unconvinced that formal rules prohibiting publication of identifying information will automatically protect them. They do not trust reporters and felt information would get out allowing them to be identified, shamed and bullied...This expectation is not limited to*

children in rural communities and is particularly relevant for those from ethnic minority communities. They also appeared unconvinced about the capacity of laws and adults to protect them.

Children and young people said the press sensationalise information, or construct bold headlines that do not reflect the content of the cases, and will 'cherry pick' bits of information. They are mostly doubtful that the press will print a truthful story..."

The context in which this report was prepared was the general concern which then existed about Part 2 of the Children, Schools and Families Act 2010 which, if implemented, set out steps designed to achieve greater transparency in the Family Court. It was an ill-thought out and deeply unpopular piece of legislation, rushed through Parliament in the final days before Parliament was prorogued.

The majority of the children and young people who took part in Brophy's survey indicated that if they knew a reporter would be in court or would have access to sensitive material such as expert medical reports, they would not be willing to talk openly to professionals. That could mean that they would withhold information which would enable professionals to assess risk and that, in turn, may lead to them not receiving the protection and care they need. Brophy says that:

"Children and young people said doctors must tell them that a reporter might be in court to hear the evidence and they must be told early – before any substantive issues are addressed, any other approach would be a betrayal of children's trust by doctors...These responses indicate a reduction – and if findings are replicated in larger samples – a dramatic reduction in the capacity of clinicians to safeguard children by providing the court with crucial information.

Family courts may face having to make crucial decisions about children, where their evidence and wishes and feelings are either missing, changed, incomplete or 'sanitised' by a child or young person in an effort to protect him/herself – and perhaps a parent – from the gaze of the press."

It is now ten years since Brophy's first report. I am not aware of any evidence coming to light during that period of instances where children and young people, having been told that a journalist may be in court to hear the evidence or that the court's judgment may be published on Bailii, have withheld relevant information from a medical expert. I accept that without further research in this area, drawing conclusions from this is inevitably speculative. However, two possible reasons why this is the case could be either because children are not being told that a journalist may be in court or that a judgment may be published (which, if true, Brophy argues would be a breach of a child's rights under Article 12 of the United Nations Convention on the Rights of the Child ('UNCRC')) or because, though they have been given this information, it does not cause the degree of concern and alarm which Brophy predicted.

The report also points out that "major fears exist about information from newspapers being transferred to the internet where they may remain indefinitely."

Brophy argues that issues relating to increased transparency will almost inevitably give rise to a breach of children's rights under Article 12 of the UNCRC. As she puts it:

> "A decision 'not to tell' children and young people [that a reporter may be in court to hear the evidence] may arguably be a breach of Article 12 of the UNCRC, while telling children a reporter might be in court – as children in this study indicate – will prevent many from feeling able to express their views freely and without pressure about decisions that will affect them – also arguably a breach of Article 12."

It is important to note the methodology used for this research. The children were all seen by interviewers who told them a story (a vignette) about a fictional child who was going through court proceedings. The child would then be asked what they thought the fictional child in the story might think and want about issues relating to access to court papers and information sharing. This approach avoided the need for the interviewee to have to talk about their own circumstances. It follows, therefore, that their answers are speculative and hypothetical and do not necessarily resonate with the child's own particular experiences. So far as I am aware there is no evidence available from children and young people who have had to face such problems themselves.

Discussing a hypothetical problem is very different from discussing a personal, lived experience. A description of how you might react if faced with a particular set of circumstances may be very different from the way you would *actually* react if you found yourself in that position.

The children and young people involved in this research expressed the fear that they may be teased and bullied if identified from media reporting. Brophy refers to this fear several times in her reports. However, it is important to be clear that the fears expressed by this cohort of children and young people are not based on their own personal experience. I am not aware of any research evidence which demonstrates that any children have in fact been teased and bullied as a result of being identified from media reporting of cases in which they have been involved. In the research carried out by Doughty, Twaite and Magrath[4] the researchers asked those who participated in their study whether they were aware of any child being adversely affected by media coverage, but none of the professionals or children's groups who participated in that study was able to identify a single instance where this had happened.

The Transparency Project organised an event at Gresham College on 5 April 2017 under the title *Reporting the Family Courts – are we doing it justice?* The event was described as 'A collaborative discussion between those working in and those reporting on the family justice system'. One of the panel members answering questions was Mr Justice (now Lord Justice) Peter Jackson. In answering a question about publishing judgments and the risk of jigsaw identification he said this:

> *"I may be out on a limb on this but I have an unease about the possibility of airbrushing abuse...I personally object to being told that I can't put in a judgment the terrible things these children have gone through. To take a particular point, the research that was referred to earlier by Julia Brophy took up one of my judgments as a very bad example of saying nasty things and that the children who read about it thought that it shouldn't have been said. The children in that case...who were teenagers, reported back that they were delighted the judgment had been published because finally someone had listened to what they had been going through."*

Other judges have had similar experiences. On 10 October 2019, His Honour Judge Dancey published a judgment in care proceedings concerning a 15 year-old girl. The judge was seriously concerned about this young person's experience of being in care and about the difficulties there had been in finding a suitable placement for her. He decided that his judgment, which set out his concerns in detail, should be published. All parties agreed. So, too, did the young person. It is appropriate to set out the first five para-

---

[4] *Transparency through publication of Family Court judgments - An evaluation of the responses to, and effects of, judicial guidance on publishing family court judgments involving children and young people - http://orca.cf.ac.uk/99141/.*

graphs of his judgment:[5]

> "1. On 12 August 2019 I made a care order and, on 30 September 2019, a final deprivation of liberty (DOLs) order in respect of a young person, A, a girl aged 15½ years.
>
> 2. I am not giving this judgment to explain why I made these orders (which nobody opposed) but because, as I suggested to A when she came to a hearing, I thought her story should be told.
>
> 3. Although I identify the local authority in this case, I am not going to name individual workers. The problems that I will describe are more about lack of suitable resources than failures by social workers.
>
> 4. I am writing this judgment in a way that I hope will be accessible for A and her family.
>
> 5. A is a bright and articulate girl. I have met with her. I will not say it was easy for she told me in no uncertain terms what she thought about things. It was quite challenging meeting with her. But I am glad to have done so and listened to her."

Ethical issues

The risk that a child or young person may not be open with a professional (for example, a psychologist) if they knew that there may be a journalist in court or that the professional's report would be made available to the media, raises some ethical issues for professionals about whether to tell, what to tell and when to tell children and young people about the possibility of media interest in their case.

In an article published in the Family Law Journal in October 2009,[6] Consultant Child and Adolescent Psychiatrist, Dr Danya Glaser, a highly respected expert witness who has regularly given evidence in the Family Court, set out her concerns about these developments. She begins by expressing the opinion that the move for greater transparency had arisen because the media wished to scrutinise the role and work of expert witnesses in the Family Court. She said:

> "Much has been said and written about the issue of media access to

---

[5] *Dorset Council v A* [2019] EWFC 62.
[6] *Media Access to Expert Reports: A Child and Adolescent Mental Health Perspective* [2009] Fam Law 911.

> *family courts. The ostensible reason for this move is to increase transparency about court proceedings in order to better inform the public and disabuse them of wrong perceptions' such as the belief that courts freely and unnecessarily remove children from their parents' care. There is an agenda, namely to scrutinise specifically the opinion and evidence of expert witnesses."*

I question Dr Glaser's use of the word 'agenda' in this context. Does she seek to imply that scrutiny of experts by the media should not be encouraged or even, perhaps, not allowed? One of the fundamentals of open justice is that in a trial that is open to the public all witnesses – and all judges – come under public scrutiny. One of the concerns of those who insist on describing the Family Court as a 'secret' court is that those who give evidence in the Family Court, including experts, those who present that evidence and those who adjudicate upon it are not open to scrutiny and are therefore unaccountable.

In the Family Court, whenever a miscarriage of justice occurs it occurs behind closed doors, out of sight of the public. Surely, a greater concern than that expressed by Glaser is that, for the reasons explained in earlier chapters, too few journalists take advantage of their right to attend hearings in the Family Court? Their failure to attend inevitably means that the public's view of the Family Court is still very restricted. Miscarriages of justice can go unnoticed.

Criminal trials take place in public. Some criminal trials rely just as heavily upon expert evidence as hearings in the Family Court. Over the last 20 years there have been some well-publicised occasions when expert medical evidence has led to convictions which were subsequently quashed in the light of new medical evidence. The names of three mothers, Sally Clarke, Angela Cannings, and Donna Anthony, for example, all come to mind.

I noted in Chapter 3 that *The Times'* journalist, Camilla Cavendish, has expressed some trenchant views on the role of experts in the Family Court. Just as the names of those who suffer a miscarriage of justice leave an indelible mark on public consciousness so, too, regrettably, do the names of some expert witnesses whose evidence has been the subject of significant judicial criticism.

Glaser goes on to express the following further concerns:

> *"...it is now proposed to allow the media to read medical and other expert reports. This will pose serious difficulties for doctors and other*

professionals acting as expert witnesses, for a number of reasons. Experts are instructed on the basis that by using their clinical skills in meeting with family members they will be able to assist the court in its decision-making. The clinical professional is therefore being used simultaneously as clinician and expert. The stock in trade of mental health professionals is their ability to converse with patients in a particular way so as to elicit information. To be of benefit to the patient and, in this case, also to the court, the context has to be one of trust – trust in the skill, expertise and integrity of the clinician by both patient and court.

One of the fundamental assumptions underpinning clinical encounters is confidentiality…[It] is inconceivable that one may now be put in a position of having to warn the patient that what is being discussed, almost invariably highly personal and often distressing, necessarily included in one's report, will also be read by the media."

The 2014 report

In February 2014 the President's guidance on transparency in the family court came into effect. The President, Sir James Munby, made it known that he regarded this as simply a first step in an ongoing process of opening up the Family Court. Concerned about the guidance on transparency and even more concerned about what next steps the President might propose, in 2014 the National Youth Advocacy Service (NYAS) and the Association of Lawyers for Children (ALC) commissioned Brophy to undertake another study. The results of this study were published in July 2014 under the title, *Safeguarding, Privacy and Respect for Children and Young People & The Next Steps in Media Access to Family Courts*. The Foreword to this report was written jointly by the Children's Commissioner for England, Dr Maggie Atkinson, and the Children's Commissioner for Wales, Keith Towler. They emphasised the importance of Articles 12 and 16 of the UNCRC. They made the point that Article 12:

> *"states all children have the right to a voice, which is both heard and taken seriously, in all decisions about them and their lives".*

They go on to say that Article 16:

> *"is crystal clear: all children have an inalienable, undeniable right to have their privacy protected, unless there are things happening in their lives that place them in danger".*

The two Commissioners said that if the media was granted even greater access to the Family Court it was "simply disingenuous to argue that a child's supposedly protected anonymity will be maintained". In their opinion, the children and young people involved in this study "raise credible doubts about the ability of the media to respect their privacy".

The sample size for this second study was extremely small. Only 11 young people were involved, aged between 16 and 25. They were not the subject of a survey (as in the 2010 report). The discussions were described as a 'group exercise'. This was, in effect, a focus group whose members were asked questions about policy. The exercise lasted for a day. In terms of the setting of policy, for my part I have significant doubts about the weight that can properly be attached to the views of this very small sample.

The sample was drawn primarily from the NYAS young people's consultation and participation group (a national group covering England and Wales). It is clear from this report that, as in the 2010 report, this small group held strong negative views about the media. The report states that 'Young people do not trust the media – in all its forms." Although the report says that some or all of this group (it is not clear which) had "personal experiences with reporters and photographers from print and televised media" the report does not indicate whether those experiences arose in the context of their involvement in proceedings in the Family Court. The report does not suggest that the fears raised by the study group in the 2010 study had been realised in the experience of any of this group of 11 young people.

As in the first study, this small group viewed the media as "a highly competitive, commercially driven industry motivated by the need to increase sales figures through populist readership." The group went on to say that the media "does not prioritise the truth."

For the members of this group:

> *"Fairness and balance are not features they identify with any part of the media: indeed they see commercial priorities as overriding – and in some cases precluding, truth telling."*

This group was unanimous in its opposition to media attendance at hearings in the Family Court. It was also unanimous:

> *"in arguing that when a court is considering media access it should first ascertain the views, interests and long-term welfare implications for any child."*

The group acknowledged that whether a particular child had the capacity to consent would depend on his or her level of maturity.

As in the earlier study, the young people in this group were strongly of the opinion that if children knew that reporters would be in court and/or would have access to court documents they would be unable or unwilling to talk openly to professionals about ill-treatment and would be likely to withhold information. They also made the point that telling children in advance about the presence of the media in court or of the media having access to court papers is not a matter of personal choice; "it is an ethical obligation in terms of truthfulness and an obligation under Article 12 of the UNCRC." They expressed concern that, with respect to this issue, at present they currently have no power and no redress.

The group was concerned about the ease with which, they believed, children and their families could be identified from information contained in a published judgment. They were concerned about the risk of jigsaw identification and of identification making them vulnerable to harassment and bullying. There was a time when printed news, however personal and intrusive, could properly be regarded as tomorrow's fish and chip wrapping. Those days are gone. The effect of the internet, especially social media, is that once news is 'out there' it remains 'out there' indefinitely

This group of young people "raised serious doubts" about allowing parents to talk to the media at the end of the case, not even to raise concerns about the conduct of professionals and/or the court. They said that "parents need to act like parents" and put children's interests first. They said that "there are other avenues to address grievances" though the report does not state what those "other avenues" might be. They were unanimous in their rejection of the proposal that reporters should have access to court documents.

It is clear that this small group saw Sir James Munby's proposals as pandering to the media. According to Brophy's report:

> *"They said the President should stop trying to please the media, not least because it will not fulfil his agenda; he should explore other mechanisms for monitoring and, if necessary, improving services and information about services."*

The report ends with an absolute rejection of any notion that increasing transparency will expose miscarriages of justice and thereby prevent or reduce the risk of future miscarriages of justice. Agreeing with the young people, Brophy said that she considered such a notion to be "naïve". Brophy concludes that:

> "As young people and others identify, the framework for this area of legal policy has to be considered against the commercial imperatives of the contemporary media and not an ideologically driven agenda about, for example, public education, which the press itself does not claim to fulfil."

Those are strong words. It is right that children's voices should be heard in this debate. It is very important that the state should "respect and ensure" their rights under the UNCRC, not in some token way, but clearly and honestly – one might say 'transparently'. However, children are not the only actors participating in the dramas which unfold daily in the Family Court. Parents have rights, too. In Chapter 3, I referred to the *Webster* case.[7] Three children, then aged 4, 3 and 1, were removed from the care of their parents and placed for adoption. The reason for their removal was a finding by the court that one or other of the parents had physically abused and injured one of the children. It was only when their fourth child was born and became subject to proceedings that further investigations were undertaken and doubts raised about the reliability of the medical evidence which had been relied upon at the hearing relating to the three older children. There appeared to have been a miscarriage of justice in the proceedings relating to the three older children.

By then, the older children had been adopted. An attempt to appeal against the adoption orders failed. It was now far too late. That story was the subject of five published judgments.[8] The mother was given permission to talk to the media. A number of documentaries were made by writer and broadcaster, John Sweeney, then working for the BBC. Can it seriously be argued that the right to privacy of the three older children (then aged 6, 5 and 3) under Articles 12 and 16 of the UNCRC somehow 'trumped' the parents right to expose what appears to have been a serious miscarriage of justice? The effect of that miscarriage of justice was that four full siblings were brought up in two homes, only one child cared for by his birth parents. That is a deeply unhappy and unsatisfactory outcome to those proceedings.

There are other cases, equally as poignant in their own way, in which, in my opinion, permitting full media coverage has not only been appropriate and

---

[7] See page 26 above.
[8] *Norfolk County Council v Webster* [2004] EW Misc 3; *Norfolk County Council v Webster* [2006] EWHC 2733 (Fam); *Norfolk County Council v Webster* [2006] EWHC 2898 (Fam); *Re Brandon Webster* [2007] EWHC 549 (Fam); *Webster v Norfolk County Council* [2009] EWCA Civ 59.

fair but has also been necessary in order to comply with the parents' own rights under, in particular, Articles 6, 8 and 10 of the European Convention on Human Rights.

Family Justice Council Debate
The 8th Annual Family Justice Council Debate took place on 11 November 2014. The motion considered was, *Transparency in family proceedings – Is the Family Court Open for Business?* The debate was chaired by Sir James Munby. Speaking for the motion were The Honourable Mr Justice Newton and Baroness Claire Tyler. Speaking against the motion were Dr Brophy and Ms Sue Berelowitz, then Deputy Children's Commissioner for England. Given the subject matter of this debate it is perhaps surprising that the four speakers did not include a media representative though there was a BBC solicitor in the audience and he contributed to the discussion which followed the presentations by the four speakers.

Brophy's contribution very much mirrored the views expressed in the two reports to which I have already referred. By now, her views were well-known. For the most part, Berelowitz's views did not vary significantly from those expressed by Brophy. She said:

> *"In our view in the Office of the Children's Commissioner, the Convention [UNCRC] requires that family proceedings fully protect the privacy of any child involved. So that whether named or identified by other details enabling jigsaw identification their views, circumstances and histories are never disclosed to the public…this is for two main reasons; firstly, the direct harm to the child that may be occasioned by identification – this could take the form of bullying, and is something that children have mentioned repeatedly; secondly, reprisals or negative effects on family relationships."*

However, answering questions from the floor, Berelowitz made this comment which appeared to be aimed specifically in the direction of the media:

> *"The point is: it is their [i.e. the children's] private stuff. Set aside reporting, they don't want you there. They do not want you listening to their private misery. They don't want you in the room at all, and that's the basic point. Reporting is a different issue, but that is their starting point, 'Please stay away'."*

I find that message surprising. That ship had sailed more than five years earlier. Since April 2009 duly accredited media representatives have been entitled to attend hearings in the Family Court. Their right to attend is a right given to them by secondary legislation.[9] It is a right that can only be taken away from the media in the same way – by rule change.

Much more controversial was a comment made by Berelowitz at the very end of her speech opposing the motion. She said:

> *"I have worked closely with profoundly distressed and damaged and troubled children all my working life. I know and understand their minds; it is my job so to do. I know how little it takes to tip a child over the edge.*
>
> *I know too that it takes only 30 seconds from when a child puts a bathrobe cord around their neck for that child to die. I genuinely fear that it is only a matter of time before this deeply misguided motion, which has at its heart, I believe, an utter disregard for the welfare and best interests of children, and is, in my view, therefore unlawful, will result in the death of a child. And who amongst us tonight says that this is a price worth paying?"*

Given Berelowitz's views on the topic under debate, it is perhaps ironic that this particular comment should have attracted the attention of the national media. On 12 December 2014, a headline in the *MailOnline* read:

> *"Opening up family courts 'will cause child suicides': Fury at claim by children's tsar in secret justice battle."*

I am not aware of the existence of any evidence that any child (or, indeed, any parent) has died by suicide either as a result of being informed that a journalist would be attending a Family Court hearing or as a result of the publication of a Family Court judgment. There is nothing in any of Brophy's reports that justify such a statement.

The 2015 report

In October 2015, again having been commissioned by NYAS and the ALC, Brophy published a report headed, *A review of anonymised judgments on Bailii: Children, privacy and 'jigsaw identification'*. Young people were concerned that anyone reading a judgment with some local knowledge may be able to identify the child referred to in that judgment, perhaps by means of jigsaw identification. The review exercise is described in the report as follows:

---

[9] The Family Proceedings (Amendment) (No 2) Rules 2009, Statutory Instrument 2009 No. 857 (L.8).

> *"Eleven young people aged between 17 and 25 years analysed a total of 21 judgments posted on Bailii between 2010 and 2015...The review was followed by a computer search for coverage of judgments/ cases by the media and social networking sites."*

Before I deal with the outcome of this study it is appropriate to express a preliminary concern about the sample size. I cannot put it better than Professor Jo Delahunty QC did in a lecture in May 2018.[10] She said:

> *"Whilst I remain concerned about the views expressed so eloquently by the 11 young people in the Brophy study I am conscious that a sample of 11 cannot tie the courts hands for the thousands it deals with every year. But consultation may be required because we can't make children the products of adult experiments with their futures. Rather than using the Brophy research to throw a grenade beneath the wheels of the transparency wagon, or, conversely, attacking the Brophy research by calling out its small sample base so as to seek to jettison its work, I think there is a need for a larger piece of research with an agreed base line and control groups of participants to understand the range of opinions amongst the children whose futures the courts are deciding. I am clear in my mind that we cannot stand still. Change must happen because the danger of ill-informed and hostile public opinion infecting the work of the family courts cannot be ignored. The scenes outside Alder Hay Hospital by Alfie's army were unacceptable. One cannot turn the family court into a war field. Action has to be taken by those who are prepared to participate respectfully in a constructive dialogue between court users before the debate is ambushed by those who are fuelled by anger rather than reason as their motivation to act."*

Brophy's report identified a number of features routinely found in judgments which would be of assistance to someone determined to try to identify the child involved in a particular case. These markers included identifying the local authority, naming the social worker (which might identify the locality where that social worker worked), naming other professionals involved in the case (e.g. doctors and health care staff, Children's Guardians), stating the child's date of birth, giving details that might identify other family members (e.g. a parent's mental health and/or drug and alcohol problems). The reality is – and it should not have needed academic research to tell us this – that every piece of information given in a judgment forms

---

[10] *Transparency in the Family court: What Goes on Behind Closed Doors?*, a lecture given by Professor Jo Delahunty QC at Gresham College.

part of a jigsaw of information. The more information that is given, the greater the possibility of the family being identified. That problem is exacerbated if there is information in the media (perhaps because of recent criminal proceedings) and/or on social media concerning the same family member. There can come a point at which the number of pieces of the jigsaw, when pieced together, is sufficient to enable identification of the family concerned.

This all makes perfectly good sense and stands as a warning to take care about the level of detail included in a judgment. However, it is equally important to note that although the study aimed 'to select judgments with a potential geographical link to the young investigators via local authority applicants', nowhere is it suggested in the report that this 11-strong group of young sleuths were, in fact, able to identify any of the children who were the subjects of the judgments that were reviewed. That should not be allowed to encourage complacency. It should, though, indicate that the response to this report needs to be thoughtful and proportionate.

Anonymisation of judgments

Brophy's study raises a concern about the anonymisation process. That issue needs to be addressed as a priority. Brophy notes on page iv of the executive summary of her report that some of the details picked up on by the young people in their review of the judgments:

> *"are arguably errors in the anonymisation process, the 'direction of travel' for such errors in a larger sample is worrying."*

Those comments resonate with observations made in the Doughty report to which I referred earlier.[11] That report contains a lengthy section under the heading 'Failures in anonymisation'. The report says that:

> *"shortly after the fieldwork began, we found instances of failure to redact identifying details in some judgments that were already online... We encountered two problems about anonymisation early in our study.*
>
> > *1. Finding some judgments that had not been fully redacted but had remained on the BAILII site for some time (apparently unnoticed). We should emphasise that we were not searching for errors*

---

[11] *Transparency through publication of family court judgments: An evaluation of the responses to, and effects of, judicial guidance on publishing family court judgments involving children and young people*, 23 March 2017, Dr Julie Doughty, Alice Twaite and Paul Magrath.

in anonymisation when reading judgments, and those we noticed were by chance. These errors were not speculation about potential jigsaw identification but simply a name being left in the judgment by mistake.

2. Being notified of a new judgment with errors in it. On two occasions early in our study we were notified by professional contacts of new judgments appearing on BAILII which appeared problematic. One of these was completely unredacted and one still contained a name of the future carer of the child. BAILII was contacted direct and took immediate remedial action...

We are aware that occasionally cases are still being published with errors that judges have failed to pick up, and that the Press Office and BAILII deal with these promptly. The Transparency Project asked the Court Service about procedures in July 2016, when they were advised that new guidance was being drafted. We understand from BAILII that about 70% of requests for judgments to be removed are made because of inadequate anonymization; about 20% where it was not actually intended to have the judgment published at all, so sent in error; and the remainder where the wrong, unredacted version was sent. These are informal estimates."

The 2016 study on anonymisation
In July 2016, funded by the Nuffield Foundation, Brophy published a paper headed, *Anonymisation and Avoidance of the Identification of Children & The Treatment of Explicit Descriptions of the Sexual Abuse of Children in Judgments Intended for the Public Arena*. If the title of the paper had ended there the paper would not have caused any controversy. However, beneath the title there appeared the words "Judicial Guidance". This created confusion. Had the guidance been approved and adopted by the judiciary? Was the guidance intended to be followed by anyone charged with anonymising judgments? The President's Practice Guidance on Transparency gives the impression that it was not expected that judges themselves would anonymise their judgments. This was to be done either by the solicitor for the applicant in the proceedings or by the solicitor for the party seeking permission to publish.

The unfortunate inclusion of the words 'Judicial Guidance' led to the President, Sir James Munby, issuing Practice Guidance making clear that this 'judicial guidance' did not have the authority of guidance published by the President of the Family Division. The publication of this 'judicial guidance' also led to criticism in a judgment by a High Court Judge, Mr Justice

Hayden.[12] He said:

> "36. ...I formed the clear impression that counsel in this case and indeed in another case that I heard recently, had overestimated the reach and scope of Dr Brophy's research. The confusion, it seems to me, lies in the title: 'Judicial Guidance'. I think the legal profession may interpret that as signalling an authority which this research does not have. The position has been clarified by the President of the Family Division's own guidance which was issued on the 18th October 2016...
>
> "37. There is no doubt that Dr Brophy's research is, as one would expect, very child focused. I am concerned however that in expressing her aim to be striking 'a better balance between the policy that more judgments should be published' and the concerns of 'young people' about 'deeply distressing' information 'in the public arena', Dr Brophy has lost sight of the legal framework that requires to be applied in any decision concerning publication. We are not concerned merely with a 'policy', to publish more judgments, rather we are applying the obligations imposed by Article 10 and Article 8 ECHR. This has been established law since the decision in Clayton v Clayton [2006] EWCA Civ 878..."

That is not the end of the story. In December 2018 the new President of the Family Division, Sir Andrew McFarlane, issued *Practice Guidance: Anonymisation and avoidance of the identification of children and the treatment of explicit descriptions of the sexual abuse of children in judgments intended for the public arena*. The Practice Guidance approved the 'judicial guidance' produced by Brophy. As Practice Guidance, compliance is not obligatory but is strongly encouraged.

It is clear from Brophy's research, and from the Doughty research, that there is a problem with the quality and consistency of the anonymisation of published judgments in England and Wales both at Circuit Judge and at High Court Judge level. It is a problem that needs to be taken seriously and addressed as a priority. A possible solution may be found from the way anonymisation of judgments is dealt with in Australia.

The introduction to Part 5 of the Family Court of Australia's 2017–18 Annual Report states that:

---

[12] *Re J (A minor)* [2016] EWHC 2595 (Fam).

> "In 2017-18, judges of the Family Court of Australia handed down judgments at both first instance and appellate levels. The decisions reflect the Court's expansive jurisdiction, the wide variety of issues that it addresses and its position as a superior specialist federal court that deals with the most complex and serious family law cases. A selection of significant and noteworthy judgments are published in this report. The Court recognises that the accessibility of its judgments to the public is important. It commits the resources required to ensure that every final judgment delivered is anonymised and published consistent with s 121 of the Family Law Act 1975 (Cth) ('the Act'). This policy has enabled the Court to better respond to community interest and concerns about particular cases highlighted in the media and demonstrates the commitment of the Court to being open and accountable for its decisions. Virtually all judgments, after anonymisation, are published in full text on the Australasian Legal Information Institute (AustLII) website.[13] There is a link to the AustLII site from the Court's website (www.familycourt.gov.au). The website provides links to recent decisions…In 2017–18, the Court published links to 1170 first instance and 262 Full Court judgments."

In *Publishing Family Court judgments: problems and solutions*,[14] Lyn Newlands[15] asks: 'How does the Court ensure that judgments are sufficiently anonymised to avoid identification of parties and their children without impacting on the integrity of the Judge's reasons?' She sets out in considerable detail the approach, and the very obvious meticulous care, that is taken. She says that:

> "When anonymising judgments, three principles need to be borne in mind – privacy of the parties and children; integrity of the Judge's reasons; and ensuring the finished product is intelligible. These principles may at times conflict with each other, requiring a delicate balancing act to achieve effective anonymisation of the judgment at hand."

Judgments from the Family Court of Australia are not anonymised by the judge (as is currently the norm in England and Wales) or by the parties' law-

---

[13] The Australian equivalent to Bailii in the UK.
[14] *http://www.austlii.edu.au/cgi-bin/sinodisp/au/journals/JlLawInfoSci/2016/6.html?stem=0&synonyms=0&query=lyn%20newlands.*
[15] Lyn Newlands is the former Judgments Publication coordinator in the Family Court of Australia. I am grateful to Virginia Wilson, Deputy Principal Registrar and National Law Registrar for the Family court of Australia for providing me with a copy of Newland's article and details of the current arrangements for anonymisation in the Family Court of Australia.

yers (as proposed in 2014 in the President's *Practice Guidance Transparency in the Family Courts – Publication of Judgments*). The Family Court of Australia currently employs two members of staff to anonymise and publish judgments. Newlands describes two different approaches to anonymisation:

> *"For courts undertaking routine anonymisation of judgments, there are two options from which to choose.*
>
> > *Partially automated anonymisation uses software designed to find and replace pre-defined words from text. This process is supplemented by a subsequent quality control check to identify and undertake any further anonymisation required. This is the option chosen by the Federal Circuit Court of Australia*
> >
> > *Manual anonymisation is a traditional 'word by word, line by line' editing process where individual words and phrases are substituted by less identifiable terms/phrases, for example, an 'electrician' might become 'skilled tradesman.' As an incidental consequence of the anonymisation process, the judgments officer undertakes an informal proof reading role whereby minor punctuation, grammatical and/or formatting errors may be corrected, and more serious problems referred back to chambers for resolution, prior to external publication of the judgment. This is the option selected by the Family Court of Australia."*

In the final two paragraphs of her paper, setting out her conclusions, Newlands says that:

> *"Since 2007 the Family Court of Australia has endeavoured to publish as many of its judgments as possible. It has provided the extra resources required to enable it to do so in compliance with the requirements of s 121 of the Act. When unforeseen problems have arisen, they have been recognised and resolved. The learning thus acquired has added to the knowledge base of the JPO and is applied constantly in the complex and challenging exercise of anonymisation.*
>
> *Online publication of its judgments enables the Family Court to make them widely accessible to the public and the profession, and logically extends the transparency inherent in its operation as an 'open' court. At the same time, parties can be reassured that the Court makes every effort to protect their privacy. Many problems have been addressed since 2007 but, given the constantly evolving online environment, I am sure there will always be more!"*

Newland's paper does not apply to the Family Court of Western Australia or to the Federal Circuit Court of Australia, both of which have their own arrangements for anonymisation. Those arrangements are similar to those for the Family Court of Australia in that judgments are anonymised centrally and not by the judge. Currently the Family Court of Australia and the Federal Circuit Court of Australia are harmonising procedures and use both the automation software and manual anonymisation. The choice of method or combination of the two methods depends on the length and complexity of the judgment. Once procedures are harmonised there should be no difference between the two courts.

The anonymisation of a judgment is an important task. Getting it right is not optional but a necessary requirement in order to maximise the prospect of achieving the objective of protecting the privacy of children and their families. In my opinion, the arrangements for anonymisation of judgments in Australia appear more professional and more likely to provide a higher level of quality and consistency than the somewhat hit and miss approach that has been the case in the Family Court in England and Wales.

13: OPEN JUSTICE IN OTHER COUNTRIES

> *"As a legal journalist of 20 years' standing, I would be happy to add my name to those supporting greater openness for family proceedings. In general, I would argue that the courts should be open to press and public, subject only to restrictions on identifying children involved in proceedings. It is patently in the public interest that justice should be done patently and in public."* (Joshua Rozenberg) [1]

In May 2009, the month after the implementation of the rule change which permitted duly accredited media representatives to attend hearings in the Family Court, the Department of Social Policy and Social Work at Oxford University published *Family Policy Briefing 5*[2] ('the Briefing paper'). Its title was *Openness and transparency' in family courts: what the experience of other countries tells us about reform in England and Wales*. Dr Julia Brophy was the lead author.

The Briefing paper begins by explaining that the paper:

> *"examines the issues surrounding public and press access to family hearings in England and Wales…It reviews the history and current position regarding press and public access to family courts in other, comparable, jurisdictions."*

The other jurisdictions considered are Australia, New Zealand, Canada (Nova Scotia and British Columbia) and Scotland. With respect to each of those jurisdictions the Briefing paper examines the position concerning public access to the courts, publication of information relating to court hearings, sanctions for breach of confidentiality and access to judgments.

After reviewing the position in each of those four countries, the Briefing paper concludes that:

---

[1] House of Commons Constitutional Affairs Committee, Fourth Report of Session 2004-2005, Volume II *Family Justice: The operation of the family courts*, page 36, Ev 199.

[2] http://transparencyproject.org.uk/press/wp-content/uploads/2015/01/Family_Policy_Briefing_5.pdf.

> "In debates in England and Wales other jurisdictions have been held up as examples of the benefits of press access. However, closer examination of what is permissible, both in press access to and press reporting of individual cases and the safeguards each jurisdiction puts in place to protect child and family privacy reveals a more complex picture with less press and public access than is commonly claimed."

It has been argued that media attendance at court would improve both transparency and legitimacy. The Briefing paper concludes that that view is not borne out by experience:

> "Following recent changes to admit the press, independent research in New Zealand found press coverage based on unsubstantiated allegations by litigants continued, written by reporters who were not in court and did not check facts with a judge. Allegations of 'secrecy' and bias continue in Australia…"

The Briefing paper disagrees with the proposition that newspaper reporting will educate the British public about family courts. The point is made that journalists argue that it is not their job to educate the public and that, in any event:

> "Surveys indicate people do not get their information about how courts work from newspapers…Educational materials and programmes from courts themselves are far more likely to meet information needs and do this accurately."

A decade on since the publication of the Briefing paper, it is appropriate to take another look at what is happening in those four jurisdictions – at any changes that have occurred and any problems that have been encountered. In addition, I shall also consider the current position in Northern Ireland and Eire.

Australia[3]

Since the enactment of the Family Law Act 1975 all but one State in Australia comes under the jurisdiction of the Family Court of Australia. That one State, Western Australia, has its own Family Court. The Family Court of Western Australia is very similar to the Family Court of Australia.

---

[3] I am grateful to Professor Patrick Parkinson, Dean of Law at the TC Beirne School of Law, The University of Queensland, Brisbane for so willingly answering my questions about the current position in Australia.

The Family Law Act 1975 deals with those cases which, in England and Wales, would be categorised as 'private law' cases. When that Act was first introduced it contained a total ban on reporting anything in relation to proceedings in the Family Court. All proceedings were to be held in closed courtrooms. It was an offence to publish any statement or report relating to proceedings or any account of the evidence in those proceedings. This was a significant departure from Australia's traditional approach of open justice. The report of a Joint Select Committee[4] noted that the reason for this departure was that:

> "15.5 ...Parliament, when reversing the usual presumption, considered that there was no particular public good to be served by exposing the private domestic conflicts of individuals to the public gaze and it was concerned that individuals involved in such disputes should not be, in any way, exploited by the press."

The practice of conducting family proceedings in closed courts was relatively short-lived. The report goes on to note that:

> "15.6 ...The privacy of the proceedings led to accusations of the court being akin to a 'star chamber'. A further problem for the court was described by the chief justice as follows:
>
>> 'Litigants who complained that they had been denied justice could make allegations concerning the court and the conduct of judges and those involved in the proceedings without these allegations being capable of rebuttal. The administration of justice in the Family Court was open to criticism by slur and innuendo and thus, from the outset, the administration of justice in the court was capable of being portrayed as being of a different category to that of other courts.'"

The Family Law Act 1975 was amended in 1983 to permit private law family proceedings to be held in open court, though still subject to restrictions on identification of the parties. Section 121[5] of that Act provides an indicative list of the kind of particulars that should be taken to be 'identifying' factors. Breach of the prohibition of publishing material which may identify a person as a party to proceedings is a criminal offence punishable by the

---

[4] *The Family Law Act 1975: Aspects of its operation and interpretation* (AGPS, Canberra, 1992), referred to by Professor Parkinson in his book, *Australian Family Law in Context: Commentary and Materials*, 7th ed, 2019 Thomson Reuters, Sydney at paragraph 7.150.
[5] See Appendix A, page 255.

imposition of a fine or a period of imprisonment.

In the report of the Joint Select Committee, it was noted that:

> *"15.8 The government of the day, in amending legislation, acknowledged the calls for the hearing of the Family Court's proceedings in open court. The Act relaxed the total prohibition on the publication of details of proceedings, severe penalties were prescribed for any account of proceedings that identified a party in connection with the proceedings, and guidelines as to what constituted identification were set down in s 121(3) [of the Family Law Act 1975 as amended]. These parameters have been criticised for setting insurmountable barriers to publication.*
>
> *15.9 The restraint on publication has been criticised, especially by the media and some interest groups. The media argues that the full reporting of legal proceedings is a fundamental pillar of democracy and that the public has a right to be informed on all matters. Some of the legal fraternity and some interest groups argue that proceedings able to be fully reported are more likely to ensure the accountability of the court – people will be able to air any grievances and judges can be scrutinised more effectively."*

The Family Law Act 1975 does not deal with child protection issues ('public law' cases as they are referred to in England and Wales). Those cases are heard in state Children's Courts (in the state of South Australia they are dealt with in the Youth Court). There is variation from state to state with respect to the attendance of the public and the media at child protection hearings. In some states, hearings take place in closed courts; in others, they take place in open court. It is unnecessary to consider the position in every state. The differences can adequately be demonstrated by considering the states of Victoria and South Australia.

The Children's Court of Victoria deals with both youth justice and child protection. Section 523 of the Children, Youth and Families Act 2005 provides that all Children's Court proceedings are to be conducted in open court unless the court decides otherwise. The media can cover cases in the Children's Court but, unless they have the permission of the President, section 534 makes it an offence to publish a report that contains any particulars likely to lead to the identification of the court, the child or any other party to the proceedings or a witness in the proceedings. Section 534(4)[6] sets out

---

[6] See Appendix A, page 257.

a detailed list of factors which are deemed likely to lead to identification. An offence is punishable by the imposition of a fine (in the case of a body corporate such as a news agency) or, in the case of an individual, a fine or a term of imprisonment. The Children's Court of Victoria publishes selected judgments from Family Division cases. The judgments are anonymised.

In South Australia the Youth Court deals with both juvenile crime and child protection cases. Section 24 of the Youth Court Act 1993 states that the public are not entitled to attend either criminal or child protection hearings. A "genuine representative of the news media" is entitled to attend criminal hearings in the Youth Court but not child protection hearings. The court has the power to admit media representatives in exceptional circumstances. There is no recollection of the media making such a request in recent years. Section 164(1) of the Children and Young People (Safety) Act 2017 provides that "a person engaged or formerly engaged in the administration, operation or enforcement of this Act" may not publish any information relating to the proceedings if the court prohibits publication of the report which "identifies or contains information tending to identify the child or his or her school". Section 164 of that Act provides that unless permitted by the court the media are unable to publish anything relating to a Child Protection hearing unless authorised by the court. There is a maximum penalty of A$10,000 for breach. The judgments given in care and protection matters are not available to the general public.

New Zealand

Section 11A of the Family Courts Act 1980 sets out a list of those who are permitted to attend hearings in the Family Court in New Zealand. That list does not include members of the public. Accredited media reporters are entitled to attend but the judge has wide discretionary powers to exclude them. Section 11B prohibits the publication of "identifying information". "Identifying information" is defined in section 11C. Breach of these provisions is a criminal offence. Breach also amounts to a contempt of court and can be punishable as such.

In August 2017, the Principal Family Court Judge, Laurence Ryan, published *A Guide for Media Reporting in the Family Court*. The reason for publishing the Guide is said to be that:

> *"In the interests of transparent justice and to ensure the court is as open and accountable as possible, it is important that court reporters do not feel these rules exclude them from the Family Court. Therefore, this guide aims to assist reporters who wish to cover Family Court proceedings in an accurate, fair and balanced way."*

It is not an exaggeration to say that for all the reasons set out earlier in this book, in England and Wales journalists *do* feel that the rules exclude them from working effectively in the Family Court in England and Wales.

It is interesting to note that the New Zealand Guide goes on to say that:

> *"News media wishing to film, record audio or take photographs in the Family Court must apply in the usual way under the In-court Media Coverage Guidelines...Under the Family Court rules 2002 (rule 429) anyone can seek permission to access court files or documents such as judges' minutes and decisions...A decision on whether to release a document or allow a file or part of a file to be viewed is made by a registrar or a judge after considering whether the applicant has a genuine and proper interest in accessing a file...Journalists who wish to interview parties to a case after it is disposed of need to be mindful that any statutory prohibitions remain in place, irrespective of a party's view about being identified. Any orders prohibiting publication also remain in force unless specifically discharged."*

I am informed by Professor Mark Henaghan[7] that in New Zealand reporters very rarely attend hearings in the Family Court involving children. As a result, very little is published in the media concerning children's cases. Professor Henaghan says that:

> *"In reality none of the news outlets in New Zealand send journalists to the Family Court. It is a rare occurrence. Stories about the Family Court come out via research that has been done and via Commissioned Reports on the Court. Stories also come out via interviews with professionals who work in the Court, interviews with academics and via interviews with clients of the Family Court. Also, when a judgment comes out on an important point the media will write it up. But, sadly, they do not regularly attend the Court. There are few media outlets who have regular court reporters even in the Criminal Court."*

Not surprisingly in those circumstances, breaches are rare. Professor Henaghan could not think of a case where the media had been charged with a breach of the provisions of sections 11A, 11B and 11C.

---

[7] I am grateful to Professor Mark Henaghan, Professor of Law at Auckland University, for providing me with information concerning media attendance at and the reporting of hearings in the family court in New Zealand.

According to Professor Henaghan, the most common criticism of the Family Court in New Zealand is via radio talk back where participants talk frequently about the 'secret' Family Court and how they have been treated.

Some judgments are published. A judgment published by the court is anonymised by the judge before publication. Although New Zealand is a small country, as a result of the low number of cases that are covered by the media jigsaw identification is not considered to be a problem.

Canada[8]

Canada is formed of 10 provinces and 3 territories. The Briefing paper refers to Nova Scotia and, more briefly, to British Columbia. Nova Scotia is the second smallest of Canada's 10 provinces. For Nova Scotia the Briefing paper provides information concerning press and public access to the family courts, the publication of information relating to family court proceedings and the sanctions for breach of confidentiality. No similar information is provided concerning British Columbia. For British Columbia the only information provided is a brief reference to the facilities for information for the wider community and some detail about access to court judgments.

The structure of the family courts in Canada is very different from that in England and Wales. It is unnecessary to go into the detail. I am concerned not with the legal system in Canada but with discrete issues relating to transparency.

In Nova Scotia, hearings in cases relating to child protection and adoption take place in public.[9] So, too, do hearings in private law proceedings.[10] In both, the judge has the power to exclude. The media, therefore, has a general right to attend family hearings in Nova Scotia though I am told that reporters normally only attend hearings in cases which have already acquired a high profile. Their attendance is rare.

In child protection and adoption cases there is a statutory prohibition against publishing any information that may lead to the identification of the child.[11] The Act specifically provides that:

---

[8] I am grateful to Professor Rollie Thompson, Professor of Law, Schulich School of Law, Dalhousie University, Halifax, Nova Scotia and to Professor Nicholas Bala, Professor of Law in the Faculty of Law, Queen's University, Kingston, Ontario for their assistance in providing information concerning the issue of transparency in the family courts in Nova Scotia.

[9] Section 93 of the Children and Family Services Act 1990.

[10] Rule 59.60 of the Civil Procedure Rules.

[11] Section 94 of the Children and Family Services Act 1990.

> *"Where the court is satisfied that the publication of a report of a hearing or proceeding, or a part thereof, would cause emotional harm to a child who is a participant in or a witness at the hearing or is the subject of the proceeding, the court may make an order prohibiting the publication of a report of the hearing or proceeding, or the part thereof."*[12]

In private law cases there is no statutory prohibition against the publication of reports about cases. However, the rules provide that:

> *"A judge may make an order prohibiting the publication of the identity of a child, or the name or a party or witness, or of any other information that would identify the child."*[13]

In England and Wales, the President's consultation paper issued in August 2014 having come to nought, there are no specific rules concerning disclosure to the media of confidential documents (for example, expert medical reports) from the court file and no encouragement for the media to apply for disclosure. If a journalist should apply for disclosure the court must balance the child's interests under Article 8 of the ECHR and the media's interests under Article 10, take account of the best welfare interests of the child and endeavour to reach an outcome that is proportionate.

In Nova Scotia, in private law proceedings, a non-party (for example, a journalist) is entitled to apply to the court for access to the court file. The position can be illustrated from a judgment published in 1997.[14] The facts can be stated shortly. In October 1996 an order was made pursuant to section 42(1) of the Children and Family Services Act placing two children in the permanent care and custody of the Department of Community Services. The order followed a lengthy hearing following the murder of the children's father. Their mother (and her brother) were involved in the death of the father. Both were charged with murder. Both were acquitted. An interim order was made prohibiting the media from attending or reporting on the proceedings relating to the children. The judge explained his position:

> *"I'm not prepared to allow the media to be present or…to report… in any fashion…on the matters before the court…at this time that, I want to be clear, [this] is subject to review, and that order would be*

---

[12] Section 94(2).
[13] Rule 59.60(2) of the Civil Procedure Rules.
[14] *The Minister of Community Services (applicant) v F A (respondent)* (1997) 159 N.S.R.(2d) 230 (FC).

that no person shall publish or make public information that has the effect of identifying a child who is a participant or subject of this proceeding or a parent or guardian or relative of the child. I think that basically means there can be no reporting whatsoever on it."

The media subsequently applied for the order to be varied to enable them to report on the children's proceedings and, for that purpose, to have access to the court file. The judge said:

"14. Each situation is different, but the court should have the ability to ensure that a child welfare hearing is neither delayed nor diverted by media-related issues. That said there is subject to ss. 93 and 94 of the Children and Family Services Act a legitimate interest in the public (through the media) having access to and the ability to comment on child welfare proceedings. Here the order I made was expressly made "subject to review". It sought to protect the interests of the trial participants at a time when there was uncertainty over who would be the long-term guardian of the children in question. Where there is uncertainty as to who will be the guardian of children, the court should be cautious in making decisions affecting their welfare. The order made sought to protect the children as the Act mandates, but allowed for "review"...."

After the children had been placed in permanent state care, the *Chronicle Herald* applied to review that order. Their application was successful. The restrictions on publication and access to the court file were varied. The first two paragraphs of the new order now read:

"1. The [Chronicle] Herald is strictly prohibited from publishing any information identifying the children or their present guardian or any other information relating to the custody and welfare of the children, their names, their background, their culture, their race, etc., or that there was a court proceeding involving the children of S.S. and F.A.;

2. The [Chronicle] Herald is granted access to, and authorized to duplicate, documents and exhibits entered in evidence at the Children and Family Services Act hearing on October 9, 1996, along with discovery transcripts, submissions of counsel, transcripts and the decision of the presiding judge;"

Anonymised judgments in children's cases are routinely published. The judge is responsible for anonymising the judgment. I am told by Professor Thompson that the two most contentious issues in England and Wales –

should the media be able to attend hearings in the Family Court, should anonymised versions of the judgments handed down in the Family Court be published – are not live issues in Nova Scotia.

In 2003, in Nova Scotia, a paper was published under the title *Discussion Paper prepared on behalf of the Judges technology advisory committee for the Canadian Judicial Council on open courts, electronic access to court records, and privacy*. The problem of having a disparate group of courts applying different laws and having different rules of procedure was laid bare in the Discussion Paper. It said:

> *"35. Some provinces and territories have passed statutes or created regulations which touch on the fundamental principle of openness to court proceedings...*
>
> - *in family court proceedings, British Columbia and Nova Scotia provide that they shall be open although the judge has the discretion to exclude any person; New Brunswick leaves it to the judge's discretion whether the proceedings are open or closed; Alberta, Manitoba, Newfoundland and Labrador, Prince Edward Island and the Yukon provide that family proceedings may be closed.*
>
> - *Newfoundland and Labrador and Saskatchewan generally restrict access to court records for family law proceedings to the parties and their lawyers; in British Columbia access is restricted to parties, their lawyers and a family justice or a person authorized by a judge in an application pursuant to the Family Relations Act; in Quebec, sworn financial statements filed with the court in relation to support applications are confidential; Alberta, Manitoba, North West Territories and Ontario do not restrict access to court records in family proceedings.*
>
> - *in child welfare proceedings, British Columbia and Nova Scotia provide that the proceedings shall be open although the judge does have the discretion to exclude any person; Alberta provides that the proceedings may be closed to the public; Manitoba, Newfoundland and Labrador, Ontario and Prince Edward Island provide that the proceedings shall be closed to the public, although in Manitoba and Ontario proceedings are open to the media unless the judge exercises discretion to exclude them.*

> - *there are dozens of statutes and regulations which limit access to court proceedings and/or court records."*

There has been one development in Nova Scotia which, in my opinion, calls for serious thought from those of us who practice family law in England and Wales and who struggle with this vexed issue of transparency. For some years Nova Scotia has had a Media Liaison Committee. The judiciary and the media are both well-represented on this committee. The committee publishes guidance on *Media and Public Access to the Courts of Nova Scotia*.

The most recent version of the guidance was published in 2019. Section 1 is headed 'Open Courts and the Right to a Fair Trial'. It reads:

> *"We live in a society that places a high value on openness in the justice system. In a 1989 Supreme Court of Canada case, Edmonton Journal v. Alberta (Attorney General), [1989] 2 S.C.R. 1326, the Court explained the value of open courts:*
>
>> *"The concept of free and uninhibited speech permeates all truly democratic institutions... As a result of their significance, the courts must be open to public scrutiny and to public criticism of their operation by the public.... the public interest in open trials and in the ability of the press to provide complete reports of what takes place in the courtroom is rooted in the need:*
>>
>> *1) to maintain an effective evidentiary process; 2) to ensure a judiciary and juries that behave fairly and that are sensitive to the values espoused by society; 3) to promote a shared sense that our courts operate with integrity and dispense justice; and 4) to provide an ongoing opportunity for the community to learn how the justice system operates and how the law being applied daily in our courts affects them."*
>
> *Accordingly, the general rule in Canada is that trials are open to the public and may be reported in full. By enabling the public to attend court proceedings and allowing access to court documents relating to trials, we educate our citizens about the law and enhance their confidence in the fairness of the legal system and the way it operates.*
>
> *The media play a crucial role in informing the general public about what goes on in our Courts. The average citizen gains knowledge of the legal system primarily through the words and images conveyed by the media in news reports about court proceedings. Both the justice*

system and the public at large are well served when media coverage of hearings and dispositions of specific cases is accurate and complete. Court officials and staff working within the justice system have a responsibility to assist the public, including the media, in obtaining the access to which they are entitled by law to report accurately on Court proceedings."

Scotland

In *Family Policy Briefing 5*, Brophy refers to the Children's Hearings system in Scotland and to the Children (Scotland) Act 1995 which then set out the law relating to Children's Hearings. That part of that Act has now been repealed and replaced by the Children's Hearings (Scotland) Act 2011. In Scotland, matters relating to the protection and safeguarding of children are normally dealt with by a Children's Hearing (a Tribunal). The hearing is conducted by a panel of three lay people. The grounds upon which a case may be referred to a Children's Hearing are set out in statute. If the grounds of the referral are accepted the panel may proceed to determine what should happen to the child. This is a welfare decision made in the child's best interests. If the grounds of the referral are not accepted the panel may either discharge the referral or refer the application to the court for investigation of the grounds. The Sheriff Court deals with all such referrals. All of this is set out in the 2011 Act.

The remaining parts of the Children (Scotland) Act 1995 are still in force. That Act is regarded as the foundational Act for matters of child law in Scotland. Part 1 of the Act deals with private law disputes relating to children and sets out the law relating to parental rights and responsibilities. Part II deals with public law issues (other than Children's Hearings). Broadly, Part II addresses the kind of issues covered in England by Part III of the Children Act 1989 including, for example, requiring a local authority to provide accommodation for a child.

So far as the issue of transparency is concerned, in public law proceedings under the 2011 Act section 78 entitles a representative of a newspaper or a news agency to attend Children's Hearings. The general public have no right to attend. Section 182 prohibits the publication of 'protected information' which includes, in particular, information intended or likely to identify a child or the child's home address or school. Breach of this provision is a criminal office punishable by a fine.

In contrast, private law cases are heard in open court. However, publication of information relating to private law proceedings is subject to the restrictions set out in section 46 of the Children and Young Persons (Scotland)

Act 1937. That section gives the court power to direct that no newspaper report of the proceedings shall reveal the name, address, or school, or include any particulars calculated to lead to identification of a child under the age of 17 and no picture shall be published of the child concerned. Unlike the provisions of section 182 of the 2011 Act, these restrictions don't apply automatically in every case but only in those cases where the court orders that they should apply. In most cases the onus is on the parties to apply for such an order. Although private law cases are heard in open court, in any action concerning children, the Sheriff will organise a preliminary Child Welfare Hearing. These hearings allow the Sheriff to speak to both parties and their solicitors, and identify what issues are in dispute. These hearings are always held in private, with only the parties and their solicitors in attendance.

That is the law – but what is the practice? I am informed by Dr Gillian Black in the Faculty of Law at Edinburgh University, that a media presence in court in a children's case (public or private) is almost unheard of and this is supported by anecdotal evidence from a senior family law solicitor and a Sheriff. Even where court proceedings are in public, the media do not attend (even though there is nothing to stop them from attending) and only rarely report on child cases.

Unlike the position in England and Wales, it would seem that the media in Scotland have little interest in the work of the Family Courts. I have not read or heard anything to suggest that the public lacks trust in the family courts in Scotland or that there are concerns about the way local authorities in Scotland go about their work or about miscarriages of justice in public law cases. In terms of media concern, the position in Scotland could not be more different from that in England and Wales. I do not know why that should be the case.

Northern Ireland

Although the position in Northern Ireland was not considered in the Briefing paper, ongoing developments there merit a mention. A review of civil and family justice in Northern Ireland has recently been undertaken. The Review Group's Report on Family Justice[15] was published in September 2019. Section 18 of the report is headed "Open Justice". The current position concerning media attendance at and reporting of family proceedings in Northern Ireland is that:

> "*18.4 Most applications in the Family Proceedings Court (FPC), the*

---

[15] *https://judiciaryni.uk/sites/judiciary-ni.gov.uk/files/media-files/Family%20Justice%20Report%20September%202017.pdf.*

Family Care Centre (FCC) and the Family Division are heard 'in private' – that is, 'in chambers'. Members of the public are not permitted to attend hearings held in private. Duly accredited members of the media are often permitted to attend hearings of family proceedings held in private in the Family Division, the FCCs and the FPCs, subject to the power to exclude them on specified grounds. This is different from hearings in camera, where neither media representatives nor members of the public can attend."

The Review Group concluded that that situation needs to change. The report states that:

"18.6 In recent years, there has been an emerging and growing consensus that the law should be reformed to ensure greater transparency in proceedings concerning the welfare of children. We must not underestimate the role that public debate, and the jealous vigilance of an informed media, has to play in exposing past miscarriages of justice and in preventing possible future miscarriages of justice. There is a compelling and irrefutable public interest in the effective operation of family justice courts, which deal with matters of the greatest importance."

The report recommended that:

"1. Relevant legislative changes to be made to provide for the rights of the media to attend fact-finding hearings and other family courts in Northern Ireland and be brought into line with the position in the rest of the UK and Ireland. We recommend the introduction of rules similar to rule 27.10(2) and rule 27.11(2) of the Family Procedure Rules (FPR) in England and Wales.

2. The law to remain that the media are unable to report what they saw, heard or read within the proceedings without permission of the court but the family court and the High Court at any stage of the proceedings should have the power to relax the prohibition on reporting on a case-by-case basis by means of a rule similar to FPR 2010, rule 12.73, save that the criteria for relaxation should be based on the court concluding that it is in the public interest to do so or for some other compelling reason why it should be published."

In June 2019 the Shadow Family Justice Board in Northern Ireland issued a consultation paper, *Media Access to Family Courts,*[16] seeking views on the setting up of a Pilot Scheme to run, initially in the Family Division of the High Court, which would allow pre-approved media representatives to attend and report on cases listed for hearing and judgment in the family courts.[17] The Shadow Family Justice Board has since considered that, in the absence of statutory rules similar to those now in force in England and Wales, it will not be practical to progress the pilot as intended."

Eire

In Eire the *Child Care Law Reporting Project* merits a brief mention. The account that follows is taken from a paper written by the Director of the project, Carol Coulter.[18] Coulter explains the background succinctly. She says:

> *"Ireland, like England and Wales, has struggled for decades with the conflicting demands of the need for transparency in the family courts and the need to protect the privacy of children and their families. For most of that time the balance was struck in favour of privacy in all family law matters, with an absolute prohibition, not only on publishing any information about such proceedings, but on sharing such information with family and friends and with disclosing it in any complaints proceedings against professionals."*

The project is very different to the media reporting we are used to in England and Wales. The Project does not publish details of individual cases. Rather, it publishes quarterly volumes of reports. The reports take the form of a synopsis of each case rather than a verbatim note of the judge's judgment, though some written judgments are published on the Court Service website. The synopsis contains much less detail than a full transcript. The courts and the parties are not identified. This method of reporting shines a light into the working of the Family Court whilst greatly reducing the risk of the parties being identified by jigsaw identification.

Coulter goes on to say that:

> *"In my view, and in the Irish experience, transparency in child protection proceedings requires a body dedicated solely to reporting on family and child care law, which then makes the reports available for re-publication by the media. Having a single unit doing so allows for*

---

[16] *https://ico.org.uk/media/about-the-ico/consultation-responses/2019/2615698/shadow-family-justice-board-sub-commitee-consultation-20190617.pdf.*

[17] The proposals for accreditation are set out at paragraphs 2.6 to 2.18 and raise some interesting issues.

[18] *https://www.childlawproject.ie/events/child-care-law-reporting-without-tears/.*

> *the reporting to be governed by a protocol that protects the anonymity of the children and their families, and that filters the information reported so that the media do not have access to identifying or sensitive information. Such a unit also in our case allowed for information not otherwise collected to be obtained for further analysis of child protection proceedings generally, leading to recommendations for change."*

This project was a pilot. Although it has been in operation for some six years there appear to be some uncertainties about its future funding. What would be the merits of operating a similar scheme in England and Wales? Although I acknowledge that the pilot appears to have worked well in Ireland there are two immediate problems in seeking to replicate this scheme in England and Wales. The first is cost. There is no budget for it. A similar scheme in England and Wales would have to be operated on a much larger scale to have any real value. The second problem is that those who are concerned about the lack of transparency in the Family Court in England and Wales, and that includes but is not limited to the media, are unlikely to be persuaded that this scheme would genuinely be able to hold judges, social workers and doctors to account. Identifying miscarriages of justice would perhaps be an unlikely outcome.

Conclusions

Considering what is happening in other countries is undoubtedly interesting. There are practices in other countries which may very well be worth considering in England and Wales. However, from my review of the current position in the countries considered by Brophy, with my addition of Northern Ireland and Eire, what struck me most was that none of these different models has been so convincing that other countries have been queuing up to follow them. If one takes the states Children's Court and Youth Court in Victoria and South Australia respectively, for example, their approaches to transparency could not be more different.

The Briefing paper comes to this conclusion:

> *"In debates in England and Wales other jurisdictions have been held up as examples of the benefits of press access. However, closer examination of what is permissible both in press access to and press reporting of individual cases and the safeguards each jurisdiction puts in place to protect children and family privacy reveals a more complex picture with less press and public access than is commonly claimed. It provides some likely answers to questions families, politicians and a wider public in England and Wales might want to ask."*

I find it difficult to disagree with that conclusion. Many people in England and Wales have a position – invariably a strongly held position – concerning the issue of transparency in the Family Court. I doubt that many have arrived at their position as a result of undertaking a thorough review of what happens in other countries. The position is more likely to be the other way around – that if you have a strong view on this issue you are likely to be able to find another country which operates a system not dissimilar from the system you would like to see in England and Wales. The value of this comparative approach is not that it enables us to decide which side of the debate we should be on but simply that it makes us think.

14: THE CHILD'S RIGHT TO PRIVACY

> *"The law relating to parent and child is concerned with the problems of growth and maturity of the human personality. If the law should impose upon the process of 'growing up' fixed limits where nature knows only a continuous process, the price would be artificiality and a lack of realism in an area where the law must be sensitive to human development and social change."* (Lord Scarman)[1]

In earlier chapters I have explored the halting progress made during the last 15 years towards increasing transparency in the Family Court. One of the key factors that has made progress so difficult has been a belief, strongly held by some, that increasing transparency whilst at the same time protecting privacy, especially the child's privacy, is a circle that simply cannot be squared. Therefore, it is argued, there should be no further increase in transparency. In this chapter, I shall explore the child's right to privacy. I want, in particular, to consider what are the limits to that right.

In Chapter 13, I considered Dr Brophy's *Family Policy Briefing 5*. The Briefing paper reviewed transparency issues in the family courts of four other countries. In particular, it considered the approach taken in those countries to questions such as whether hearings relating to children should take place in public or in private; if in private, whether the media should be allowed to attend and, if so, what, if anything, they should be allowed to report, what penalties there should be for breaching reporting restrictions and whether family court judgments should be published? Although the approach taken in response to these questions varies from country to country, the common denominator was concern for the child's right to privacy.

I set the scene for this chapter with two quotations. The first is from a judge in Western Australia, supporting greater transparency. The second is from an academic in New Zealand, opposing greater transparency.

The first quotation comes from a recent judgment given by the Chief Justice of the Family Court of Western Australia, Chief Justice Thackeray. Some of his comments echo sentiments expressed in this country by the imme-

---

[1] *Gillick v West Norfolk and Wisbech Area Health Authority and Another* [1985] UKHL 7.

diate past President of the Family Division, Sir James Munby. In *Seven Network (Operations) Limited v Aaron Philip Cockman and Attorney General of Western Australia*,[2] Chief Justice Thackray said:

> "47. It is important that I repeat here what I said in *Cuzens*[3] after adopting Duncanson' J's analysis of the law:
>
>> 'As the Chief Justice of the court, I would much prefer that the public be given full information concerning what actually happens in the Family court day-in, day-out. This would help to dispel the many myths and misunderstandings about the work of the court. It would also expose the blatant lies of a small number of litigants who use social media and other means to give their side of their experience in the court and to blacken the name of their ex-partner.'
>
> 48. The routine presence of the media in Family Courts around Australia, and wide reporting of the activities of hardworking judiciary at all levels would also assist the public, the press and politicians to critique data about judicial efficiency gathered by bureaucrats and accountants who have no real perception of the work of the courts and what each of their pieces of data represents. To be useful, data requires rigorous analysis by experts without an agenda. Critical public analysis of data requires a well-informed public. And I accept that a well-informed public relies upon a well-informed, free and balanced press.
>
> 49. I hope these remarks, and all those I have made in earlier judgments in which I have permitted publication of proceedings, make clear that I approach these applications with a desire to allow the public an insight into the workings of their family law system and with nothing to hide from viewers/readers who rely upon the applicants to keep them informed. That said, my judicial oath requires me to administer the law by reference to the word and spirit of a carefully considered statute, and not by my own preferences as a court administrator exasperated by the ill-informed commentary that often passes for public debate in this area. Instead, I must keep firmly in mind that my wishes as an administrator cannot prevail over the interest of litigants who come before the judges confident in the expectation that their private lives will not be laid bare to the general public."

---

[2] [2018] FCWA 108.
[3] *West Australian newspapers Ltd and Channel 7 Perth Pty Ltd and Cuzens* (2016) FLC 93-690.

The second quotation comes from New Zealand. In *Privacy Issues in the Family Court*,[4] Associate Professor Pauleen Tapp[5] expresses views which resonate with those expressed in this country by those who oppose any further increase in transparency in the Family Court in England and Wales. These are her key conclusions:

> *"It is the thesis of this chapter that the nature of disputes which proceed to a hearing in the Family Court is such that no amount of openness in the system could meet the needs of the aggrieved litigants who use social and print media, politicians and public protest to criticise the Court and who by their actions encroach on the privacy of other members of their family. Nor would openness provide the answer to the complaints about the system which commonly form the basis of claims that greater transparency in the system would provide for greater accountability...*
>
> *General accountability is provided by the placing of anonymised judgments on the Family court website and in law reports, the media releases made by the Court in relation to decisions of special public interest, the ability of accredited news media representatives to attend and report on most Family Court hearings and the publication of comment about the system in professional and academic literature...*
> *It is argued that accountability would not be advanced, certainly not to the degree necessary to balance the harm which would occur to the child's welfare, by opening up the Court to the general public, permitting the media to access court documents and permitting the media to publish reports of the proceedings identifying the people involved. A report of a particular hearing provides the public with a mere snap shot in time of a dynamic situation. A report by a person who is required to write the report within a word limit in a restricted time and who is unlikely to have the specialised knowledge to fully understand what has occurred, cannot be a useful accountability mechanism...*
>
> *Families, especially children, involved in Family Court processes are, by virtue of the disagreement which brings them into the system, vulnerable. Privacy for the family is essential if the family is to be able to focus on repairing relationships so that they can move forward. There are appropriate mechanisms which provide for the accountability of the Family Justice system without breaching the privacy of the child."*

---

[4] This paper appears as Chapter 12 in *Privacy Law in New Zealand* 2nd edition, 2016, Stephen Penk and Rosemary Tobin (eds), Thomson Reuters.
[5] Associate Professor of Law at the University of Auckland.

In considering those two very different positions, I propose to begin by considering Articles 12 and 16 of the United Nations Convention on the Rights of the Child ('the UNCRC').

United Nations Convention on the Rights of the Child
On 20 November 1989 the UN General Assembly unanimously adopted the text of the Convention on the Rights of the Child. The treaty was signed by the United Kingdom on 19 April 1990, ratified on 16 December 1991 and came into force on 15 January 1992. It is the most widely ratified of all human rights instruments. Unlike the European Convention on Human Rights and Fundamental Freedoms, the UNCRC has not been incorporated into domestic law.

In a report published in March 2010, *The United Nations Convention on the Rights of the Child: How legislation underpins implementation in England*,[6] it is said that:

> "4. The Government is fully committed to children's rights and the continued implementation of the UNCRC to make the Convention a reality for all children and young people living in the UK.
>
> 5. Since ratification of the UNCRC in 1991, implementation of the Convention has been pursued through legislation and policy initiatives, including the Children Act 1989, Children Act 2004, Every Child Matters and policy for 0-19 year olds set out in the Government's 2007 Children's Plan.
>
> 6. In general, the UK does not incorporate international treaties directly into domestic law.[7] Instead, if any change in the law is needed to enable the UK to comply with a particular treaty, the Government introduces legislation designed to give effect to that treaty. As set out in this document, existing legislation and policies give effect to the rights and obligations in the UNCRC and regard is given to the UNCRC when developing any new legislation or policy."

The failure of the UK Government to incorporate the UNCRC into domestic law continues to be a contentious issue. The 25th Report of the UK Parliament's Human Rights Joint Committee,[8] entitled *Children's Rights*, was

---

[6] https://assets.publishing.service.gov.uk/government/uploads/system/uploads/attachment_data/file/296368/uncrc_how_legislation_underpins_implementation_in_england_march_2010.pdf.
[7] A notable exception to this is the European Convention on Human Rights which was incorporated into UK law by the Human Rights Act 1998.
[8] https://publications.parliament.uk/pa/jt200809/jtselect/jtrights/157/15702.htm.

published in October 2009. The report states that:

> *"20. The UN Committee[9] has recommended that the UNCRC should be incorporated into UK law, a point echoed by numerous witnesses to our inquiry.*
>
> *21. All four of the Children's Commissioners [England, Scotland, Wales and Northern Ireland] called for the UNCRC to be incorporated into UK law."*

The committee noted that there is no direct legal remedy which could be relied upon in respect of any breach of the UNCRC. The UK meets its obligations under the UNCRC through a combination of legislation, policy initiatives and guidance. The committee did not consider that to be adequate. The committee's conclusion and recommendation were clear:

> *"5. The Government has not persuaded us that children's rights are already adequately protected by UK law, nor that incorporation of the UNCRC is unnecessary. We agree with those witnesses who emphasised the benefits of incorporation, accompanied by directly enforceable rights. It is significant that all four Children's Commissioners in the UK, with their extensive experience of working with children, think it would make a real practical difference to children if the UNCRC were incorporated into UK law. However, we recommend that further information be given by the Government about the extent to which the UNCRC rights are or are not already protected by UK law."*

That report was published more than a decade ago. The position remains unchanged.

The fact that the treaty obligations have not been incorporated in domestic law does not mean that the rights set out in the UNCRC are of no value to children in the UK. In his book, *The Rights of the Child: Law and Practice*,[10] MacDonald says that:

> *"The central message of this book is that the [UNCRC] can be relied on before the domestic courts, tribunals and decision-making bodies*

---

[9] This is a reference to The United Nations Committee on the Rights of the Child (CRC) which is the body of 18 Independent experts that monitors implementation of the Convention on the Rights of the Child by its State parties.

[10] Alistair MacDonald (now the Honourable Mr Justice McDonald), (2011), Jordan Publishing Limited at paragraph 3.2.

of this jurisdiction notwithstanding that it has not been formally incorporated into domestic law."

Articles 12 and 16 are the key provisions of the UNCRC relied on by those who are opposed to any greater transparency in the Family Court. It is also appropriate to have regard to Article 3, and in particular to Article 3(1):

Article 3

1. In all actions concerning children, whether undertaken by public or private social welfare institutions, courts of law, administrative authorities or legislative bodies, the best interests of the child shall be a primary consideration.

Article 12

1. States Parties shall assure to the child who is capable of forming his or her own views the right to express those views freely in all matters affecting the child, the views of the child being given due weight in accordance with the age and maturity of the child.

2. For this purpose, the child shall in particular be provided the opportunity to be heard in any judicial and administrative proceedings affecting the child, either directly, or through a representative or an appropriate body, in a manner consistent with the procedural rules of national law.

Article 16

1. No child shall be subjected to arbitrary or unlawful interference with his or her privacy, family, home or correspondence, nor to unlawful attacks on his or her honour and reputation.

2. The child has the right to the protection of the law against such interference or attacks on his or her honour and reputation.

All three of these Articles are clearly relevant to any discussion concerning transparency and openness in the Family Court. What is less clear is, firstly, the impact of Article 3(1) on Articles 12 and 16 and, secondly, whether there are any limits to the reach of Articles 12 and 16 in the context of the debate concerning transparency in the Family Court and, thirdly, if there are, what those limits are.

The Child's Right To Privacy

There is an obvious and important difference between Article 3(1) of the UNCRC and section 1(1) of the Children Act 1989. Article 3(1) provides that: "In all actions concerning a child ... **the best interests of the child shall be a primary consideration**." Section 1(1) of the Children Act provides that when the court determines any question with respect to the upbringing of a child: "**the child's welfare shall be the court's paramount consideration**."

With respect to Article 3(1) of the UNCRC, in *ZH (Tanzania) v Secretary of State for the Home Department*,[11] Baroness Hale made the point that:

> *"In making the proportionality assessment under Article 8 [of the ECHR], the best interests of the child must be a primary consideration. This means that they must be considered first. They can, of course, be outweighed by the cumulative effect of other considerations."*

It follows, therefore, that in considering issues relating to transparency and openness, and in particular in considering the voice of the child and the privacy of the child, the best interests of the child must be considered first; but they are not paramount.

Article 12 has been described by the Committee on the Rights of the Child as:

> *"a unique provision in a human rights treaty; it addresses the legal and social status of children, who, on the one hand lack the full autonomy of adults but, on the other, are subjects of rights. [Article 12(1)] assures, to every child capable of forming his or her own views, the right to express those views freely in all matters affecting the child, the views of the child being given due weight in accordance with age and maturity."*[12]

In this country, even before that Committee had reported, the importance of the rights set out in Article 12 had already been underlined by Baroness Hale in an appeal considered by the House of Lord in 2006.[13] She made the point that:

---

[11] [2011] UKSC 4 at paragraph 33.
[12] Report of the Committee on the Rights of the Child, Fifty-first session, Geneva, 25 May – 12 June 2009: General Comment No. 12 (2009), *The Right of the child to be heard*.
[13] *Re D (A Child)* [2006] UKHL 51 at paragraph 57.

> *"there is now a growing understanding of the importance of listening to the children involved in children's cases. It is the child, more than anyone else, who will have to live with what the court decides. Those who do listen to children understand that they often have a point of view which is quite distinct from that of the person looking after them. They are quite capable of being moral actors in their own right. Just as the adults may have to do what the court decides whether they like it or not, so may the child. But that is no more a reason for failing to hear what the child has to say than it is for refusing to hear the parents' views."*

It is clear from that passage that although listening to the voice of the child is important, the views expressed by the child are not necessarily binding on the court. The court must take account of all relevant evidence. Article 12 requires that the child *be given the opportunity* to be heard in any judicial and administrative proceedings affecting them and that their views *be given due weight* in accordance with the age and maturity of the child. The voice of the child is a primary consideration but it can be outweighed by the cumulative effect of other considerations. As Lyon and Parten have said:[14]

> *"Children must be allowed to make an independent input to discussions concerning them although their views may be superseded by the views of others and/or overtaken by other considerations. Children are entitled to have a say in matters affecting them but not the final say. The provisions of [the Children Act 1989] offer children qualified autonomy but fall well short of allowing children full consequences of action."*

With respect, it would appear, therefore, that in her foreword to Dr Brophy's report in March 2010,[15] Dr Atkinson seeks to place greater weight on the words of Article 12 than those words are capable of bearing or, indeed, were ever intended to bear.

Similarly, although Article 16 requires that: 'No child shall be subjected to arbitrary or unlawful interference with his or her privacy, family, home or correspondence' and that: 'the child has the right to the protection of the law against such interference', a judicial decision to publish a judgment or to publish any of the evidence in the case (appropriately redacted and anonymised) is neither an arbitrary nor an unlawful interference with the

---

[14] *Children's Rights and the Children Act 1989*, Lyon and Parton in *The Handbook of Children's Rights*, Bob Franklin (ed), London, Routledge, 1995, pp 40-55 at p 42.
[15] See Chapter 13 page 174.

child's rights under Article 16. Assessing the child's right to privacy is a primary consideration but it can be outweighed by other factors. It seems to me that those 'other factors' include the rights of the media or a parent under Article 10 ECHR and the importance of open justice in the circumstances of that particular case.

The publication of judgments in family cases is not a practice that is of recent origin. Although it has only been since February 2014 that Circuit Judges have been encouraged to publish their judgments in Children Act cases, judges sitting in the Family Division of the High Court, the Court of Appeal and the Supreme Court[16] have been publishing judgments in family cases relating to children for many years. They have done so without any of the furious opposition that has been voiced since February 2014. Indeed, so far as concerns appeals, not only are judgments routinely published, the appeals are normally heard in open court.

It is clear from the language used in Articles 12 and 16 that the rights there set out are not absolute. They are, though, rights which should be taken into account when considering children's rights under the European Convention on Human Rights and under the general law.

The European Convention on Human Rights

In addition to the right to privacy set out in Article 16(1) of the UNCRC, children also have the right to respect for their private and family life set out in Article 8 of the ECHR.[17]

Two preliminary points need to be made. First, the rights under Article 8 are not just adult rights. They are children's rights, too. That is also the case with respect to rights under Article 6 (the right to a fair trial), and Article 10 (the right to freedom of expression). These are rights which children have, not because they are the children of adults who have those rights but because they themselves, as individuals, are entitled to those rights from birth.

Second, some of the rights set out in the ECHR, including the rights under Articles 8 and 10, are not absolute rights but qualified rights. Those rights are qualified by the words set out in Articles 8(2) and 10(2). Similarly, the right set out in Article 16 of the UNCRC not to be "subjected to arbitrary or unlawful interference with his or her privacy, family, home or correspondence" is also a qualified right. A child's right under Article 16 UNCRC is no

---

[16] The Supreme Court came into being on 1 October 2009. Before that date the final right of appeal was to the Appellate Committee of the House of Lords.
[17] The terms of Article 8 are set out in Chapter 2 at page 16.

wider than the child's right under Article 8(1) of the ECHR.

In Chapter 2, I noted that where rights under Article 8 and Article 10 of the ECHR are in conflict, a balance must be struck. I noted the guidance given by Lord Steyn on the approach that should be taken when balancing rights.[18] Notwithstanding the fact that the points made by Lord Steyn were made in the context of a criminal case, it is generally accepted that they apply equally in the civil and family jurisdictions.[19]

Those who emphasise the child's right to privacy under Article 16 UN-CRC and Article 8 ECHR seek, by doing so, to encourage the view that the child's right to privacy always takes (or should always take) precedence over the Article 10 rights of the media or a parent. That begs the question whether, when balancing the Article 8 rights of the child against the Article 10 rights of the media, the child's welfare is the court's paramount consideration. In my opinion it is not.[20]

The rights already accorded to the media
For the last decade, since the rule change in 2009, duly accredited media representatives have had the right to attend some hearings in the Family Court. This is sometimes misrepresented as a right which the judge gives to journalists on a case by case basis as an exercise of judicial discretion. That is not correct. The Family Procedure Rules 2010 give the media the right to attend. Duly accredited journalists do not need permission from the judge.

---

[18] *In re S (A Child) (Identification: Restrictions on Publication)* [2004] UKHL 47 - see page 17 above.

[19] The original hearing took place before Mr Justice Hedley in the Family Division of the High Court. He dismissed an application for an injunction restraining the publication by newspapers of the identity of a defendant in a murder trial which had been intended to protect the privacy of her (the defendant's) son who was not involved in the criminal proceedings.

[20] The Court of Appeal has recently suggested that there is a lack of clarity on this point. In *Re W (Children)* [2016] EWCA Civ 113 at paragraphs 41 to 43. Lord Justice McFarlane said:
> "In the process of preparing this written judgment...I have come to the preliminary view that there may be a conflict, or at least a tension, between the apparently accepted view that welfare is not the paramount consideration on an issue such as this, on the one hand, and Court of Appeal authority to the contrary on the other hand."

As it was not necessary for the Court of Appeal to answer that question in order to determine the outcome of this particular appeal, and having heard no detailed submissions on the point, the Court of Appeal left the point to be determined on another occasion. However, there is an argument for saying that the Court of Appeal has, in fact, already determined the outcome to this question. In *Re X (A Minor) (Wardship: Jurisdiction)*, Roskill LJ said:
> "I cannot accept the argument that the interests of the child should be allowed to prevail over the wider interests of freedom of publication, whatever may be thought about the merits or demerits of the passages objected to..."

The Child's Right To Privacy

That is a subtle but important distinction. That right derives from Article 10 of the ECHR and is given effect by the state through the Family Procedure Rules. The judge has the power to exclude journalists from attending all or part of a particular hearing. That power may only be exercised when it is proportionate and necessary to do so and must be on one of the grounds set out in the rules.[21]

I note in passing that soon after that rule change in April 2009, there was a suggestion that the rule change was open to challenge in the court and that such a challenge had a significant prospect of success. In *Media Access to Family Court and Article 8 Compliance*[22], Nuala Mole argues that:

> *"The Court has, in other circumstances, taken the opportunity to criticise the UK for permitting the press and public to attend court proceedings involving children. In T v UK [2000] 30 EHRR 121 the children's ability to participate effectively in the proceedings was held to have been violated because the trial was held in open public court and there was massive press attention given to the trial. As far as we are aware no challenge has yet been mounted in Strasbourg to the changes which have already occurred earlier this year permitting media access to court proceedings in Children Act cases. However, it seems likely – given the detailed consideration given by the Court to the government's arguments at the time in B and P*[23] *and the court's acceptance of those arguments – that such a challenge would have significant prospects of success. It is difficult to see how the Court would accept as 'necessary in a democratic society' the government's complete volte face from the position they so recently persuaded the Strasbourg Court to accept as essential to safeguarding children. It is even more likely that the same approach would be taken by the Strasbourg Court as was taken in B and P on permitting the press access to documents on the court files in child protection cases."*

Despite that confident prediction about the likely denouement of the rule giving media representatives the right to attend hearings in the Family

---

[21] Family Procedure Rules 2010, rule 27.11(3) sets out the grounds upon which a judge may exclude a media representative from a hearing.
[22] Nuala Mole, the Aire Centre, published in January 2010 in [2010] Fam Law 78. The Aire Centre (Advice on Individual Rights in Europe) is a registered charity which provides free legal advice and representation particularly to EEA nationals and their family members on free movement rights, representing them in front of domestic immigration and social security tribunals on issues around their right to reside, access to benefits, healthcare and housing.
[23] *B and P v UK* [1985] UKHL 7.

Court, there has been no such challenge. The rule remains in force. It has now been in force for more than a decade. It is difficult to imagine that a challenge at this late stage would have the remotest prospect of success.[24]

Mole goes on to express the opinion that the provisions in Part 2 of the Children, Schools and Families Act 2010, which would have allowed the media access to view sensitive documents in children's cases, would not be compatible with Article 8 of the ECHR (or, presumably, with Article 16 of the UNCRC). Part 2 was subsequently repealed without ever having been brought into force.

Allowing the media to have sight of confidential documents such as expert medical reports is another controversial issue. Mole speculates that any such change in practice would not be allowed to stand. She says that:

> *"The information contained in the files which are put before a court in family proceedings is sensitive personal information about the child and others which is in principle entitled to the highest possible protection from disclosure. Any dissemination to the press constitutes an interference with the right to respect for private life guaranteed under Art 8 ECHR. Such an interference must identify one of the six permitted aims in Art 8(2) and must be proportionate to that identified aim. There is no general right of access for the media to personal information about individuals. Any disclosure of information about specific cases for the purpose of conducting judicial proceedings must be no more than is strictly necessary for the efficient conduct of those proceedings. Both Arts 6 and 8 permit the exclusion of the press in the interest of juveniles."*

Mole was not the only person to hold strong views on this issue. In an article published in 2010, *Opening up the Family Courts – what happened to children's rights?*,[25] Dr Julie Doughty, too, was critical of Part 2 of the Children Schools and Families Act 2010. She said that:

> *"both the premise and the consultation process on these reforms have ignored and infringed a range of children's rights…Analysing the reform process, and the particular nature of cases heard in family courts, it is concluded that children's rights have been overridden by adult interests."*

---

[24] It is also appropriate to note in passing that medical cases relating to children are normally heard in open court.
[25] An article by Julie Doughty published in *Contemporary Issues in Law* in July 2010.

The Child's Right To Privacy

I noted in Chapter 12 that in her 2010 report, Brophy said that the children and young people interviewed in that study:

> *"are unconvinced that formal rules prohibiting publication of identifying information will automatically protect them. They do not trust reporters and felt information would get out allowing them to be identified, shamed and bullied..."*

It is not clear whether it was explained to those children and young people that a journalist who breached the statutory restrictions on publication would be in very serious trouble. He or she would be in contempt of court and at risk of being sent to prison.

Even before the rule change in 2009, judges had the power to allow journalists to attend hearings in the Family Court. They did so on a case by case basis when persuaded there was good reason why the media should attend. The rule change in 2009 reversed the burden. What caused so much angst with the 2014 consultation paper on 'Next Steps'[26] was that Sir James posed the question whether the burden should also be reversed with respect to the disclosure to the media of medical and other expert reports. In the consultation paper, he said:

> *"Thirdly, I am seeking views on further guidance...dealing with the disclosure to the media of certain categories of document, subject, of course, to appropriate restrictions and safeguards...[T]he next step might be a pilot project...under which the disclosable documents would fall into two categories:*
>
> > *(1) Documents prepared by the advocates, including case summaries, position statements, skeleton arguments, threshold and fact-finding documents.*
> >
> > *(2) Some experts' reports, or extracts of such reports.*
>
> *I view category (1) as the logical next step. I envisage that advocates will prepare the documents in a form that can be released to members of the accredited media. The purpose will be to facilitate their understanding of the case and to assist them in performing their watchdog role. If a case summary is available for members of the media to read, they will be able to decide quickly whether the case is one they*

---

[26] https://www.judiciary.uk/wp-content/uploads/2014/08/transparency-the-next-steps-consultation-paper.pdf.

would wish to attend, as they are entitled to do.

I envisage that...until it has been possible to evaluate the outcome of the pilot, documents disclosed in this way will remain confidential, unless the judge orders otherwise, so that any copying or onwards transmission or disclosure by members of the media of the documents or their contents would be a contempt...

Category (2) is more complicated and more controversial...It will not be every expert's report that will be released but only those identified by the judge, having heard submissions. In some cases, consideration may have to be given as to whether the report should be redacted or anonymised...I propose that in the first instance disclosure be confined to reports in the 'hard sciences'. Again, the purpose will be to facilitate the media's understanding of the case and to assist them in performing their watchdog role. Again, I would envisage that at least initially...documents disclosed in this way will remain confidential, unless the judge orders otherwise, so that any copying or onwards transmission or disclosure by members of the media of the documents or their contents would be a contempt. I propose that where such disclosure is being considered, the expert should be informed prior to disclosure."

Sir James Munby was not the first judge to propose that the media be allowed access to experts' reports. As I noted in Chapter 8,[27] in a judgment given in 2011 Sir Nicholas Wall, then President of the Family Division, directed that, in that case, a redacted and anonymised version of the medical report which was the subject of that hearing, should be published.[28] He also made the point that he would:

"like to see a practice develop, in which expert reports would be routinely disclosed, and the media able to comment both on the report and on the use to which they were put in the proceedings. This would mean that the views of the judge on the expert evidence would also be disclosed."[29]

In their foreword to Brophy's second report, published the month before publication of the President's consultation document and therefore perhaps

---

[27] See page 128 above.
[28] Notwithstanding the apparently mandatory terms of that order, that medical report was never published.
[29] *X, Y, and Z & Anor v A Local Authority* [2011] EWHC 1157 (Fam) at paragraph 94.

to be regarded as a pre-emptive strike, the Children's Commissioners for England and Wales argue that:

> *"Firstly, Parliament should have the opportunity to scrutinise proposals to increase media access and reporting of family cases...Secondly...the proposals should also be subject to a proper public consultation exercise, accompanied by widespread publicity making it clear what is proposed..."*

I have no difficulty with the proposal that the media should have access to some of the documents drafted by advocates, in particular to case summaries. It would enable the media to identify cases they wished to cover and give them a better grasp of the issues in the case. In my opinion, this would not require a rule change. However, I take a different approach to the disclosure of experts' reports. Just as the right of media representatives to attend hearings in the Family Court was given by secondary legislation (a rule change), so, too, should any change which gave the media an entitlement or an expectation that they should be able to have access to experts' reports. In my opinion this can only be achieved by a rule change.

The child's right to privacy is encapsulated in Article 16 of the UNCRC and Article 8 of the ECHR. Allowing the media to have access to reports containing sensitive and highly personal information relating to a child amounts, potentially, to a significant interference with the child's right to privacy. If disclosure of such material to the media is to become routine, that change should be approved by the state by way of an appropriate rule change. The rule change should be preceded by a consultation involving all relevant stakeholders. Absent a change in the rules, such disclosure should not become routine or automatic and neither, indeed, should refusal become automatic. Judges should continue to be able to allow disclosure of confidential material to the media (for publication if appropriate) on a case by case basis, as at present. Currently, such orders are only made when the judge is persuaded that disclosure in that particular case is proportionate, justified and appropriate notwithstanding that the disclosure would interfere to some extent with the child's right to privacy.

I noted in Chapter 12[30] that in an article published in the Family Law Journal in 2009, Dr Danya Glaser expressed concern about expert medical reports being disclosed to the media. She made the point that: "One of the fundamental assumptions underpinning clinical encounters is confidentiality." In her opinion, allowing the media into court or, worse, allowing the

---

[30] See page 178.

media to publish confidential information about a child, would lead to the doctor being in breach of his or her duty of confidentiality.

It is clear from guidance published by the General Medical Council that the doctor's duty of confidentiality is not absolute.[31] That guidance makes it clear to doctors that the civil courts "have powers to order disclosure of information in various circumstances". Doctors are told: "You must disclose information if ordered to do so by a judge…".[32]

Having disclosed information to the court, it is for the court and not the doctor to determine what should happen to that information. It is open to the judge to quote from that information in his or her judgment and to give permission for the judgment to be published, suitably anonymised. It is also open to the judge to direct that the information be disclosed to the media on whatever terms the judge considers to be appropriate.[33] Contrary to the uninformed opinions sometimes expressed in the media (including social media), orders of that nature are not made by judges on a whim but only if such a direction is considered to be proportionate and justified on the facts of the particular case. In arriving at that decision, the judge would be bound to consider the child's right to privacy under Article 16 of the UNCRC and Article 8 ECHR. The key point, however, is that those rights under the UNCRC and ECHR are qualified and not absolute and must be balanced against the media's Article 10 rights in accordance with the guidance given by the House of Lords in *In re S (A Child) (Identification: Restrictions on Publication)*.[34]

Children's rights under Article 13 UNCRC and Article 10 ECHR
Brophy's research makes clear the hostility towards the media of those children who participated in her studies. I noted at page 177 that there is evidence that that is not a view universally held by children and young people. The context for the discussion in Brophy's reports has been of adults (judges, parents, the media) making decisions about the publication of private sensitive information relating to a child contrary to the wishes (and, as the adults may well say, best interests) of the child and without prior consultation with the child. What Brophy's reports do not do is to acknowledge that children and young people have their own right to freedom of expression and sometimes wish to exercise that right in a way that is contrary to the wishes of their parents and the instincts of the judge. Depending upon the

---

[31] *Confidentiality: Good practice in handling patient information*, published January 2017, came into force April 2017.
[32] Paragraph 90.
[33] As occurred in *X, Y, and Z & Anor v A Local Authority* [2011] EWHC 1157 (Fam).
[34] [2004] UKHL 47.

age, capacity and maturity of the child it may well be the case that the decision of a competent child should be respected and should prevail.

Article 13 of the UNCRC provides that:

> *(1) The child shall have the right to freedom of expression; this right shall include freedom to seek, receive and impart information and ideas of all kinds, regardless of frontiers, either orally, in writing or in print, in the form of art, or through any other media of the child's choice.*
>
> *(2) The exercise of this right may be subject to certain restrictions, but these shall only be such as are provided by law and are necessary:*
>
> *(a) For respect of the rights or reputations of others; or*
>
> *(b) For the protection of national security or of public order (ordre public), or of public health or morals.*

Article 10 of the ECHR provides that:

> **Freedom of expression**
>
> *(1) Everyone has the right to freedom of expression. This right shall include freedom to hold opinions and to receive and impart information and ideas without interference by public authority and regardless of frontiers. This Article shall not prevent States from requiring the licensing of broadcasting, television or cinema enterprises*
>
> *(2) The exercise of these freedoms, since it carries with it duties and responsibilities, may be subject to such formalities, conditions, restrictions or penalties as are prescribed by law and are necessary in a democratic society, in the interests of national security, territorial integrity or public safety, for the prevention of disorder or crime, for the protection of health or morals, for the protection of the reputation or rights of others, for preventing the disclosure of information received in confidence, or for maintaining the authority and impartiality of the judiciary.*

So far, I have considered the right to freedom of expression in the context of the media (or perhaps even a parent) seeking to assert that their Article 10 rights should take precedence over the child's Article 8 rights. I noted in Chapter 12 that Brophy's research suggests that children do not want the media to attend court to hear, and less still to be able to publish, sensitive, private information relating to them and their family. I have noted that there is another group of young people who don't object to their story being told in the media and whose views ought to be made clear to the judge. There is a third group of children and young people who want to be allowed to make their own approach to the media to tell their story and who are prepared to waive their right to privacy in order to do so.

Angela Roddy became pregnant when she was just 12 years old. The putative father was the same age. The local authority issued care proceedings in respect of both the baby and Angela. Care orders were made. The baby was placed for adoption. Subsequently an application was made for the care order relating to Angela to be discharged. She was then aged 17. Angela herself contacted the media and applied to the court for permission to tell her story to the media. In a witness statement she said that she wanted to talk about her experience of the care system and is doing this "because I want people to know what it is like to go through the care system and the consequences of having unprotected sex." She says, "I am happy to be named and photographed for the purposes of the newspaper article, and I have considered the consequences of this." She relied on her rights under Article 10 ECHR and, though not specifically mentioned in the judgment, presumably also her rights under Article 13 of the UNCRC.

In his judgment, Sir James Munby said:[35]

> *"34. A child is, of course, as much entitled to the protection of the Convention – and specifically of Articles 8 and 10 – as anyone else...*
>
> *46. ... Are we to recognise that Angela should in relation to her Convention rights enjoy the same autonomy, the same decision-making power, as she will undoubtedly have when she reaches the age of 18 in just one year's time? Are we to trust Angela to decide for herself whether that which is private (and not merely private – what we are talking about here is something extremely personal and intimate) should remain private or whether it should be shared with the whole world? Are we, in other words, to take children's rights seriously and as our children see them? Or are we to treat children as little more than the largely passive objects of more or less paternalistic parental or judicial decision-making?...*
>
> *57. ... And we do not recognise Angela's dignity and integrity as a*

---

[35] *Re Roddy* [2003] EWHC 2927 (Fam).

human being – we do not respect her rights under Articles 8 and 10 – unless we acknowledge that it is for her to make her own choice, and not for her parents or a judge or any other public authority to seek to make the choice on her behalf."

Angela's application was not opposed either by her parents or by the local authority. Sir James Munby made it clear that he would have allowed the application even if it had been opposed.

Notwithstanding the strong opposition of some to the prevention of the media from seeing and reporting any confidential information relating to a child or young person, there must also be factored into the equation the fact that children and young people not only have a right to privacy but also a right to freedom of expression. Tapp points out that:[36]

"Where the right to freedom of expression is claimed by the child, the Court will be required to consider not only the nature of the general public interest in the matter but also the relative importance of the child's welfare of respect for their autonomy and respect for their privacy."

With respect to disclosure to the media of confidential information relating to a child, account needs to be taken of the three stages that children go through. The first stage is where they are too young to be able to express a view or to have any understanding of the issues or of the consequences of the decision that has to be made. The second stage is where the child is old enough to express a view but does not have the level of insight required to make an informed decision or to understand the consequences of the decision. Children falling into the second group should be encouraged and supported in expressing their views. The voice of the child is plainly a matter which the court must weigh in the balance.

The third stage is where the child or young person is not only old enough to express a view but also old enough and sufficiently capacitous to be able to understand the issues and the consequences and make an informed decision. With respect to a decision which requires the balancing of Article 8 and Article 10 rights, whilst the court plainly has the authority to make the decision in respect of a child or young person in any of those three groups, it seems to me that the court should be slow to make a decision concerning a young person in the third group which is contrary to the expressed views and wishes of that young person.

---

[36] Ibid page 346.

If authority is required for that last proposition it is to be found in the House of Lords decision in the case of *Gillick*[37] almost a quarter of a century ago. Lord Scarman said:

> *"Parental rights clearly do exist, and they do not wholly disappear until the age of majority. Parental rights relate to both the person and the property of the child – custody, care, and control of the person and guardianship of the property of the child. But the common law has never treated such rights as sovereign or beyond review and control. Nor has our law ever treated the child as other than a person with capacities and rights recognised by law. The principle of the law, as I shall endeavour to show, is that parental rights are derived from parental duty and exist only so long as they are needed for the protection of the person and property of the child.... The law relating to parent and child is concerned with the problems of the growth and maturity of the human personality. If the law should impose upon the process of "growing up" fixed limits where nature knows only a continuous process, the price would be artificiality and a lack of realism in an area where the law must be sensitive to human development and social change... The modern law governing parental right and a child's capacity to make his own decisions was considered in Reg. v. D. [1984] A.C. 778. The House must, in my view, be understood as having in that case accepted that, save where statute otherwise provides, a minor's capacity to make his or her own decision depends upon the minor having sufficient understanding and intelligence to make the decision and is not to be determined by reference to any judicially fixed age limit."*

Conclusions

I said at the beginning of this chapter that I proposed to explore the child's right to privacy and consider whether there are any limits to that right. I well understand that there are those who consider that a child's right to privacy should automatically outweigh the Article 10 rights of both the media and the parents. For those who reluctantly accept that that is not the case and that rights must be balanced, I equally well understand that many are likely to consider that an order permitting the disclosure to the media of confidential, private information concerning a child should only be made in circumstances that are wholly exceptional.

The media's right to freedom of expression is a right which exists not for the benefit of the media but, through the diligent and honest exercise of

---

[37] *Gillick v West Norfolk and Wisbech Area Health Authority and Another* [1985] UKHL 7.

that right by the media, for the benefit of society in general. The existence of a free press is an essential part of a free society. The right to privacy is, as I noted earlier, of equal value to the right to freedom of expression. In any particular case, the task for the court, invariably an anxious task, is to balance those two rights in the way that I have described in this and earlier chapters. Sometimes the balance will come down in favour of the Article 10 rights of the media. Sometimes it will come down in favour of the child's UNCRC and ECHR right to privacy. The important point to be clear about is that neither right is presumptively greater than the other. Both are equal. As a matter of law, both rights have their limits. It is also appropriate to make the point that balancing rights under Articles 8 and 10 does not necessarily lead to an all or nothing outcome. There may be circumstances in which some modest interference with one right may make it possible for the two rights to be satisfactorily balanced rather than one right being substantially suppressed. For example, there may be circumstances where publication can be facilitated if certain identifying or sensitive information is excluded.

15: REFLECTIONS

"From such crooked wood as man is made, nothing perfectly straight can be built." (Immanuel Kant)[1]

The title of this book is in the form of a question: *The 'Secret' Family Court – Fact or Fiction?* Now that we have reached the final chapter, I need to give an answer. However, before I do, I want to ask another question. When people refer to the Family Court as a 'secret' court, what do they mean by 'secret'?

On 5 January 2020, an article published in *The Guardian*, written by journalist Louise Tickle, had the headline: "In our secret family courts, judges still don't understand what rape means." Tickle was referring to a recent appeal hearing before a High Court Judge. I shall return to that case later in this chapter. For the moment, as Tickle is one of many journalists who during the last 15 years have referred to the Family Court as a 'secret' court, I simply want to ask: what does she mean by 'secret'? That has been the subject of a dialogue between us. Tickle argues that:

> "the Cambridge English Dictionary definition of 'secret' is 'a piece of information that is only known by one person or a few people and should not be told to others'. The media use that word because while we may know what goes on, we know it cannot openly be talked about under threat of very stiff sanctions. That is what a secret is – it is something that is known, but cannot be talked about, or known by other people. In the description 'the secret Family Court' the word secret is being used according to its correct dictionary definition and in the way that most people in society would normally construe it."

I accept that explanation as far as it goes. However, I still want to know whether the use of the word 'secret' is intended to suggest that because the Family Court is a 'secret' court we should be deeply suspicious about it, that there is something darkly sinister about the Family Court in the sense that it does not want you to know what it does. Are we talking about a deliberate attempt to hide what goes on in the Family Court, to keep the public

---

[1] From *Idea for a Universal History from a Cosmopolitan Point of View*, an essay by Immanuel Kant, 1784.

in the dark? That may not be what is intended but it is, in reality, how the charge of 'secrecy' is often perceived.

Tickle expanded on her original explanation. She said that in her opinion the sensitivity about the use of the word 'secret' from those working in the family justice system arises out of a misunderstanding that the media is attacking the *motivation* for privacy, when in fact its criticism is about the damaging result of privacy's *effects* – i.e. the media's resulting lack of ability to scrutinise state power exercised through the family courts. That is a very important distinction and one which I accept. However, it is a subtle distinction and I fear it is not one that would immediately be understood by the proverbial 'man or woman on the Clapham omnibus'.[2]

It is not just those working in the family justice system who are concerned that the media's use of the word 'secret' is an attack on the *motivation* for privacy – it is the public at large. This seemingly harmless argument about whether the Family Court is 'private' or 'secret' is actually profoundly important because it shapes the way people think. The man or woman on the Clapham omnibus who has never had any dealings with the Family Court before and suddenly finds themselves involved in, say, care proceedings, is likely to be concerned about whether they are going to get a fair hearing in this 'secret' court. I would want to question whether the repeated use of the word 'secret' to describe the Family Court actually makes the point that journalists (I am content to accept Tickle's views as representative of the general body of journalists) want to make.

In 2013, Sir James Munby made the point that:[3]

> *"The family lawyer's reaction to complaints of 'secret justice' tends to be that the charge is unfair, that it confuses a system which is private with one which is secret. This semantic point is, I fear, more attractive to lawyers than to others. It has signally failed to gain acceptance in what Holmes J famously referred to as the "competition of the market": Abrams v United States (1919) 250 US 616, 630. The remedy, even if it is probably doomed to only partial success, is – it must be – more transparency; putting it bluntly, letting the glare of publicity into the family courts."*

---

[2] *The man or woman on the Clapham omnibus* is a hypothetical ordinary and reasonable person, referred to by the courts in English law where it is necessary to decide whether a party has acted as a reasonable person would. *The man or woman on the Clapham omnibus* is a reasonably educated, intelligent but nondescript person.
[3] *Re J (A Child)* [2013] EWHC 2694 (Fam) at paragraph 34.

The reality is that the argument about whether the Family Court is a secret court has not been an argument about the difference between the *motivation* for privacy (secrecy), and the *effect* of privacy (secrecy). The argument has descended into a semantic debate about whether the Family Court should be described as 'secret' or 'private'. That debate is nothing more than a distraction. It is arid and pointless.

Whether intended or not, used in the context in which the media has used them, 'secret' and 'secrecy' are not neutral words. Those words have been used pejoratively, as a means of criticising the Family Court. In Chapter 3, I set out a number of headlines given to articles in *The Times* by Camilla Cavendish and in *The Telegraph* by the late Christopher Booker. The words 'secret' and 'secrecy' in those headlines are plainly being used as a point of criticism. They focus more on words than principles. If the repeated use of the words 'secret' and 'secrecy' were going to achieve a greater degree of openness and transparency in the Family Court, one might have thought that after 15 years of almost constant use, there would be some sign of it reaping dividends. There are none.

In fact, in my opinion, the greatest achievement of the use of the word 'secret' has been to undermine public trust and confidence in the family justice system – and in particular to cast doubt on the ability of the system to deal fairly, sensitively and reliably with some profoundly difficult issues concerning the welfare of children and the abilities of their parents.

What really matters, surely, is that much of what happens in the Family Court is not 'open justice' in the sense in which that expression has been used and understood for more than a century? That needs to change. The whole focus of the debate needs to change. There needs to be greater openness, greater transparency, about the work of the Family Court. Transparency should be the default position for cases heard in the Family Court as much as for cases heard in any other court. 'Transparency' means one of two things – either that hearings are heard in open court or that the media be given the right to report what goes on in the Family Court – the right which they mistakenly believed was being given to them in April 2009. In any situation in the Family Court where transparency and openness are deemed not appropriate there needs to be clear, rational, cogent reasons, publicly stated, why that should be the case.

So, how do I answer the question in the title of this book? The answer I give is *my* answer and I accept and respect that *your* answer may be different. As I have spent the last 12 months writing this book, the more I have read, the more people I have spoken to, the more I have reflected, the more I am confirmed in the view I held at the beginning of this journey: that it is neither accurate nor appropriate to describe the Family Court as a 'secret' court. In my opinion, that description is a fiction which diverts attention away from the real point. What matters, as Tickle's article, if not its headline, makes crystal clear, is that there is a lack of adequate scrutiny of what goes on in the Family Court.

The rules give the media the right to attend most hearings in the Family Court – but they rarely come. The rules allow the media to apply for reporting restrictions to be lifted or varied – but they rarely apply. Although the media may not take advantage of those entitlements, they are nonetheless available to every media outlet. Given those entitlements, how can this properly be described as a 'secret' court?

The reality is that, largely as a result of section 12 of the Administration of Justice Act 1960, what I have just described as the media's 'entitlements' are at present little more than a mirage. The charge of 'secrecy' is, in truth, a full-frontal attack on section 12 of the Administration of Justice Act 1960. Viewed in that way, the media's attack is fully justified. If only the media had spent the last 15 years campaigning for that section to be repealed rather than continually banging the drum of secrecy we may not now be in the position we are in, responsible reporting may be much easier and public trust in the Family Court may be significantly higher than it is.

Having made that point, I now return to the court case which gave rise to Tickle's recent headline. Tickle's article related to a finding of fact hearing which took place in August 2019. The complainant (the mother) alleged that she had been the victim of serious domestic abuse by her partner (the father). The complaints included allegations of rape. The hearing took place before a Circuit Judge, His Honour Judge Tolson QC. The judge found against her.

The finding of fact hearing took place in private. The complainant appealed. In December 2019 her appeal was heard in open court by a High Court Judge, Ms Justice Russell. Judgment was handed down on 22 January 2020. The appeal was allowed. Ms Justice Russell ordered that the finding of fact hearing should take place again before a different judge.

Tickle's article was written after the hearing of the appeal but before the judgment was handed down. When she wrote it she had the benefit of agency copy prepared by Brian Farmer of PA Media. She was aware of the criticisms that had been made about the way the judge had conducted the finding of fact hearing. In her article she pulled no punches. She said:

> *"The fact that the family law system in this country is hidden behind a veil of secrecy means that these offensively vintage attitudes to rape and domestic violence can persist in courts that tens of thousands of separating couples must pass through every year. And it raises the question: what other outrageously sexist decisions are being made by out-of-touch judges behind closed doors?"*

She has a point. Ms Justice Russell's judgment demonstrates that she has a point. What was particularly striking about this judgment was Ms Justice Russell's excoriating criticisms of Judge Tolson. She said:

> *"17. ...along with Judge Tolson's conduct of this case any broad analysis of his judgment, and approach to the fact-finding is so flawed as to lead to the conclusion that it is unsafe and wrong."*

She went on to say:

> *"37. This judgment is flawed. This is a senior judge, a Designated Family Judge, a leadership judge in the Family Court, expressing a view that, in his judgment, it is not only permissible but also acceptable for penetration to continue after the complainant had said no (by asking the perpetrator to stop) but also that a complainant must and should physically resist penetration, in order to establish a lack of consent."*

So far as concerns the question asked in the title of my book, and more particularly the issues of openness and transparency which lie behind that title, this case highlights four important points.

First, the initial finding of fact hearing in August 2019 took place behind closed doors. The media were entitled to attend. The general public were not. Unless they had been tipped off in advance about the issues raised in this case, perhaps by the mother or her solicitor, it is unrealistic to expect that there would have been a media presence in court. This underlines the importance of a point I have made in earlier chapters. The way cases are described on the court list makes it impossible for a journalist reading the list to have any idea of the nature of the cases that are to be dealt with on any particular day. That, in turn, makes it well-nigh impossible for a journalist to decide whether there is any point in going to court. The effect of not letting the media know what cases are coming up is tantamount to shutting them out.

Second, had the mother not appealed against the decision made by the Circuit Judge in August 2019, it is highly unlikely that the details of this case would ever have come into the public domain. There can be no doubt that it was entirely appropriate that the appeal judgment in this case should have been made public. The fact that it might not have been underlines the point Tickle makes about the damaging result of privacy's *effects*.

Third, until October 2016 the hearing of an appeal against the decision of a Circuit Judge in a private law Children Act case was dealt with in the Court of Appeal. Since October 2016 such appeals have been heard by a High Court Judge of the Family Division. In the Court of Appeal, appeals are normally heard in open court. Until recently, the hearing of a family appeal by a High Court Judge normally took place in private (though I am told that there are a very few examples of individual appeals being heard in public at the discretion of the appeal judge). Since October 2019, as a result of an amendment to the rules,[4] such appeals should now 'ordinarily' be heard in public and will 'ordinarily' include an order restricting the publication of information concerning the proceedings. But for that rule change, the hearing of this mother's appeal would almost certainly have taken place in private and, in all probability, the facts would never have come into the public domain.

Fourth, the context for this finding of fact hearing was private law proceedings between parents concerning their child (aged 4 at the relevant time). The finding of fact hearing was necessary in order to enable the court to consider whether the mother's allegations of domestic violence and abuse were true. If found to be true, that behaviour would clearly have been relevant in determining the future relationship between the child and the father. The fact-finding process was a discrete issue. The child had no part to play in that hearing. The child was neither a direct victim nor a witness. In principle, therefore, there is no reason why that hearing could not have taken place in public.

Had the mother's allegations of rape been heard by a criminal court the hearing would have been in open court and the mother's identity protected. Had the mother's allegations been the basis for a civil claim for damages for the harm suffered, the hearing would have taken place in open court. There are grounds for doubting whether the civil court would have granted

---

[4] See Family Proceedings Rules 2010 rule 30.12A and Practice Direction 30B.

her anonymity.[5] Why, then, should a finding of fact hearing in a private law Children Act case routinely be heard in private (as they are at present)?

This mother was clearly a vulnerable person. She could (and, as Ms Justice Russell made clear, should) have been given protection by the making of a 'participation direction'.[6] Steps could have been taken to protect the rights of the child (the subject of these proceedings) under Article 8 ECHR and Article 16 UNCRC. The court could have imposed reporting restrictions. In the unlikely event that the number or conduct of any members of the public or media attending the hearing was likely to impact on the parties' ability to give their best evidence, the court could have revisited its decision to sit in public throughout. On the basis of the limited facts available it would seem at least arguable that this was a hearing that could have taken place in public.

Tickle's question (which I paraphrase) about what else is happening in the Family Court in private which the public does not get to hear about is, I regretfully accept, a reasonable question. Some issues of concern come into the public domain as a result of an appeal (as in the case I have just considered).[7] How many issues of concern about the conduct of a family hearing such as this remain invisible because the hearing takes place in private and

---

[5] See *Justyna-Zeromska-smith v United Lincolnshire Hospitals NHS Trust* [2019] EWHC 552 (QB). As a result of clinical negligence a mother's baby was still-born. The mother suffered very severe psychiatric injury. She brought a claim for damages. Shortly before the trial she applied for anonymity. The judge, Mr Justice Martin Spencer, refused her application. He said:

> "20. In the present case, the revelation of the matters personal to this claimant and her family are inherent and intrinsic to a claim of this nature, relating as it is to psychiatric injury suffered by the Claimant from the stillbirth of her daughter. Having chosen to bring these proceedings in order to secure damages arising out of that tragedy, the Claimant cannot avoid the consequences of having made that decision in terms of the principle of open justice and the consequent publicity potentially associated with such proceedings being heard in open court."

[6] See Family Procedure Rules 2010 rule 3A and Practice Direction 3AA. A 'participation direction' is a direction made by the court to assist a vulnerable witness to give their best evidence. It could include, for example, a direction that a party or witness should sit behind a screen in court so that they cannot see or be intimidated by another party or witness, or a direction allowing a party or witness to participate in a hearing by giving their evidence by live link – e.g. from a different room in the court building or even, perhaps, from a completely different location.

[7] See, for example, the following cases referred to on Bailii: *Re G (Children: Fair Hearing)* [2019] EWCA Civ 126; *Re S-W (Children)* [2015] EWCA Civ 27; *Re A (Children)* [2015] EWCA Civ 133.

the media do not attend?[8]

On 25 January 2022, in an article by another journalist writing for *The Guardian*, Sonia Sodha, the point is made that:

> *"The only reason this case is in the public domain is because the woman in question appealed to the high court. Family court proceedings are heard in private and subject to stringent reporting restrictions that limit parents' ability to talk publicly about what happened. This is to safeguard children's privacy, but the sheer weight of the shroud of secrecy that engulfs the family courts means attitudes such as [the attitude of this judge] can persevere without scrutiny."*

As I noted in Chapter 1, Sonia Sodha also observed that:

> *"Family court judges have an unenviable responsibility: they have to make balance-of-probability rulings about what happened between two parents behind closed doors, sometimes on limited evidence, that determine how much, if at all, contact those parents have with their children, whose safety is paramount."*

It is right that judges exercising such powers are open to scrutiny. It is right that this case received the publicity it did; it illustrates the importance of the public's right to know what happens in the Family Court. But that case is exceptional. My experience of judges working in the Family Court at every level is that they care deeply about the children and families in whose lives they are often called upon to make life-changing decisions. Judges want to achieve an outcome that is not only legally correct but, more importantly, is a proportionate decision made in the child's best welfare interests. They are dedicated and committed people who take on this immense burden of responsibility out of a genuine concern for the welfare and well-being of the children and families they deal with. They do not take the charge of

---

[8] Tickle and the media are not alone in making that point. In a lecture given on 30 January 2020, *Can the law keep up with changes in society?* Professor Jo Delahunty said: "It does the family 'justice' system no favour to have judges sitting in cases in which such manifestly out of date and dangerous attitudes are held with the attendant risks that poses to the victim and the children. It is no wonder that this case attracted widespread press interest and public condemnation. But I ask: had there not been an appeal (which was heard in public) to a senior and robust judge would we have had such a robust denunciation of the conduct of a colleague and a strong recommendation as to what to do to avoid repetition of his mistakes? The question this case will inevitably raise is 'in how many other cases has this happened where the victim has not had a robust lawyer prepared to take the matter up on appeal?'" - *https://s3-eu-west-1.amazonaws.com/content.gresham.ac.uk/data/binary/3225/2020-01-30_JoDelahunty-ChangesInSociety-T.pdf.*

'secrecy' easily.

Although I accept that there are many hearings which take place in the Family Court which should be heard in private, there are some which could be heard in public. In my opinion, those hearings which could safely take place in public should take place in public. With respect to those which should continue to take place in private, the media's right to attend is a right to act as the eyes and ears of the public (for whose benefit the Family Court exists). This *must* be a meaningful right. The media *must* be allowed to do their job. That means that unless there are cogent reasons to the contrary, they must be allowed to publish a story about what they have observed in court even if, for good reason, the judge should decide to place some restrictions on what they can report.

Some progress has been made over the last ten years since the media were permitted to attend some hearings in the Family Court though, in truth, they have proved to be small steps. As a result of the Practice Guidance on Transparency issued in February 2014, more Family Court judgments are being published. As a result of the Practice Guidance on anonymisation and the avoidance of the identification of children, issued by the President of the Family Division in December 2018, there should have been an improvement in the quality and reliability of the anonymisation of judgments.[9]

In October 2019 the President issued *Guidance as to Reporting in the Family Courts*. The purpose of this guidance was to assist the media by making it clear that a formal application is not required when applying to the court for it to consider whether to publish its judgment, or for reporting restrictions to be lifted after the hearing is over.

Most recently, in the *View from the President's Chambers* published in December 2019, the President set out details of his intention to undertake a transparency review. In his 'View' the President says:

> "**Transparency Review**
>
> As trailed in the May 2019 'View', I have now gathered together a small panel to assist me in undertaking a review on the issue of transparency in the Family Court, with a view to informing my own policy, as President, on this important and sensitive issue. The panel

---

[9] Though I am not aware of any study having been undertaken to ascertain whether that is, in fact, the case.

members are:

Dr Eia Asen (Child and Adolescent Psychiatrist)

Anthony Douglas CBE (formerly CEO of CAFCASS)

Clare Dyer (former *Guardian* legal editor)

Nicola Shaw CBE (Executive Director of the National Grid)

The Panel, which meets for the first time on 18 December, is likely to call for evidence from any interested parties to be submitted by the end of February 2020. Thereafter key contributors may be invited to attend an oral evidence session. The Panel may also gather evidence from other jurisdictions. It is my intention that the Panel process will enable me to publish a statement describing my concluded view on the issue of transparency by the end of May 2020."

On 3 February, the President issued a 'Call for Evidence' inviting any person or agency who wishes to submit evidence, advice or other material for consideration within the Transparency Review to do so by 2 March.

This is a very welcome step forward. However, we have a long way to go. And unless we are prepared to go forward together, those who, like me, firmly believe that the Family Court is a caring and compassionate court seeking only what is best for the children and families it serves, we will continue to be bogged down by the distraction of an arid, semantic debate about secrecy and privacy. Unless we are prepared to make that journey we are going to have to accept the inevitability that the charge of being a secret court will continue even though, as I would contend, it is neither true nor helpful.

Writing this book has taken me on a journey. It is a journey that has persuaded me that, so far as concerns the issue of openness and transparency in the Family Court, there are things that are wrong which need to be put right. I therefore intend to make some recommendations. They are set out at the end of this chapter. Whether they will win support or withering condemnation I know not. However, as the sun rapidly goes down on my own career as a Family Court judge I am grateful to have this opportunity to make a contribution to a debate which, at present, appears to have no end.

Recommendations

Section 12 of the Administration of Justice Act 1960

On 16 December 2008 the then Secretary of State for Justice and Lord Chancellor, Jack Straw, made a statement to Parliament.[10] In the course of his statement, he said:

> *"For entirely legitimate reasons, the privacy of parties to family proceedings must be properly protected. That is of enormous importance to adults, and is an overwhelming imperative in cases involving children. At present, with some exceptions, neither the public nor the media are permitted to witness proceedings in these courts. However, many argue that the current provisions to safeguard privacy and confidentiality go too far, leaving family courts unfairly open to accusations of bias or even injustice."*

He went on to say:

> *"I have been actively considering how we can shed more light on family courts while preserving the imperative of the welfare of the child. The Government have now reached their conclusion, and I am therefore announcing today that the rules of court will be changed to allow the media to attend family proceedings in all tiers of court... The overall effect of these changes will be fundamentally to increase the openness of family courts, while protecting the privacy of children and vulnerable adults."*

I have no doubt he genuinely believed that the measures he proposed would "fundamentally ... increase the openness of family courts". But he was wrong. He was wrong because he and his advisers had failed to take account of section 12 of the Administration of Justice Act 1960. Even before the rule change came into effect judges pointed out that legislation already in place (section 12) would severely restrict what the media could publish.

In Chapter 4, I argued that section 12 is an anachronism which, in modern parlance, is well past its sell-by date. It is having an effect neither imagined nor intended at the time the Act was passed 60 years ago. The journalists I spoke to are all of a common mind: section 12 should be repealed. Sir James Munby said just that in an article published in 2010.[11] He said it again, in clear, compelling and uncompromising terms, shortly before he

---

[10] Hansard, 16 Dec 2008: Column 980.
[11] See page 60.

retired in 2018. In a lecture given in Edinburgh[12] he said:

> "A vital aspect of the ongoing transformation in the family justice system has to be reform of our still creaking rules about access to and reporting of family cases. Nothing short of radical reform will enable us to rid ourselves of the relentlessly repeated and inevitably damaging charge that we operate a system of private – some say secret – justice. The task is massive, the complexity of the law is quite astonishing – itself a reproach to any reputable system of justice – and the differences of view as to what should be done run deep and in some respects seem almost unbridgeable. Statutory reform is essential – the Administration of Justice Act 1960 which remains the foundation of the modern law is no longer fit for purpose in the world (unknown in 1960) of the internet and social media. The history of attempts at reform is unpromising: consider the origins and fate of Pt II of the Children, Schools and Families Act 2010, never implemented and now repealed. But it would be scandalous if in 10 or 20 years time we were still having to try and muddle along as we do at present."

Sir James has said it again since he retired. In a talk given in Edinburgh on 10 February 2020, Sir James referred to: "The restrictive provisions of the now elderly and hopelessly obsolescent section 12 of the Administration of Justice Act 1960…". He goes on to refer to the "suffocating effect of section 12."

Sir James says that:

> "there is an urgent need to address the problems associated with section 12. It has become increasingly clear that section 12 should be repealed, to be replaced, no doubt, with much less restrictive, more narrowly drawn and more focused legislation better suited to the modern world."[13]

I agree with the problem Sir James identifies and the remedy he proposes. Something must be done. Change is long overdue. It cannot be right that a statutory provision, the breach of which could lead to a journalist or a parent being sent to prison, can only be fully understood by the finest legal minds in the country. If people's liberty is being put on the line they are

---

[12] *Changing Families: Family Law Yesterday, Today and Tomorrow – a View from South of the Border* [2018] Fam Law 538.
[13] *The Guardian's* headline for this article was *Reporting restrictions turning family courts into black hole, says ex-judge* – in the circumstances, an entirely appropriate headline.

entitled to understand clearly what it is that they can and cannot do; what it is that may lead to them being committed for contempt.[14]

Since December 2019 we have had a government with a substantial majority in the House of Commons, almost certain to remain in power for a full five-year term. There has never been a better time to press for change. That opportunity should not be allowed to slip by.

Recommendation 1: that immediate steps be taken to seek to persuade the Government of the urgent need to repeal section 12 of the Administration of Justice Act 1960.

Publication of judgments

In addition to allowing duly accredited media representatives to attend hearings in the Family Court, the last Labour Government also recognised the importance of increasing the volume of information coming out of the Family Court. In his statement to Parliament on 16 December 2008, Jack Straw went on to say:

> *"As well as allowing the media to attend family proceedings, there is a need to increase the amount and quality of information coming from the courts. At present, anonymised judgments of the Court of Appeal, and in some instances of the High Court, are made public, but that is not the situation for the county courts or the family proceedings courts, which deal with the bulk of family law cases.*
>
> *We have therefore decided to pilot the provision of written judgments when a final order is made in certain family cases. The courts in the pilot areas – Leeds, Wolverhampton and Cardiff – will, for the first time, routinely produce a written record of the decision for the parties involved. In selected cases, where the court is making life-changing decisions for a child, it will publish an anonymised judgment online, so that it can be read by the wider public."*

From this came the Family Court Information Pilot. Despite the goodwill and commitment of those directly involved in the planning, execution and evaluation of this pilot, it was not a success. I discussed this in Chapter 5.

A more robust approach to the publication of judgments was introduced

---

[14] The position in Australia, for example, is much clearer – see Appendix A and compare these two legislative provisions with section 12 of the Administration of Justice Act 1960 which is set out in Chapter 4 on page 47.

in the Practice Guidance: *Transparency in the Family Courts – Publication of Judgments*, published by the then President of the Family Division, Sir James Munby, on 16 January 2014. I discuss the guidance in Chapter 6 and evaluate it in Chapter 7. My assessment is that this Guidance has only had a limited impact. As Chapter 7 makes clear, although the Guidance led to an initial surge in the number of Family Court judgments published by Circuit Judges, over time the number began to fall. Even when the number of judgments being published was at its peak, there was still a significant number of Circuit Judges, including several Designated Family Judges, who did not publish any judgments at all. Their reasons varied. Some took the view that as Practice *Guidance*, compliance was optional. Some fundamentally disagreed with the publication of judgments because of the risk of the child being identified. Some were concerned about whether the media could be trusted to act responsibly when writing articles about published judgments. Some were concerned about the time commitment to produce (or approve) a judgment in publishable form.

My position on this issue of publishing judgments is well-known. Before my retirement I did my best to comply with the Practice Guidance. I published judgments regularly. Although I have in the past expressed reservations about whether the media can be trusted,[15] and even in this book have expressed a degree of exasperation at the way the print media, in particular, have covered some of the judgments I have published,[16] those concerns are outweighed by my concern to protect the integrity of the family justice system and increase the public's confidence and trust in the work of the Family Court by making it more open. In saying that, I have well in mind the regrettable fact that miscarriages of justice are still happening and, even more disquieting, are still happening behind closed doors. Whether a miscarriage of justice comes to the notice of the public is, at present, very much a matter of chance. That is unacceptable. The publication of judgments is an important corrective. I continue to be persuaded that some (not all) Family Court judgments should be published. However, some important issues need to be addressed.

Anonymisation
The most important part of the process of publishing a judgment is to ensure that the judgment is properly anonymised in order to reduce the risk (I don't think it is possible to guarantee the total eradication of the risk) of a family being identified. One of the issues raised by Doughty, Twaite and

---

[15] See my article *Can the Press be Trusted?* published in the Family Law Journal in [2011] Fam Law 260.
[16] See Chapter 10 at page 160.

Magrath in their evaluation of the President's Practice Guidance on Transparency[17] was that anonymisation errors in judgments published on Bailii were a significant problem that needed to be addressed. In Chapter 12, I referred to Dr Brophy's study concerning anonymisation[18] and her guidance on the steps that should be followed in order to achieve high quality anonymisation. In December 2018 the President of the Family Division, Sir Andrew McFarlane, published *Practice Guidance: Anonymisation and Avoidance of the Identification of Children and the Treatment of Explicit Descriptions of the Sexual Abuse of Children in Judgments Intended for the Public Arena*. The Guidance includes two checklists which are based on the recommendations made by Brophy in 2016.

Although the Guidance is intended to be a useful tool to assist the process of high quality anonymisation of judgments it, in fact, highlights a very serious problem. It is a matter of public knowledge that the Family Justice system is in crisis. Over recent years the volume of work has gone up. That has not been matched by an increase in resources. Family Circuit Judges are under intense pressure to get through the increasing volume of work. In his 'View from the President's Chambers' published in December 2019, the President acknowledged "The unremitting pressure of work in the Family Court".

The President said that he was:

> "acutely concerned about the impact of this unremitting burden upon all those who work within the Family Justice system, whether as lawyers, social workers, CAFCASS/CAFCASS Cymru officers, HMCTS staff, magistrates and judges."

This is highly relevant to the issue of anonymisation. Notwithstanding the expectations in the Practice Guidance on Transparency that it would be lawyers and not judges who would anonymise judgments, it is my belief that there are many family judges (and I was one) who anonymise their own judgments. Why is that the case? I can only speak of my own experience. I typed all of my own judgments. In each case I routinely asked the advocates to read through the judgment with care and point out any errors. Some proved to be very good at doing this. Others were not. I was therefore reluctant to leave something as important as the anonymisation of a judg-

---

[17] *Transparency through publication of family court judgments: An evaluation of the responses to, and effects of, judicial guidance on publishing family court judgments involving children and young people* published by Cardiff University in March 2017.
[18] *Anonymisation and Avoidance of the Identification of Children & The Treatment of Explicit Descriptions of the Sexual Abuse of Children in Judgments Intended for the Public Arena*.

ment to the advocates in the case. The ultimate responsibility for the publication of the judgment rests with the judge. I, therefore, anonymised my own judgments. I accept that the reality today is that family Circuit Judges simply do not have the time to do this. That is not going to change in the foreseeable future. Undertaking the process of anonymisation by following the Brophy checklists in the President's December 2019 Practice Guidance (which run to 18 sides of A4 paper) is a painstaking process which cannot be done at speed.

There is already evidence of inadequately anonymised judgments being posted on Bailii. I am not aware that this issue has been the subject of any analysis since the report by Doughty, Twaite and Magrath was published. I do not know whether the situation has improved or deteriorated since their report was published. There is a consensus amongst judges that those firms which transcribe judgments that have been digitally recorded are, to put it charitably, of mixed quality when asked to deal with anonymisation. There is, therefore, no consistency in either standard or approach. The risk of inadequately anonymised judgments being placed on Bailii is a real risk. It is an unacceptable risk. It needs to be taken seriously. It needs to be addressed.

Recommendation 2: that there should be an urgent review of all Family Court and Family Division judgments posted on Bailii in the last 12 months to assess whether there has been any improvement in the overall quality of anonymisation since the publication of the report by Doughty, Twaite and Magrath.

I noted in Chapter 12 the arrangements for anonymisation of judgments in the Family Court of Australia. The benefits of having a similar system in England and Wales would be that:

- the anonymisation of all judgments would be undertaken by fully trained, dedicated staff;

- it is likely that there would be a significant increase in consistency of approach;

- it is likely that there would be a significant reduction in the number of errors; and

- it would remove from judges a task which they simply do not have time to perform and may well, as a consequence, lead to an increase in the number of judgments anonymised and published.

Recommendation 3: that the anonymisation of judgments be recognised as a specialist task, that an Anonymisation Unit be created following the Australian model and that the staff allocated to work in these units be adequately trained and resourced.

Disclosure of documents
In his statement to the House of Commons on 16 December 2008, Jack Straw said that:

> *"The consequences of family proceedings are so significant that the parties involved will sometimes need to seek advice or support from a range of people, including legal advisers, family members, medical practitioners and Members of Parliament or other elected representatives. To do so, they must be able to discuss and share information about their case. In 2005, we made changes to the rules of court to allow people to disclose certain information to specified individuals, but after two years it became clear that those rules remained unnecessarily restrictive and too complicated. Following a consultation last year, the Government have now decided to relax the rules on the disclosure of information in family proceedings."*

The Conservative MP for Arundel and South Downs, Nick Herbert, made an important point to the Justice Secretary followed by a question:

> *"A key concern for families is that they are unable to raise their cases with the media, but it appears that the Government's proposed rules for disclosure will still prevent them from doing so. Will the Justice Secretary confirm that, and explain why he believes it is right to maintain that restriction?"*

The Justice Secretary was somewhat Delphic in his response. He said:

> *"The Hon. Gentleman asked me some specific questions about disclosure by families to the media. We have to put the detail of the changes to the rules committee, and I am actively considering that issue."*

I dealt with issues relating to communication of information in Chapter 3. Nothing has happened to address this particular issue since that exchange in Parliament in December 2008. Parents are caught by section 12 of the Administration of Justice Act 1960 and are therefore still unable to disclose any 'information relating to the proceedings' to a media representative without obtaining the prior permission of the court. It is difficult to understand the rationale for this restriction. A journalist who is given 'information relating to proceedings' by a parent would be bound by the provisions of section 12. Breach could lead to contempt proceedings. The journalist would be in exactly the same position that he or she would have been in had the court sanctioned disclosure of documents to the media. I am reliably informed that some parents do already discuss their case with the media and allow journalists to read case papers. Everyone knows that is happening. What is the point of holding the sword of committal over a parent's head? It simply adds to what are likely to be the already high stress levels felt by parents. It is an unnecessary and illogical restriction. The alternative – which is to continue to turn a blind eye to the fact that this is happening – simply makes a mockery of the law. The Family Procedure Rules 2010 should be amended to remove that restriction.

Recommendation 4: that Family Procedure Rules 2010 Practice Direction 12G be amended to make it permissible for a party to Children Act proceedings to share information relating to proceedings with duly accredited representatives of news gathering and reporting organisations (including permitting such persons to read any papers relating to the case which may be in that parent's possession) and/or with legal bloggers.

The media – what needs to change?
In my opinion there are a number of changes that need to be considered in order to improve trust, confidence and working relationships between the judiciary and the media.

First, I noted in Chapter 4 the steps taken in 2011 by the then President of the Family Division, Sir Nicholas Wall, and Bob Satchwell, then Executive Director of the Society of Editors, to set up a group to consider what might be done to achieve greater transparency in the Family Court. So far as I am aware that group has been defunct for several years. In Chapter 13, I noted the steps that have been taken in Nova Scotia to set up a Media Liaison Committee on which both judges and the media are well represented. In England and Wales there is no similar structured forum for ongoing dialogue between the judiciary, the media and senior HMCTS staff. There is clearly a role for a similar committee in England and Wales.

Recommendation 5: that a national Media Liaison Committee be formed, the constitution of which should include representatives of the print and broadcast media and senior members of the judiciary. It may also be appropriate for such a committee to include representatives from public interest journalism and/or public legal education bodies and perhaps from the press regulators.

Second, as I noted in Chapter 10, when the rules were changed in 2009 to permit accredited media representatives to attend hearings in the Family Court, the Justice Secretary had to come to a decision about what was required in order to be 'accredited'. He determined that an 'accredited' journalist should be any journalist with a UK Press Card. That did not require journalists working in the Family Court to have any knowledge or understanding of the work of the Family Court. The financial state of the newspaper industry is such that there is little money or time available for in-service training and little opportunity to undertake any form of training. There are few opportunities for journalists to meet with family judges. It seems to me that it is in the interests of the public and the judiciary that we should have not just a free press but also an informed press.

Recommendation 6: that consideration be given to whether the current criteria for being a 'duly accredited representative' of a news gathering or reporting organisation are adequate or whether there should be a requirement for some additional form of accreditation for journalists working in the Family Court. This issue should be referred to the Media Liaison Committee.

Third, as I noted in Chapter 10, newspapers, both national and local, have an online presence in addition to their traditional print format. When publishing a report about a judgment in the Family Court it would be very simple for the online version to contain a link to the law report published on Bailii. In that way members of the public interested in doing so could very easily access the full judgment and read what the judge actually decided and why rather than relying exclusively on the inevitably brief account of the judgment written by a journalist. The journalists I spoke to agreed that this would be easy to achieve and most could see no reason why that should not happen.

Recommendation 7: that an approach be made to the media to seek their agreement to including in any online news story relating to a published judgment a link to that judgment on Bailii. This issue should be referred to the Media Liaison Committee.

Fourth, as I noted in Chapter 4, the group of journalists and lawyers put together by Sir Nicholas Wall and Bob Satchwell commissioned two barristers, Adam Wolanski QC and Kate Wilson, to prepare a paper setting out a comprehensive review of the law relating to what might broadly be referred to as transparency issues. This is now nearly ten years old. It would be helpful if an updated version could be published. That could be achieved quickly.

Recommendation 8: that steps be taken to update and publish the report prepared by Wolanski and Wilson in 2011.

Transparency – the Next Steps

In Chapter 14, I considered the Consultation Paper issued by the President of the Family Division on 15 August 2014. None of the responses to the consultation have been published. The consultation paper sought responses on four issues.

First, views were sought on the impact and the working today of the Practice Guidance on transparency. I dealt with that issue earlier in this chapter.

Second, views and suggestions were sought as to whether any steps can be taken to enhance the listing of cases in the Family Division and the Family Court so that court lists can, as the media have suggested, be made more informative than at present as to the subject matter of the cases. This is an issue I took up with the journalists I interviewed. They made the comparison with the Crown Court where journalists can find out what cases are before the court the next day. In the Family Division and the Family Court no such helpful information is available. As a result, we have created a situation where the media are entitled to attend hearings in the family court but cannot find out in advance what cases are being heard, do not know at the start of a hearing how much, if anything, the judge will allow them to publish and, without the judge's permission, are not entitled to have access to any of the case papers. The media's description of the rule change in April 2009 as a con is, at the least, understandable. The President's consultation paper on Next Steps made some suggestions on how this issue might be addressed. There is a basis here for discussions with the media. It is regrettable that five years on, nothing has happened. It is, in my opinion, something that could easily be addressed. It is a quick fix. We should fix it.

Recommendation 9: that, in consultation with the media, the listing of cases in the Family Division and the Family Court be changed (in so far as this can be achieved without breaching the confidentiality of each case listed) to enable the media to identify, with respect to every case listed, the type and nature of the case.

Third, views were sought on the disclosure of certain categories of documents to the media. I dealt with this in Chapter 14. It is clear from my conversation with journalists that it would be extremely helpful to them to have a copy of the case summary. In care proceedings a case summary is prepared for the vast majority of hearings. It would be very simple for case summaries to be prepared in anonymised format and for journalists to be given a copy. For the reasons set out in Chapter 14, in my opinion the disclosure of other material to the media is an issue which should be considered by the Family Procedure Rule Committee.

Recommendation 10: that the President of the Family Division be invited to consider the appropriateness of issuing Practice Guidance with respect to the preparation of case summaries in public law cases, in an anonymised form, on the basis that such case summaries should be made available not only to the court and the parties in the case but also to the media.

Recommendation 11: that the President of the Family Division:

(i) be invited to consider issuing a consultation paper concerning the possibility of confidential reports in care proceedings (for example, paediatric reports and psychiatric reports) being made available to the media;

(ii) be requested to publish the results of the consultation; and

(iii) if the outcome of the consultation supports such disclosure, he be requested to refer the matter to the Family Procedure Rule Committee to consider the drafting of appropriate amendments to the Family Procedure Rules 2010.

Fourth, the President sought "preliminary, pre-consultation views about the possible hearing in public of certain types of family case." In my opinion, the responses to this issue from the original consultation should be published. As we are now more than five years on, the consultation on that issue should be repeated and the results published. Earlier in this chapter I suggested that there may be some hearings in the Family Court which could take place in public subject to appropriate safeguards being in place. I suggested, in particular, finding of fact hearings in some private law Children Act cases.

Recommendation 12: that, with respect to the proposal to consider the hearing of certain family cases in public, the response to the consultation in 2014 be published and that the consultation exercise be repeated to ascertain whether there has been any shift in the opinions of relevant stakeholders during the last five years. If the balance of opinion supports the possible hearing in public of certain types of family cases, the President be requested to refer the matter to the Family Procedure Rule Committee.

Training

Some of the subjects I have covered in this book raise training issues. For example, issues relating to when, when not, and how to publish a judgment, how to anonymise a judgment ready for publication, how to deal with an application by the media for disclosure of case papers (including expert reports) and how to deal with an application by the media to publish information which is not automatically permitted by Practice Direction 12G.

I am informed that in the last academic year the Judicial College included a 90-minute talk on "Transparency and legal blogging in the family courts" given by Lucy Reed (Chair of the Transparency Project) and journalist Louise Tickle. The purpose of this training was said to be: "To introduce the work of the Transparency Project, to explain the legal blogging pilot and to explore issues arising from the attendance of legal bloggers and journalists at court". I am told that this session was well received.

It is good that training has been provided. My concern is about whether it is broad enough to address all of the issues judges may have to deal with.

Recommendation 13: that issues relating to transparency and openness in the Family Court, both law and practice, be included in all family law Judicial College training courses.

I make one final point. I raise it for consideration and not, at this stage, for recommendation. The Judicial College depends heavily upon external speakers from a wide variety of different disciplines. I know from personal experience that this can be invaluable. It is one of the strengths of the training provided by the Judicial College. If the media are to assist in the training of judges, is there any scope for judges to offer assistance in the training of journalists? I simply ask the question!

Appendix A

Family Law Act 1975 (Australia)
Section 121 Restriction on publication of court proceedings

(1) A person who publishes in a newspaper or periodical publication, by radio broadcast or television or by other electronic means, or otherwise disseminates to the public or to a section of the public by any means, any account of any proceedings, or of any part of any proceedings, under this Act that identifies:

   (a) a party to the proceedings;

   (b) a person who is related to, or associated with, a party to the proceedings or is, or is alleged to be, in any other way concerned in the matter to which the proceedings relate; or

   (c) a witness in the proceedings;

   commits an offence punishable, upon conviction by imprisonment for a period not exceeding one year.

(2) A person who, except as permitted by the applicable Rules of Court, publishes in a newspaper or periodical publication, by radio broadcast or television or by other electronic means, or otherwise disseminates to the public or to a section of the public by any means (otherwise than by the display of a notice in the premises of the court), a list of proceedings under this Act, identified by reference to the names of the parties to the proceedings, that are to be dealt with by a court commits an offence punishable, upon conviction by imprisonment for a period not exceeding one year.

(3) Without limiting the generality of subsection (1), an account of proceedings, or of any part of proceedings, referred to in that subsection shall be taken to identify a person if:

   (a) it contains any particulars of:

      (i) the name, title, pseudonym or alias of the person;

      (ii) the address of any premises at which the person resides or works, or the locality in which any such premises are situated;

(iii) the physical description or the style of dress of the person;

(iv) any employment or occupation engaged in, profession practised or calling pursued, by the person or any official or honorary position held by the person;

(v) the relationship of the person to identified relatives of the person or the association of the person with identified friends or identified business, official or professional acquaintances of the person;

(vi) the recreational interests, or the political, philosophical or religious beliefs or interests, of the person; or

(vii) any real or personal property in which the person has an interest or with which the person is otherwise associated;

being particulars that are sufficient to identify that person to a member of the public, or to a member of the section of the public to which the account is disseminated, as the case requires;

(b) in the case of a written or televised account or an account by other electronic means – it is accompanied by a picture of the person; or

(c) in the case of a broadcast or televised account or an account by other electronic means – it is spoken in whole or in part by the person and the person's voice is sufficient to identify that person to a member of the public, or to a member of the section of the public to which the account is disseminated, as the case requires.

Appendix A

Legislation in the State of Victoria
Section 534(4) of the Children, Youth and Families Act 2005

(4) Without limiting the generality of sub-sections (1) and (3), the following particulars are deemed to be particulars likely to lead to the identification of a person –

- (a) the name, title, pseudonym or alias of the person;

- (b) the address of any premises at which the person resides or works, or the locality in which those premises are situated;

- (c) the address of a school attended by the person or the locality in which the school is situated;

- (d) the physical description or the style of dress of the person;

- (e) any employment or occupation engaged in, profession practised or calling pursued, by the person or any official or honorary position held by the person;

- (f) the relationship of the person to identified relatives of the person or the association of the person with identified friends or identified business, official or professional acquaintances of the person;

- (g) the recreational interests or the political, philosophical or religious beliefs or interests of the person;

- (h) any real or personal property in which the person has an interest or with which the person is otherwise associated.

Bibliography

Baggini, Julian, *A Short History of Truth*, 2017, Quercus Editions Ltd.

Bellamy, His Honour Judge Clifford, *Can the Press be Trusted?* [2011] Fam Law 260.

Brooke, Heather, *Your right to know*, 2007, Pluto Press, London.

Brooke, Heather, *The Silent State*, 2010, William Heinemann, London.

Brophy, Dr J and Roberts, C, *'Openness and transparency' in family courts: what the experience of other countries tells us about reform in England and Wales*, 2009, Family Policy Briefing 5, University of Oxford.

Brophy, Dr J, Doughty, J, Johal J, Owen, Scanlan, Dr L, Tomlinson, J, and Turnbull, D, *The Children's Commissioner for England's report on The views of children and young people regarding media access to family courts*, 2010, The Oxford Centre for Family Law and Policy Department of Social Work, University of Oxford.

Brophy, Dr J, *Safeguarding, Privacy and Respect for Children and Young People & The Next Steps in Media Access to Family Courts*, 2014, National Youth Advocacy Service and Association of Lawyers for Children.

Brophy, Dr J, Perry, K, Harrison, E, *A review of anonymised judgments on Bailii: Children, privacy and 'jigsaw identification'*, 2015, National Youth Service and Association of Lawyers for Children.

Brophy, Dr J, *Anonymisation and Avoidance of the Identification of Children & The Treatment of Explicit Descriptions of the Sexual Abuse of Children in Judgments Intended for the Public Arena*, Judicial Guidance 2016, Association of Lawyers for Children.

The Calcutt Report: Review of Press Self-Regulation (1993).

Cathcart, Professor Brian, *Trust, Newspapers and Journalists: A Review of Evidence*, 2017, published in the journal 'Radical Statistics', Issue 118.

Confidence and Confidentiality: Improving transparency and privacy in family courts, October 2006, Department for Constitutional Affairs, CP 11/06.

Confidence and Confidentiality: Improving transparency and privacy in family courts, March 2007, Department for Constitutional Affairs, CP(R) 11/06.

Confidence and Confidentiality: Openness in family courts – a new approach, June 2007 Ministry of Justice, CP 10/07.

Confidentiality: Good practice in handling patient information, 2017, General Medical Council.

Cretney, S, *Family Law in the Twentieth Century: A History*, 2003, Oxford University Press.

Curran, J and Seaton, J, *Power without Responsibility*, 2010, 7th edition, Routledge, London.

Curran, J and Seaton, J, *Power without Responsibility*, 2016, 8th edition, Routledge, London.

Davies, Nick, *Flat Earth News*, 2009, Vintage.

Delahunty, Professor Jo QC, *Transparency in the Family court: What Goes on Behind Closed Doors*, a lecture given at Gresham College, London, 24 May 2018.

Delahunty, Professor Jo QC, *Can the law keep up with changes in society?* A lecture given at Gresham College on 30 January 2020.

Denning, Lord, *The Road to Justice*, 1955, Stevens & Sons.

Dodd, M and Hanna M, *McNae's Essential Law for Journalists*, 24th Edition, 2018, Oxford University Press.

Doughty, J, *Opening up the Family Courts – what happened to children's rights?* July 2010, published in *Contemporary Issues in Law*.

Doughty J, *Confidentiality in the Family Courts: Ethical Dilemmas for Health and Social Work Practice*, 2013, in: Priaulx, Nicolette Michelle and Wrigley, Anthony eds. Ethics, Law and Society, Vol 5. Farnham: Ashgate.

Doughty, J, Twaite, A and Magrath, P, *Transparency through publication of family court judgments: An evaluation of the responses to and effects of, judicial guidance on publishing family court judgments involving children and young people*, March 2017, Cardiff University.

Doughty, J, Reed, L and Magrath, P, *Transparency in the Family Courts: Publicity and Privacy in Practice,* 2018, Bloomsbury Professional, Haywards Heath.

Eekelaar, J and Maclean, M, *Family Justice – The Work of Family Judges in Uncertain Times.*

Equality and Human Rights Commission, *The impact of LASPO on routes to justice* (Research Report 118), September 2018.

Family Justice in view, December 2008, Ministry of Justice CP(T) 10/07.

Fionda, Julia, *Legal Concepts of Childhood*, 2001, Hart Publishing.

Franklin, R, Hamer, M, Hanna, M, Kinsey, M, and Richardson, J, *Key Concepts in Journalism Studies*, 2005, Sage Publications Ltd, London.

Hale, Baroness, *Openness and privacy in family proceedings*, 10 May 2018, the Sir Nicholas Wall Memorial Lecture.

Hanna, Mark, *Irreconcilable Differences: The Attempts to Increase Media Coverage of Family Courts in England and Wales*, 2012, Vol 4 Issue 2 Journal of Media Law 274-301.

Hedley, Sir Mark, *The Modern Judge: Power, Responsibility and Society's Expectations*, 2016, LexisNexis, Bristol.

Hershman McFarlane, *Children Law and Practice*, 2019, Bloomsbury Professional.

House of Commons Constitutional Affairs Committee, *Family Justice: the operation of the family courts*, Fourth Report, Session 2004, 8 November 2004.

House of Commons Constitutional Affairs Select Committee, *Family Justice: the operation of the family courts revisited*, Sixth Report, Session 2005-2006, 6 June 2006

House of Commons Justice Committee a report on the *Operation of the Family Courts*, 14 July 2011.

House of Commons Public Accounts Committee, *Efficiency in the criminal justice system*, 23 May 2016.

Judge, Lord Igor, *The Safest Shield: Lectures, Speeches and Essays*, 2015, Hart Publishing.

Judicial Studies Board Annual Lecture, *Open justice unbound?*, Lord Neuberger, 16 March 2011.

Leveson Inquiry – Report into the culture, practices and ethics of the press, 29 November 2012, London, The Stationery Office.

Lyons, C and Parton, N, *Children's Rights and the Children Act 1989*, 1995, in *The Handbook of Children's Rights*, Bob Franklin (ed), London, Routledge.

Maclean, M with Kurczewski J, *Opening up the Family Courts: The Media, the Ministry and the Children, Schools and Families Act 2010*, chapter 5 in *Making Family Law: A Socio Legal Account of Legislative Process in England and Wales, 1985 to 2010,* 2011, Hart Publishing, London.

MacDonald, Alistair, *Media Access to Expert Reports: A Child and Adolescent Mental Health Perspective*, [2009] Fam Law 911.

MacDonald, Alistair, *Bringing Rights Home for Children: Transparency and the Child's Right to Respect for Private Life*, [2010] Fam Law 180.

Maclean, M, *Openness and Transparency in the Family Courts: A Policy Journey 2005-2011*, a chapter in *Fifty Years in Family Law – Essays for Stephen Cretney*, 2012, Intersentia Publishing Limited, Cambridge.

Masson, Professor J, QC, *Reforming Care Proceedings in England and Wales: Speeding Up Justice and Welfare?* in *Family Law in Britain and America in the New Century, Essays in Honor of Sanford N Katz* (pp 187-206), J.Eekelaar (Ed.), [12] Netherlands: Brill Academic Publishers.

Ministry of Justice, *A study of the impact of changes to court rules governing media attendance in family proceeding*, Summary of responses to stakeholder feedback, January 2010.

Munby, Lord Justice, *Lost opportunities: law reform and transparency in the family courts*, an article based on the Hershman-Levy Memorial Lecture given on 1 July 2010, subsequently published in the Child and Family Law Quarterly, vol 22, No 3 pp 273-289.

Munby, Sir James, *The Crisis in Private Law in the English Family Court*, a lecture given in Edinburgh on 10 February 2020.

Bibliography

Nel, François, *Laid off: What do journalists do next*, An exploratory study by François Nel, Director of the Journalism Leaders Programme at the University of Central Lancashire, Preston, UK, in collaboration with Journalism.co.uk.

Newlands, L, *Publishing Family Court judgments: problems and solutions*, 2016, 24(2) Journal of Law, Information and Science 81.

Parkinson, Professor P, *The Family Law Act 1975: Aspects of its operation and interpretation* (AGPS, Canberra, 1992), referred to by Parkinson in his book, *Australian Family Law in Context: Commentary and Materials*, 7th ed, 2019, Thomson Reuters, Sydney.

Rayden and Jackson on Divorce and Family Matters, 16th Edition, 1991, Butterworths, London.

Report of the Committee on the Rights of the Child, Fifty-first session, Geneva, 25 May – 12 June 2009: General Comment No. 12 (2009), *The Right of the child to be heard*.

Review of Civil and Family Justice in Northern Ireland, Review Group's Report on Family Justice, September 2017.

Sambrook, Richard, *Delivering trust: impartiality and objectivity in a digital age*, Reuters Institute for the Study of Journalism, July 2012.

Shoesmith, S, *Learning from Baby P: The politics of blame, fear and denial*, 2016, Jessica Kingsley Publishers, London.

Tapp, P, *Privacy Issues in the Family Court*, Penk, S and Tobin, R (Eds), 2016, *Privacy Law in New Zealand* 2nd edition, 2016, Stephen Penk and Rosemary Tobin (eds), Thomson Reuters.

Temple, M, *The British Press*, 2008, McGraw Hill.

The Family Court Practice 2019, LexisNexis.

The Secret Barrister – Stories of the Law and How It's Broken, 2018, Macmillan.

Wall, Lord Justice, *Justice for children: welfare or farewell?*, a keynote address for the National Conference of the Association of Lawyers for Children, Manchester, 20 November 2009.

Wall, Sir Nicholas, *Opening up the Family courts: a personal view*, Association of Lawyers for Children annual lecture in memory of Allan Levy QC and David Hershman QC, June 2006.

Index

A

Accredited media representatives 40, 109, 131, 145, 184, 220, 245, 250, 251

Accuracy of reporting by the media 104, 106, 135, 153, 157, 160, 162

Administration of Justice Act 1960

    section 12 20, 24, 37, 39, 44, 47–62, 55, 55–62, 117, 123, 125, 146, 151, 243

    section 12(1) 55

    section 12(2) 55

Admission of the media and the public into Family Court hearings 16, 25

Adoption and Children Act 2002 52

    section 50 52

    section 51 52

    section 144(4) 52

Adoption applications 52

Adoption of Children Act 1926 52

Advance notice of cases 136, 140

Anonymisation of judgments 35, 60, 67, 69, 70, 74, 92, 96, 101, 102, 151, 187–192

    burden on judges 102

    extent of 71

    failures in 187

Anonymity 36, 61, 91, 114, 145, 181

    child 16, 21

    expert witnesses 125–129

    local authority 86, 114–117

    no automatic right to 117, 123, 125

    social workers 117–123

Association of Lawyers for Children 36, 67, 109, 136, 180

Atkinson, Dr Maggie 173, 180, 218

Authorised lawyers 167

B

Baby P case 120–122

Bailii 69, 70, 76, 77, 91, 93–104, 157, 175

Balancing child's and media's rights 16, 17, 36, 90, 150

Battered baby syndrome 50

Berelowitz, Sue 184

Berg, Sanchia 7

Blair, Tony 162

Booker, Christopher 157, 160, 235

Brooke, Heather 19

Brophy, Dr Julia 173, 184, 193

Brophy: 2010 report 173–177

Brophy: 2014 report 180–184

Brophy: 2015 report 185–188

Brophy: 2016 study on anonymisation 188

Burden of proof on the local authority 51

Burden of responsibility on judges 102

Butler-Sloss, Dame Elizabeth 11

C

Cairncross Review 132

Care orders 5, 26, 27, 33, 72, 114, 134

Cathcart, Professor Brian 147

Cause lists 46, 133, 252

Cavendish, Camilla 26–32, 179, 235

Child protection 50, 77, 126, 127, 155, 164

Children Act 1948 51

Children Act 1989

section 1(1) 3, 75, 217

section 1(3) 75

section 31(2) 75

section 44 114

section 45 114

section 97(2) 24, 55, 58–59, 59, 146

section 97(6) 58, 59

Children Act 2004

section 62 24

Children and Families Act 2014

section 13(8) 90

Children and Family Court Advisory and Support Service 68

Index

Children, Schools and Families Act 2010   67, 77, 172

    Part 2   77, 79, 172, 175, 222

Children's rights under Article 13 UNCRC and Article 10 ECHR   226

Child's right to privacy   219

Child's right to privacy   151, 172, 183, 211, 219, 220, 225, 226

Child Support Act 1991

    section 24   56

Civil Legal Aid (Procedure) Regulations 2012   4

Cleveland Inquiry   51

Committal proceedings

    for breach of a reporting restrictions order   58

    for breach of the provisions of section 12 of the Administration of Justice Act   57

Communication of information   23, 24, 25, 56, 159

Contempt of court   6, 28, 37, 44, 47, 49, 55–58, 148, 151, 156, 197, 223

    penalty for   25

Contempt of Court Act 1981

    section 14   25

Court of Protection: Transparency Pilot   46

Craft, Sir Alan   126

Crime and Courts Act 2013

    section 17   7, 81

    section 17(4)   78

Criminal Justice Act 1982

    section 37(2)   59

Current state of the media   131

Curtis, Polly   8, 148

D

Dancey, His Honour Judge   177

Delahunty, Professor Jo   155, 186, 240

Denning, Lord   45

Designated Family Judges   84

Digital recording of judgments   88, 248

Disclosure of information to the media 23, 24, 25, 38, 62, 136, 137, 139, 148, 223, 225, 229, 249, 252, 254

Dodd, Mike 8, 55, 133, 145, 157

Domestic violence 4, 75, 110, 237, 238

Donaldson, Lord 54

Doughty, Dr Julie 86, 93, 172, 177, 222, 246, 248

Doughty research 93, 101

Doughty, Steve 86, 113

Dugan, Emily 8, 44, 151

'Duly accredited' representatives *See* Accredited media representatives

E

Editors' Code of Practice 150, 160

Emergency Protection Order 114

Enforcement 58, 59

European Convention on Human Rights 9, 219

    Article 6 9, 11, 32, 184, 219

    Article 6(1) 18

Article 8 9, 90, 117, 184, 189, 200, 217, 219, 220, 222, 225, 226, 239

Article 8(1) 16, 220

Article 8(2) 16, 219

Article 10 9, 62, 76, 117, 184, 189, 200, 219, 220, 221, 226, 228, 231

Article 10(1) 16

Article 10(2) 17, 219

Article 12 57

Expert evidence 29

Expert medical evidence 29

Expert witnesses 3, 29, 86, 90, 113, 125–129

Extempore judgments 69, 70, 88, 89

F

Facebook 154

Falconer, Lord 38

Family Court Information Pilot 67, 79, 173

Family Court of Australia 189, 190

Family Justice Council Debate 184

Index

Family Justice Review 79

Family Justice: the operation of the family courts 1, 24, 193

Family Procedure Rules 2010
7, 15, 25, 148, 220, 250, 253

    PD 3AA 239

    PD 12G 25, 55, 250

    PD 12I 56

    PD 27B 148

    PD 36J 167

    Rule 3A 239

    Rule 12.73(2) 25

    Rule 27.11(3) 221

    Rule 27.11(7) 148

    Rules 37.13-37.15 58

Family Proceedings (Amendment) (No 2) Rules 2009 25, 185

Family Proceedings (Amendment) (No 4) Rules 2005 24

    Rule 10.20A 24

Family Proceedings Rules 1991 15, 24, 25

    Rule 10.28 40

Farmer, Brian 8, 45, 63, 236

G

Gibb, Frances 30, 32

Glaser, Dr Danya 178, 225

Government consultations/responses 36

    Confidence and confidentiality: Improving transparency and privacy in family courts 37

    Confidence and confidentiality: Openness in family courts - a new approach 38

    Disclosure of Information in Family Proceedings Cases Involving Children 23

    Family Justice in View 39

H

Hailsham, Lord 61

Hale, Lady 19, 159

Hanna, Mark 8, 44, 55, 59–63, 138, 149, 164

Hayden, Mr Justice 188

Hayhurst, Claire 8, 137, 149

Hemming, John 81, 107

Henry, Sylvia 121

Herbert, Nick 249

Hobhouse, Lord	159
House of Commons Constitutional Affairs Select Committee	1, 2, 24, 25
Hughes, Simon	83

I

Independent Inquiry into Child Sexual Abuse in Rotherham	51
Independent Press Standards Organisation	150, 151
Instagram	155
Internet and social media	152

J

Jackson, Lord Justice	177
Jigsaw identification	69, 102, 117, 187
Journalistic techniques	
sensationalism	161, 164
vilification	161, 164
Judge, Lord	110
Judicial concerns	32
Judicial guidance	64
Judicial responses to survey	97

K

Keane, Fergal	143

L

Legal aid, removal of	4
Legal Aid Sentencing and Punishment of Offenders Act 2012	4
Legal blogging	167
Leveson report	144, 152, 155, 162
Lieven, Mrs Justice	123
Litigants in person	4

M

MacDonald, Mr Justice	172, 215
Maclean CBE, Mavis	68
Magrath, Paul	103
Major, Sir John	162
Marriage (Same Sex Couples) Act 2013	52
Masson QC, Professor Judith	122
McFarlane, Sir Andrew	6, 39, 189
Media	43
attendance at hearings	40, 44, 71, 181, 194, 198

reliability and trustworthiness of	8	Newton, The Honourable Mr Justice	184
role of	104, 146	Nicholls, Lord	160
Media firestorm, being caught up in	120	Norgrove, Sir David	79

O

Miscarriages of justice	1, 3, 26, 28, 35, 63, 133, 141, 160, 168, 179, 182–183, 206, 246	O'Neill, Baroness Onora	147
Misleading headlines	105, 149	Online news reports	132, 150, 154, 156, 251
Mole, Nuala	221	Open justice	11, 15
Moses, Sir Alan	159	Open justice in other countries	
Munby, Sir James	6, 28, 32–36, 48, 57, 59, 60, 74, 92, 102, 114, 118, 134, 137, 158, 180, 182, 184, 223, 228, 234, 243	Australia	194
		Canada	199
		Eire	207

N

Naming		New Zealand	197
expert witnesses	90, 125–129, 136	Northern Ireland	205
		Scotland	204
local authorities	46, 90, 114–117	Openness of the Family Court	32, 38

P

other professionals	123–124		
social workers	90, 117–123	Paramountcy of child's welfare	75
the child/parents	55, 58	Participation directions	239
National Youth Advocacy Service	180	Phone hacking scandal	145

Pilot Scheme: Transparency (Attendance at hearings in private)	167	**R**	
		Recommendations	243–255
Potter, Sir Mark	6, 17, 30	Reed, Lord	12
Practice Guidance on Transparency	79, 84–92, 87, 188	Reed, Lucy	168
		Reporting restrictions order	44
impact of	93–97		
Prentice, Bridget	39	breach of	56
Prior notice of cases	38, 46	on journalists	44
Publication of judgments	7	Rights of parents	51
analysis	93–99	Rodger, Lord	76
anonymisation of	7	Rozenberg, Joshua	193
lack of resources	99	Rubric	56
personal safety of judges	110	breach of	57
		Russell, Ms Justice	236
pressure of time	99	Ryder, Lord Justice	81
risk	110	**S**	
types of cases	109		
views of young people	102	Sambrook, Richard	153
		Satchwell, Bob	64
Public law orders	75	Scarman, Lord	211
standard of proof	75	Shaw, Lord	14
threshold	75	Shoesmith, Sharon	120
Public trust in journalists	146	Simon, Sir Jocelyn	48

Single Family Court 81

Social media and the internet
15, 52, 69, 82, 111, 122, 124, 152–157

Sodha, Sonia 4, 240

Steyn, Lord 17

Straw, Jack 39, 243

Sumption, Lord 14, 15

Survey of judges 96

Sweeney, John 1, 8, 36, 138, 145, 183

T

The Times' campaign 26

The Transparency Project
vii, 107, 108, 167

Tickle, Louise 8, 44, 134, 141, 149, 233

Time pressures on judges 101

Tolson QC, His Honour Judge 236

Training

    journalists 60, 148, 251, 254

    judges 254

Transcript of judgments 88, 97, 105, 108

Transparency and Accountability Bill 82

Transparency in the Family Courts: Publicity and Privacy in Practice 6

Transparency - The Next Steps: A Consultation Paper 92

Twitter 155

Tyler, Baroness Claire 184

U

United Nations Convention on the Rights of the Child 9, 214

    Article 3 216

    Article 3(1) 216, 217

    Article 10 227

    Article 12 9, 176, 180, 182, 183, 214, 216

    Article 13 226, 227, 228

    Article 16 9, 180, 183, 214, 216, 219, 220, 222, 225, 226, 239

    Article 16(1) 219

V

Victoria Derbyshire show 1, 3, 5

View from the President's Chambers 84

Voice of the child   8, 218, 229

W

Wall, Lord Justice   6, 26, 36, 64, 67, 80, 108, 128, 136, 171, 224

Welfare checklist   75

White, Josh   8, 133, 146

Wilson, Kate   64

Wilson, Lord Justice   27

Wolanski QC, Adam   64